The Restoration of All Things

of All Things

My continuing journey
beyond beyond

Mike Parsons

The Restoration of All Things

First published in the United Kingdom in 2021 by
The Choir Press
in conjunction with
Freedom Apostolic Ministries Ltd.

ISBN 978-1-78963-200-2 Paperback
ISBN 978-1-78963-201-9 eBook

Contents

Introduction

In my previous book, *My Journey Beyond Beyond*, I shared my life story on the quest for true reality in my relationship with God as my Father. This book continues the journey to where beyond was taking me. The previous four threads were woven together to create a rich tapestry expressing the pure joy and delight of a child discovering true reality for the first time. This journey, full of surprising revelations and experiences, unveiled further dimensions and depths beyond beyond once again. My encounters took me deeper into the Father's loving heart, unveiling and revealing His Oracles for creation's restoration. There will probably need to be three volumes to cover the vastness and extent of my journey but let's begin.

My beyond beyond experiences were an ongoing process of encounters that created such cognitive dissonance that the God that I thought I knew evaporated into nothingness. The true reality of who They (Father, Son and Spirit) truly are emerged from the rubble that was my deconstructed mind into the glorious light of revelation. My experiences and encounters with their true reality exploded my limited and restricted understanding that had been framed by my mind's religious constructs. I am now an atheist to the god I previously worshipped as he never existed other than as a figment of my religious imagination. The glorious true loving God who is Love, Light, Spirit and Fire emerged from the destruction of my orthodox belief systems. The encounters, like explosions of truth, destroyed my religiously framed construct to reveal a God who is I AM that I AM: pure, unadulterated, unconditional love.

As my great friend and fellow traveller, Lindy Strong has said, "My past self of ten years ago would probably call my present self a heretic" and that was my own experience on this journey. If that is not all our experience then we have ceased the journey, content with our systematic theological understanding of a God who is infinite, creating a box for that God that is only a prison for our minds. I am a happy heretic, enjoying skiing down the slope of orthodoxy to discover and explore a whole new vista beyond the limits of my understanding.

The further and deeper this rabbit hole journey has gone, the more convinced I am of God's desire and passion for the restoration of all things of creation. Creation itself will inevitably be set free from its bondage and slavery to the corruption of our sonship by the revealing of the true mystic sons of God who have arisen and are shining with love's light.

For He rescued us from the domain of darkness, and transferred us to the kingdom of His beloved Son, in whom we have redemption, the forgiveness of sins. He is the image of the invisible God, the firstborn of all creation. For by Him all things were created, both in the heavens and on earth, visible and invisible, whether thrones or dominions or rulers or authorities—all things have been created through Him and for Him. He is before all things, and in Him, all things hold together. He is also head of the body, the church; and He is the beginning, the firstborn from the dead so that He will come to have first place in everything. For it was the Father's good pleasure for all the fullness to dwell in Him, and through Him to reconcile all things to Himself, having made peace through the blood of His cross; through Him, I say, whether things on earth or things in heaven (Colossians 1:13-20).

Are all things actually all things? I discovered the answer to this is yes and no. Yes, all things that Jesus created out of the desire of the Father's heart in the power of the Spirit; but no to everything we have created from the DIY independent path of the knowledge of good and evil that has been cursed.

All things came into being through Him, and apart from Him nothing came into being that has come into being (John 1:3).

"The Father loves the Son and has given all things into His hand." (John 3:35).

"For the Father loves the Son, and shows Him all things that He Himself is doing; and the Father will show Him greater works than these, so that you will marvel." (John 5:20).

"My sheep hear My voice, and I know them, and they follow Me; and I give eternal life to them, and they will never perish; and no one will snatch them out of My hand. My Father, who has given them to Me, is greater than all; and no one is able to snatch them out of the Father's hand. I and the Father are one." (John 10:27-30).

Jesus, knowing that the Father had given all things into His hands, and that He had come forth from God and as going back to God... (John 13:3).

"But the Helper, the Holy Spirit, whom the Father will send in My name, He will teach you all things, and bring to your remembrance all that I said to you." (John 14:26).

"All things that the Father has are Mine; therefore I said that He takes of Mine and will disclose it to you." (John 16:15).

"...and all things that are Mine are Yours, and Yours are Mine; and I have been glorified in them." (John 17:10).

After this, Jesus, knowing that all things had already been accomplished... (John 19:28)

Chapter 1. The Great Shift

My journey to go beyond restoration has had many milestones, the key '*kairos* time' moments; but as the restoration of all things is the focus of this book, I will share the salient encounters that created the opportunity to choose at each fork in the road.

During 2020 a great shift took place both in my life and in creation as a whole. I was made aware of this coming shift in July 2017, though at that time I was unaware of its creational significance beyond my own personal world. This shift was to destroy the trap of normalcy and reshape the landscape of spirituality, opening up the possibilities of sonship to a whole new generation. There was personal preparation for this shift but, as I discovered, the whole Joshua Generation was also to undergo the great shaking to be prepared *for a time such as this* (see Esther 4:14).

In fact, from 2018 to 2020, I engaged with Esther many times, sometimes at her instigation and others at mine. The first time she appeared during a Sunday gathering (when we had those, before the deconstruction of the Ekklesia), she came to remind us that we were called to the kingdom royalty as sons of God for a time such as this. Intrigued, I went into the heavenly Court of the Upright to seek Esther for more revelation. We had a conversation that opened my mind to the process of preparation we often unknowingly go through to prepare us for our destiny. Such preparation is not always one we would choose for ourselves. Esther informed me that she resisted the process which she was enduring, as a young Hebrew girl, to become a concubine of a foreign, pagan king. She revealed that, like many of us, she did not know her destiny until she was in the midst of its unfurling. Esther often appeared in conferences and gatherings I was part of, in various places around the world, as a reminder to embrace the process of transformation and change necessary to fulfil our destiny.

Here are some of my journal entries that unveil the preparation I went through to be ready for this great shift in 2020. I was not aware of the wider shift as I started with my own life – figuratively, my Jerusalem – but in reality, the great shakings that took place went beyond to touch my family, community and the whole of the earth. This was a global and cosmic shift that is to become the catalyst for the restoration of all things message becoming more widely accepted and embraced. I will add my comments in brackets throughout the conversations I had with the Father, during 2017 and 2018 particularly.

18 May 2017

"Son, get ready for a shift to take place in 2020. You have two and a half years to be ready for the great shakings that will take place, both corporately and globally." (I did not see this clearly but treasured it in my heart).

"Son, fully restored sons will lead to the restoration of all things as per Our original intention and design. Fully restored relationships, family, planet, universe, dimensions, reality; dichotomies, God to man, man to man, man to creation, heaven and earth, was, is and is to come; spirit soul body, the angelic realm, everything that is separated, paradise restored and beyond. (At this time these statements were stretching my consciousness as I had not yet had the testimonies that confirmed these conversations).

"Son, you have been called and chosen and your destiny unveiled as a chancellor of heaven and a legislator on earth. Son, you are an ambassador for the Joshua Generation: it is time to make representation for mercy and grace, as the times and seasons are about to shift focus for the forerunners. Justice according to the judgment of the 70 will continue but grace must begin to be called forth. Grace, manifold grace and grace upon grace are the seasons to come forth, beyond the capacity of your present experience to explain or understand. Beyond normalcy will stretch your imagination so you must now start to engage beyond beyond, not just in the reality of your mind's consciousness, which is currently spiritual nonlinearity, but eventually in your physical nonlinear experience.

"Son, get ready and be prepared for the things that will suddenly appear to become your normality. The physical laws are about to be rewritten from beyond beyond and you have been chosen with other forerunners to be part of this process. Son, it is time to arise and shine like stars as the mountain of the house of the Lord rises from the wilderness prison to the place of prominence governmentally.

"Son, the circles of the deep and the deep within the deep must be aligned, that is why twelve ambassadors represent the twelve ages of creation order. Son, call them to prepare for the shift that is coming, that will weaken and fracture space-time continuums to then unify all things in one Son, who will sum up and be all in all.

"The dimensional boundaries must be removed and the gates opened for full restoration to be accomplished; there can be no barriers or boundaries, everything must become all in all. Son, the balance of probabilities is beginning to shift away from what has been to what will be. Unifying and restoring the past will release the future from the curse of normalcy." (This is what began to occur during the great shift of 2020 when men's trust in the humanistic systems they had created began to fail and things would never be the same again).

"I will come upon the Ekklesia and shift it to feel My heart for those who are to belong. The 'you' that you now know will not be the same, so you must be prepared for a radical shift of focus and be willing to embrace the changes and not fight them. The shift from justice to grace for the Joshua Generation will be a subtle change but a discernible change that will increase through desire until it becomes a radical change.

"Son, go back to your journals and engage grace because now you are ready to see what it was impossible to see back in 2010. The limitations and restrictions that have been and will continue to be removed will make it possible to engage grace, manifold grace and grace upon grace as a reality, first within your consciousness and then within your created reality. 2020 will be a significant time, for you and globally, so creation itself can be made ready for restoration."

6 November 2017

"Son, great shifts and shakings will start to take place in the transition between the old season and the new. You will not be shaken if you are standing on the true foundation of your original design. Trust in the world's or the religious systems will not keep you standing firm when the great shakings begin in 2020.

"Son, these shakings are the moving of My heart aligned to the groans of creation and the desires of My sons for freedom. Creation is quaking in response to the manifestation of the sons of God taking their places. When My sons begin to know their true origin and identity then creation will begin to throw off its yoke to bondage.

"The freedom from the yoke of religious oppression and suppression will begin to bring creation itself into liberty. The shifts will reflect the revelation of true sonship as the sons of God arise, throwing off the tyranny of the old order, and embrace the new order of freedom. Creation itself will flex as it begins to emerge out of darkness into the light of the rising of the sons of God.

"Reality itself will shift once the religious veils have been removed from the minds of the sons of God. There will be shakings, manoeuvrings and exposings within the hierarchies of the Moses generation that will cause another exodus out of the wilderness.

"The great commissioning is being prepared for the sons to take their heavenly governmental positions with new mantles, scrolls, weapons and discoveries."

27 November 2017

"It is an opportunity to connect to your eternal destiny and be part of a great shift that is coming in 2020. The river is flowing with grace and faith to restore your identity and equip you for new positions of kingdom governmental authority. I am calling you to shift your focus away from the wilderness and its valley of decision to Egypt and its valley of decision which reaches beyond death to the grave." (I did not know the full implication of this statement as I had only just begun to engage in helping to rescue people from the consuming fire of God's love).

5 December 2017

"Son, prepare now for what is about to come and be ready. Stir my people to become my children so they recognise their sonship and take their places in the government of heaven.

"Prepare for the shift that is coming in 2020 by seeking for and looking into Wisdom's pillars and engaging with the assemblies of heaven where the times and seasons are being set."

2 January 2018

"Son, if the old generation fails to respond I will keep calling to them to come out from the coverings of men's religious mountains but I want you to shift your focus and prepare for the new challenges ahead that will be fully realised in 2020.

"Son, get ready to reveal who I truly am to the world who cannot see Me yet as this will all change in 2020."

30 January 2018

"Son, focus on preparing your blueprint for the shift that is coming in 2020." (This was when the restoration of all things truly began to take a grip and captivate my heart).

"Call forth the government to arise: release the blue light that will draw people out of the old to come to you, those who will be key governmental figures. In preparing the local blueprint, the wider ministry will be able to increase and your focus will shift from local to global and dimensional taking you beyond beyond. You must shift from the earthly to the heavenly over the next 2 years as you learn to function there with new levels of authority.

"The council sits in 2 days. Your spirit will be engaging but over the next 2 years your soul will become more actively participating and you will become more cognitively aware of the activities and functions of the council within the affairs of the circle of the spheres." (I began to take my ambassador's role more seriously and the ability to function simultaneously in multiple dimensions began to bear fruit).

8 March 2018

"Son, do you feel it? Do you sense it? Do you hear it? Can you see it? The dawning of a new day, the beginning of a new season, a new vista with a new horizon." (I could not envisage this at that time but the challenge to feel, sense, hear and see was a stimulus to pursue a deeper intimacy with the eternal now of the Father's heart).

"Can you not hear? Can you not see? Then feel the wind shift, feel its intensity increase as you move towards 2020 and the great shift that will take place."

8 May 2018

"Son, it is not your responsibility what others do. Keep your heart right and don't be despondent." (I had become more aware of the deepening divisions within the so-called mystic movement and the opposition to the restoration of all things message that was forming). "Trust in Me and in My destiny and purposes for your life and I will fulfil your dreams and desires. I told you to prepare, for in 2020 there will be the shift and you need to be ready."

9 May 2018

"Son, in January 2020 I want you to shift your focus fully onto Freedom Apostolic Ministries and complete the 'Engaging God' Programme by resigning from all other duties and positions during 2020. Prepare the materials for the growth of restoration to be ready for 2020." (The end of 2018 into 2019 was a very challenging time in which I experienced betrayal from some of those close to me, which put in jeopardy my ability to step out of my local governance roles. But God shaped me and others during this period and provided individuals to step forward, as He promised He would in January 2018).

17 May 2018

"Son, this will need a radical shifting through mindquakes of increasing intensity so that only the truth of My kingdom remains. The tree of life must be the source for Our sons, as no other source can expand the consciousness of sonship necessary for co-creating through the power of creative thought. Son, choose who you will serve because you will serve and be influenced by someone or something. Present the opportunities to My children for their minds to be renewed by a radical shift of quake proportions. This will culminate in 2020 when the great global shift and awakening will take place."

4 July 2018

"Son, the times and the seasons are shifting and the wheels within wheels within wheels are being aligned to open the Chancellors' Houses for grace to come out of justice.

"Increase in governmental authority will be the result when the sons of God arise to be seated, enthroned, and ready to bring agreement as gateways of heaven into the earth.

"New earthly foundations must be laid and the atmosphere must be cleared so that the everlasting doors can be opened and the glory of the children of God can be displayed through sonship on earth as it is in heaven.

"Issue the call; re-energise the blue light call for the sons of God to arise and take their places of responsibility within the tree of life."

– I call for the light to shine to penetrate the veils of darkness and deception over those under the coverings of men.

– I call for the angelic messengers to go forth with the call to cross over beyond the veil into inheritance and birthright.

– I call for those whose hearts are beginning to ask the question 'there must be more than this?' to connect with the blog, YouTube, Engaging God and the book, and rise up and take their places within the Joshua Generation.

– I call for the frequency of sonship to call the sons of God to arise and resonate with their destiny scroll to tune into destiny's call and hear the cry of God's heart.

– I call for true love to release the true identity of sons and for their true heavenly positions be unveiled and revealed.

– I call for the scandal that has twisted the character and nature of God to be revealed so that love can penetrate the religious systems, both Catholic and Protestant.

– I call for love to be poured out and love bombs to be exploded to expose the lies that have shrouded the reality of God's true essence and man's full inclusion.

– I call for heaven's light to shine, to burn brightly, to attract sons like a moth to a flame.

– I call for the revolution of the circle of the deep to begin the new season.

"Son, the time for action is here; and as your focus shifts, so will the desire of your heart, to function as an ambassador for the Joshua Generation.

"I have reserved you a place within the 70 but your role as an ambassador must become more of a priority and more strategic as you present your cases for nations and people groups.

"I have My gifts and callings for the families of the earth that have been lost but it is time for restoration to begin.

"Send out the blue light call that carries the resonance of My heart so deep will call to deep to connect the ambassadors with the families within the Father's heart."

– I call for the restoration of family within the government of heaven for the Joshua Generation.

– I call for the ambassadors to respond to the frequency of God's heart.

– I call for the hearts of God's children to be turned back to their identity and destiny as ambassadors.

– I call for the sound of the trumpet to resonate within the EG Programme to reach, engage and connect with those who have been called so that they can be gathered, equipped and released.

– I call for the angelic messengers of the Joshua Generation to go forth to engage the wilderness and release the desire for those seeking and searching to cross over.

– I call for the message to equip the Joshua Generation with the 'Engaging God' programme to break into new territories.

29 August 2018

I shared with others what God told me about the shift that was coming for me in 2020 which would not just affect me. I shared that I would be stepping down from my governmental roles, both spiritual and in governance, to focus on the restoration of all things. This created some shock waves locally and I stepped down immediately from my local Bench of Three role. This enabled many things to come into the light as the other two of the Bench of Three also stepped down and the spotlight fell on our local Bench of Seven, exposing many shortcomings. The deconstruction of the local Ekklesia concept and the format and function of our gatherings began to accelerate from this point.

In 2018 the Father directed me to establish Ambassadors' groups within the 'Engaging God' programme in 2019, to be ready for the global shift that was coming in 2020.

15 February 2018

Son, see from this place of rest, empowered by My presence, on My right hand. Here is where you use your legislation effectively with the sceptre of your government. See the intent and desire of My heart in manifest vision. I began to see the clouds of the atmosphere clear and then the light of heaven radiating from the embassy of heaven that is established over our area. I saw the light of people's destiny shining with activity, abundance and overflow. I saw love as an atmosphere, a fragrance, radiant with wellness, wellbeing, peace, wholeness, unity, and oneness. I saw the power of love in action, fuelling the city with light energy. I saw the vibrational energy of heaven's life resonating with the glorious convergence of heaven and earth. I saw a dome of energy extending around the spiritual atmospheres where the principalities, powers and rulers are enthroned and administrating heaven's government into the earth.

Image by Gerd Altmann from Pixabay.

"Son, you have a global mandate for governmental equipping to establish new order Ekklesia and Embassies of heaven within the nations and families of the earth. Raise ambassadors for the Joshua Generation and the 'Engaging God' programme within nations and people groups who will partner with you at a strategic level. Son, remember I showed you the network of arcs forming benches encompassing the globe: now call it into being and legislate for its manifestation. (Nancy Coen has been sharing a similar image and concept for many years.)

21

6 January 2020

"Son, I know that the shift is going to take you out of your comfort zone, so be at rest by trusting in Me. Son, you don't have to do anything. Remember you are pleasing to Me already, just as you are, but I have so much more for you. The Oracles of My heart are just the beginning of the journey that will reveal who I am as love. Let Me take you deeper into My heart to reveal sonship's rest; that will re-envision you." (I will go into the significance of these oracles in the next chapter).

"Son, I am within all things and all things are within Me, feel it in the immanence of creation's groaning. Feel My connection with all things as part of all things. Feel the lostness, disconnection and hopelessness of creation. Son, My sons are the hope for creation: when they discover their identity they will be the sound and light that restores hope. The frequency of sonship is the way transcendence and immanence can converge and the hope produced by love's light can be restored.

"Son, you can make the shift from justice to grace if you rest in Me and trust in My love. I have been preparing you for the great shift that is about to take place for your whole life, bur specifically over the last three years, so you can be ready.

8 April 2020

"Son, the shift that you were warned to prepare for is here. The last two and half years have seen great changes, preparation, deconstruction and renewal of your mind. You have introduced ambassadors, deconstructed the Ekklesia, deconstructed the gatherings and expanded your consciousness to accept the restoration of ALL things. Your experiences with love's light, going deeper into love, have revealed the Oracles of Our heart and you have become an oracle of restoration by engaging the dimensions beyond beyond. You have seen the four streams flowing together to converge into a mighty river of restoration. You have embraced energy frequency healing and introduced crystal bowls to the Joshua generation. You have released the 'Sons Arise!' call through the engaging God programme and conference and the book. You established Restoration conferences and formed strategic relationships and the cosmic bench and have become a heavenly ambassador for the Joshua generation and restoration. You have aligned the chancellors' houses and released new mantles, weapons and commissions to converge time and the eternal now for this shift.

"All these things have been preparing you for the shift so that you would be ready to be a forerunner at this juncture in history. Son, you have responded to the call to be ready personally and have facilitated a measure of corporate readiness with those who have resonated. Now is the time to mobilise the sons to arise and shine love's light into the darkness to dispel and overcome it with love. All the networks that have been forming around the world that you are now in relationship with can be mobilised to take advantage of the great shift that is taking place to be ready for the new landscape after this period of shaking comes to an end: Global Ascension Network, Marketplace Ministries, Company of Burning Hearts, Freedom Apostolic Ministries, 'Engaging God' programme, Global Community in Yeshua, Kingdom Talks, Freedom, Ambassadors, Bath, Glory Company, Ekklesia Mumbai, Business network, New

Renaissance ministries, Heart Math, NW Ekklesia, Morgan Group, Toronto Ekklesia, River 24:7 Winnipeg, Dallas, Beyond the Courtrooms of Heaven, Quantum Ministries International, Liebusters, The Hub Texas, New Orleans.

"Son, it is time to issue the call to cosmic convergence for life and immortality to come to light in the restoration of all things reality.

"Son, you have come through the fire and embraced the pain of transfiguration for a time such as this; now embrace the shift and be ready for a global and cosmic transformation."

April 9 2020

"Son, the great shift that We have been preparing you for is upon you but you are ready to seize the season of a great opportunity that is about to dawn. The new vista will present many challenges but also many opportunities to bring about a true cosmic awakening to the true reality of human existence in relationship with Our very essence and being as love. This shift is a cosmic awakening to love, light, spirit and fire to unveil and reveal the sons of God onto the cosmic dimensional stage. The great enlightenment of true rest as revealed through the engagement with the oracles of Our heart will accelerate the ascension development of Our children to an age of great enlightenment. The ages to come are beginning to converge and expand from this point where time and the eternal now intersect. This great convergence will bring unity and blessing to those who resonate with Our heart and the four streams of restoration will begin to flow together as a mighty river to water the earth through the opening of the age-enduring doors between the earth and the heavens.

"Son, it is time to strategically mobilise those who will resonate with heaven's sound to begin to answer creation's groaning by establishing global networks and embassies of heaven on the earth. Global and cosmic councils will need to be established to nurture the foundations of this new age of limitless grace beyond the shift. The next age shift is upon you but you are ready and prepared for this new adventure, as are others who will be drawn together for this momentous shift.

"Son, release the sound, the call for the sons of God to arise and shine with love's light at this moment of great darkness and fear for the peoples so that the true glory of Our essence will radiate throughout the earth. Son, call the children of God who are wandering the wilderness of religion into the promised land of their inheritance, to come beyond the veil into true intimacy and immortality.

"Proclaim the message of hope that death has been abolished and life and immortality have been brought into the light. The fear of death has been abolished and a new age of freedom for mankind has been announced as the true jubilee of jubilees.

"Mankind has sought immortality through magic, ritual and technology but now the truth of immortality through relationship is unveiled, so all can know the truth of their inheritance and be free from their slavery to the fear of death."

Therefore, since the children share in flesh and blood, He Himself likewise also partook of the same, that through death He might render powerless him who had the power of death, that is, the devil, and might free those who through fear of death were subject to slavery all their lives (Hebrews 2:14-15).

14 April

"Son, share your heart and love encounters to reveal the limitless grace that is who We are as I AM that I AM. This revelation of the truth and true reality is the message that you carry as an Oracle and a legislator to converge time and the eternal now, heaven and earth. The shift needs to be administrated but also nurtured and protected in its infancy as people free from normalcy will feel insecure and will default back to the comfort of old religious systems and patterns.

"Legislate and govern in the unity of heart and mind to call Our children into the fullness of their inheritance. Legislate with the Elementals for the planets to be at rest during this tumultuous period of great shifting and shaking. Legislate for the safe release of pressure, building up as a result of the fear Our children are feeling.

"Son, perfect love will cast out the fear; so keep releasing the love frequency through Our oracles into the spiritual atmosphere around the world and your spheres. Knowing love by personal experiences and encounters, as you have, is the only way Our children will have the revelation of their sonship, through knowing fatherhood and true fathering. Son, Our ultimate desire and goal is for all Our children to become ascended fathers, capable of loving their creation with limitless grace and mercy.

"Son, remind Our children that this shifting period is not Our negative judgment upon them but Our love bringing good out of what is being reaped because they have sown injustice, division, strife and enmity. Our mercy always triumphs over the consequences of following the DIY tree path of independence out of the knowledge of good and evil. Our love will not allow Us to watch passively as Our children suffer the consequences of their corrupt government of creation. Our loving essence is constantly and continually at work to bring good out of every situation and circumstance, although many do not see Our handiwork because of the suffering they are experiencing. Son, We do not remove the rights of Our children to choose but We do work within those choices to restore balance in the creation and fulfil Our original desire and intention creatively through Our children's choices.

"Son, this is not fate or fatalism but constant micro-course corrections to facilitate all the choices that are being made throughout time and space. The more the sons of God mature, arise and take their places alongside Us in heavenly Kingdom government the more restoration will be the result. Our sons and heirs are in tutoring and training for becoming the co-creators they are destined to be so all of the dimensions realities can be fully restored and expanded.

"Son, strategic fallen ones need to be engaged during this shifting period as the hope of sonship is beginning to penetrate light into their darkness and hopelessness. Seek to engage with those who were in opposition to the knowledge of life and immortality being revealed in the light, as they will give you insight into those areas and beings you need to target with love so they can be restored from darkness to light.

"The light of truth is rising like the sun from the darkness of night through a new dawn to shine in the brilliance and radiance of continual noon.

"Son, align the circle of the deep with Our precepts for restoration to release the new mantles, weapons, scrolls and commissioning needed for the discovery house to be opened and the affairs of the nations to change the culture.

"Son, administrate grace within justice and judgment for mercy to be released at unprecedented levels so the sons of God can enter a season of rest that will bring peace to the elements.

"Son, a global government will need to work within the seasons of heavenly government, judgment, justice, grace and mercy, but can administrate seasons within seasons as the circle of the deep is aligned. The 12 High Chancellors' Houses will need to be engaged and opened to release the resources needed for heavenly government to manifest on earth. All heavenly government must be based on the eternal now foundations of Our precepts which represent Our heart, Our statutes which represent Our mind and Our laws which represent Our voice. Only with this alignment can the ordinances of heaven begin to be released into the earth.

"The ordinances of heaven will release the new mantles of authority in love to use the new weapons of love to unveil the scrolls for the commissioning of sons into new roles and positions of mature government."

15 April 2020

"Son, today marks a new era of unity which is the beginning of the end of the old systems of empire and wilderness life for so many of Our children. The coverings of the Old Covenant systems are being removed and many of Our children are starting to see the light that is shining. Today that light will shine more brightly and its radiance will begin to affect Our children on a global scale. Son, as you gather today with those of one heart and mind towards restoration the veils of darkness will be penetrated by unity of heart, mind and purpose on an unprecedented scale. The unity and trust which will be demonstrated by turning from independence will become a catalyst to great changes that will transform the landscape of true Ekklesia forever. The end of competition and the beginning of true cooperation will change reality and begin a new era of restoration and expansion of the Kingdom on earth as it is in heaven.

"Son, this example of what can be accomplished by a few people with one heart operating in unison will be the model example to mobilise Our children around the world to arise and shine. Empower Our children to know their identity and fulfil their destiny and release them to outwork their mandates.

"Son, prioritise your focus and seek for the heavenly strategy and a clear blueprint and mandate. The key is unity, not uniformity; and whatever you do together, ensure you are motivated by love and function in the opposite spirit to that which is opposing you. The Oracles of Our heart are to be your motivation, not militancy, so mobilise the global relationships, connections and influences to love not war. Son, this is so important as this shift that is taking place is to reveal who We are as I AM that I AM, as love. As the sons of a God arise and shine from their heavenly positions, the whole of creation will begin to see Our true essence as love, light, fire and spirit. Son, you will become beacons of light as Oracles and Legislators of the heavenly government of kings and priests into the earth. It is time for heaven and earth, time and the eternal now to converge together and the four streams that I have revealed to you to become one mighty river of restoration. It is time the everlasting doors are opened around the earth to pour out the blessing that this unity will command.

"Son, do not get side-tracked by individual agendas, by always seeking Our heart together as one and always acting as one with no individualism. The converging of hearts and minds will facilitate the merging of individuals into one body to lose the independence of the tree of the knowledge of good and evil for the path of the tree of life. The creation will respond to the revealing of the sons of God and now is the time to rule over the seven weather systems and the nine tectonic plates to establish peace. As you arise and shine love's light together the darkness and fear will need to be dispelled to reveal Our loving heart towards all Our children and all creation for restoration.

"The restoration of all things is Our agenda. Do not lose sight of that for individual agendas – but the different agendas within restoration can be dealt with better together, by supporting and encouraging through what each part brings to the whole.

Restoration Government Engagement

I engaged with Unity, Wisdom and Prudence. They spoke with one voice and stated that this is a time of alignment and convergence of time and the eternal now, heaven and earth. This an alignment with the Father's heart to reveal His Precepts (heart) Statutes (mind) and Laws (voice) to release the ordinances of heaven as scrolls, mandates and strategies. They invited us to engage the 12 High Chancellors and enter their houses (Precepts, Statutes, Laws, Ordinances, Mantles, Weapons, Scrolls, Discoveries, Commissioning, Culture, Affairs of the Nations, Treasury). We have been invited to align the 12 High Chancellors' Houses around the circle of the deep to the times and seasons of Judgment, Justice, Grace, Mercy and Rest. We are called to be Oracles who carry the oracles of the Father's heart and legislate from rest.

They gave me a scroll titled 'Restoration Government Collaboration with the Father's Heart'. It said, "Join together in unity of heart and mind and become strong by the merging of your hearts together where each one has a part to play, just as a body is one with parts having different functions."

Unity said, "Mobilise globally and release people into their identity and positions and empower their mandates with honour and love in unity, operating in the opposite spirit from the opposition we face."

16 April 2020

"Son, as you function as collaborators with Our heart in unity, you will pulse with the rhythm of Our beating heart. As you are in oneness with Our heart, you will expand to become that shield, continuously energised by that unity and oneness. Unity continually infuses you with the knowledge of Our heart from which you act as one. Your mandate for Restoration government authorises you to be the shield that protects from outside influences; but the priority is to turn to look into the earth sphere, and from your positions and thrones around the earth, to release the sound, by being the Oracles and Legislators of Our heart. You all carry the frequency of sonship for restoration, focus that merged and combined energy to target the specific obstacles and hindrances to restoration that We will show you heart to heart. Son, remember, this is not warfare, this is the exercise of governmental authority with honour, love and unity that will enable you to operate in the opposite spirit to that which opposes restoration.

"The great shift, both personal and global, is something We have been preparing you for; do not minimise or underestimate the scale of this shift, as the ripples of the great shaking are touching the dimensions. Encourage everyone to evaluate everything in light of this opportunity for change and transformation: their priorities in daily life, their focus of attention, their relationship priorities, their beliefs and mindsets, their vision for the future, their passions and priorities for creation, their opportunities for government and legislation. Son, encourage everyone not to default back to previous normalcy but to be transformed and never go back but forward with a global perspective.

"It is time to be world shapers who will shape the landscape of spirituality globally to reveal Our true loving nature and character to a world of Our children who will be desperately insecure and looking for comfort and solace. Now is the time for the Sons of God to arise and shine with love's light to draw Our children out of the wilderness of religion and out of the Egypt of the pathway of the DIY tree of the knowledge of good and evil.

"Son, only the unconditional love that is I AM that I AM can restore all things; let it begin with you and never end in its expansion through government and peace.

"Son, you are an opener of doors so that others can go in, so be content to be the doorkeeper who opens the doors through your experiences and beckons and welcomes Our children to enter sonship and go beyond.

20 April 2020

"Son, do not be intimidated by those whose minds are blinded by race or religion. You live in a New Covenant where all Our promises and covenants are fulfilled in Christ. Son, there are so many who are influenced by dispensationalism and do not even know it. They are bewitched and fooled to live under the influence of what were meant to be only types and shadows of the New Covenant that is now in force. Son, all these shadows lessen the fullness of the new by drawing Our children back to the inferior covenant of works where festivals and Jewish dates and systems place them under bondage, not liberty. All the Jewish religious and ceremonial observances such as Passover, Booths, Rosh Hashanah, Pentecost and Hanukkah were just pale reflections of the true Way Truth and Life which is one new man in Christ, who is the true Israel and Lion of the tribe of a Judah that you are all included in. All the festivals are just men's attempts to satisfy their own need to appease Us by their self-effort. Son, let me state it plain and clear: all the promises for natural Israel and Judah are fulfilled in Jesus, who made and established the New Covenant with his blood; that blood is now permanently recorded in the heavens.

"This issue has the potential to polarise and distract those seeking to establish restoration government, so be careful and always act with love, honour and unity and never let relationship be sacrificed to doctrines. Never hold back from speaking the truth in love when and where you have a mandate to challenge the mindsets that hold so many of Our children in bondage to religion of all or no kind.

"Son, you can see it from this elevated position, seated and enthroned in the heaven of heavens; keep looking to where there are absences of light and focus your attention on restoring light and truth, no matter what the personal cost to you. Son, you have no reputation or position to lose, so keep arising and shining the light and truth of restoration into the darkness that veils Our children from their true inheritance towards creation.

"Son, the four streams that are converging together as the river of restoration each have mindsets that create separation and division from each other. Challenge those mindsets through teaching but also by legislating to release frequencies of truth that will penetrate the veils and deconstruct those false beliefs. Demolishing strongholds of thinking that separate and divide is a priority but always do it with love and honour with the goal of unity. This is not a theological debate with an argument to be won but a sincere desire to remove the barriers and hindrances to true unity for the desire of a restored creation."

I legislated into the darkness of mindsets that divide and separate with love's light.

– I call for lightning bolts of heavenly truth and revelation to be released to penetrate and demolish strongholds that limit, divide and separate.

– I call for angelic messengers to visit those who are influencers within each stream with dreams and visions that will unveil the truth.

– I release the frequency of truth as love's light to call them out of the darkness of limitation and restriction.

– I release love bombs to explode around those influencers who need the revelation of the oracles of the Father's heart concerning restoration.

– I call realised eschatologists to follow the sound towards universal restoration.

– I call the universal restorationists to follow the sound towards realised eschatology.

– I call the mystics to follow the sound towards universal restoration and realised eschatology.

– I call the energy and frequency healers to follow the sound towards universal restoration, realised eschatology and true mysticism.

– I call for all the streams to become a mighty river of restoration to free creation from its bondage to corruption.

– I release the frequencies of the Oracles of the Father's heart towards each stream to create a passion and burning desire for creation's freedom from its groaning.

– I call for the harmonious symphony of creation to be restored to the primordial state of oneness.

"Son, use all the weapons at your disposal in this love quest and align the circle of the deep to release new mantles and weapons for Our limitless grace and mercy to be poured out into creation.

21 April 2020

"Son, come walk with Me." We walked in the realm of perfection within the dark cloud of the person of the Father. The Father's presence walking with me felt very familiar, yet it was also very different. There was a depth to His presence that was drawing me deeper, as it felt like I was sinking, being enveloped in pure love, tangible rest. Although we appeared to be going deeper, we were ascending higher and the darkness was light at a level or wavelength that I could not comprehend. The Father's presence made me feel safe and secure but I was excited and exhilarated as the cocoon around us appeared to get brighter and brighter. The light seemed to explode into beauteous splendour that reveals the Father's Person. The increasing light intensity felt like love, joy, peace, patience, goodness, kindness, gentleness, and faithfulness that revealed myself like I had never known before. I felt those qualities and characteristics at another level and they revealed, heart to heart and mind to mind, who He is and who I am within this amazing light of oneness.

We had ascended through the dark cloud of Perfection into the light of Eternity and it felt like I was emerging out of the chrysalis of metamorphosis as a new creation being like my Father. I then looked beyond the emotions I felt to the light of truth I was experiencing to see the wondrous sight of myself reflected in his face. That pure blue light that seemed to be vibrating, pulsating with frequency, colour, emotion, sound and pure sacred geometrical beauty was reflecting my transformed image as an ascended father. Then His comforting, familiar voice – the same but more intense – filled my mind with a vast number of pure thoughts that I could have never hoped to contain but my mind was expanding my consciousness, absorbing those amazing thoughts. This was beyond beyond yet again but so far beyond my previous grid of reference that it would have been incomprehensible except for my consciousness having expanded to accommodate the truth of this new reality of being.

I heard the familiar, comforting sound of my Father's voice: "Son, this is who you are and who you are ascending to become. This is your true identity: allow this knowledge to direct and guide you on your quest to become who you are. Son, this is truly beyond but it is your destiny to travel this path towards rest and enlightenment. This is a path that all will have to follow if they are to be. Son, there are many twists and turns still to come but you now know where this journey ends, to become another new beginning. Son, I am well pleased: you are My heart's delight, my beloved son, who is always willing to go beyond.

"Son, the circle of unity where you are expanding and contracting globally will increase in number to twelve and other circles will form. There will be a circle for the earth realm and another circle for the dimensional realm and other circles of oneness that will form until all creation has a restoration government in positions of heart responsibility. This is the beginning of the end and the end of the beginning for Our sons to become the guardians and governors of creation reality as ascended fathers. Son, now you have seen what is Our heart's desire, the Oracles will take on a new level of meaning and their frequency will increase in intensity.

"Son, the way to ascension is to rest and learn to be gentle and humble in heart at a whole new level of being. Son, be, be, be, be, be, be..." on and on, echoing in my mind. Those words resonated within my expanded consciousness; vibrating with pure love, light pulsing and pulsating into every facet of its manifoldness.

22 April 2020

"Son, as you collaborate with Our heart, contracting into Us, you can expand around the earth, shielding the earth from external and dimensional influences. Positioned globally, you can in unity focus your attention on Our priorities and contract to surround that issue. Once focused, you can release the opposite spirit into the opposition to restore the redemptive purpose that has been corrupted and perverted. Son, this is not to be a war but a series of restoration events that will restore those of Our children that have been deceived into opposing Our intentions.

"Son, the key is not just to treat each other with honour and love but to bless those who are operating in the curse; so trust that they can be returned to the fold and have their identity restored. Our children's destiny has been twisted and perverted. That is why they have been deceived, but every crooked path can be made straight and every mountain of self can be made low in humility and every valley of bondage on earth can be lifted up.

"Son, You have been given limitless grace to release limitless mercy so that Our mercy can triumph over all of man's DIY judgment and justice. Son, let mercy flow down like a mighty river of love from your position of collaboration with Our heart. Bless those who have been in opposition into submission with the same unconditional love that We have lavished upon you. Son, restoration government rules and overcomes through love expressed as mercy in forgiveness. Son, forgive them for they do not know what they are doing in the darkness of their lost identity.

"Son, gather to deal with global issues and mobilise and release others to deal with local, regional and national issues.

"Son, I call you to focus on and prioritise the restoration of all things mandate with conferences, webinars and books, to see a great reformation take place in this season of great shifting and shaking. This message must go forth to captivate the hearts of the sons of God so they become oracles and legislators of Our heart to all of creation. Only those who carry the Oracles of Our heart and become living oracles will be revealed to creation because they are shining and radiating love's light as transfigured sons. Son, embrace the continual process of transfiguration to become who you are, transfigured by love to be love's light; and arise and shine with creative light as a mature son, ascended in the realms of glory, looking upon Our face, reflecting the radiance of Our express image and likeness."

I was suddenly overwhelmed by intense feelings of love through the oracles as waves rolling and breaking over me. Waves of passion, burning desire, intense joy, deep compassion, overwhelming love, unity of oneness and lavish, abundant blessing. As each wave crashed over me I felt deeply for a different aspect of creation in bondage. People of all kinds and categories in bondage to death and corruption, the fallen ones in their hopeless deception, the dimensional beings trapped in hopeless desire and deprivation, the Elementals enslaved to corrupt motivations, the groaning of the earth and the physical universe itself. I felt the pain of lost identity wrapped up in heavy hopelessness and despair but love rose in me, overcoming all the negative emotions I was empathising with in an explosion of glorious love that makes restoration inevitable. Love wins because it has always won. It is the 'deeper magic', as C. S. Lewis put it.

23 April 2020

"Son, rest; and from your position seated in the heaven of heavens, look and see the created universe and the 12 constellations you know as the cosmos or the Mazzaroth. As a group united in oneness of heart, mind and purpose this is where I am calling you to expand from. The boundary that you set is ever-increasing: so must your consciousness be, ever-enlarging and increasing in government and peace. From the outer rim of the circle of the deep, look in and declare "we are here for you" just as you have declared that from your position as guardians of the earth. This is where the restoration government administrates the restoration of all things, as all things are contained within this boundary or can be accessed from within the twelve constellations and their portals. Son, fill this sphere with your love so your songs can be the catalyst for the harmonious symphony that restoration will result in. The groaning of creation can be heard and felt from this boundary and your frequency will begin to entrain creation as your collaboration with Our heart produces a resonance that cannot be resisted. This resonant pulsing to the rhythm of Our heartbeat will release the rest of love, joy and peace so that the oneness of unity will bless the whole created order, releasing the hope of restoration to all things within its sphere.

"Son, each of you just has to be because it is in your being that this rhythm will be produced from the honour, love and unity that you are. Being, not more doing, is what creation needs in this season to bring it to rest from which restoration will begin to spread like an infection of hope through the shining of love's light. The rest of your oneness, where there is no competition, strife and enmity within your circle, will become contagious, spreading peace and ease (not disease). Son, do everything from the opposite spirit and the contradictory position by being the oracles that express Our passionate, burning and deepest desire for creation's freedom and restoration.

27 April 2020

I had a significant encounter with the Father that took me to another level of experience of how restoration is my destiny.

"Son, I, as your Father, have been preparing you for this moment, to be one of those forerunners who converge *chronos* and *kairos*, time and eternity, heaven and earth, man with creation. You have been called for a time such as this, as it is your destiny given to you before the foundation of the earth.

Son, I am well pleased with you as you have been willing to let go of the old and focus single-mindedly on the new, which is just the restoration of what was always meant to be. Your passion for restoration has developed throughout the journey of your life as the circle of the deep was aligned for the time and seasons and *kairos* moments that directed your path: your childhood love of nature, your pursuit of the unknown and desire for adventure, your unwillingness to accept the obvious, your thirst for answers to the difficult questions that We presented to you, your willingness to let go of career and embrace spirituality, your curiosity to look beyond for deeper meaning to the mysteries of creation.

Son, your journey has been an adventure that has needed the characteristics that you have been given so that you are not confined to the normal that limits others to maintain the status quo. Now is the moment for who you really are to be revealed to creation to a fuller extent, to keep the balance as this great shift shakes that which can be shaken. Son, open your heart to the greater possibilities that exist beyond the limits of reason and the quests that you have received will be expanded to reveal their full purpose. We have held back much of their true meaning, giving you only glimpses that have drawn you beyond, as you were not mature enough. Son, you have been faithful within the limitations and now the restrictions are going to be removed so you can truly go beyond beyond; that is true destiny. You have not allowed the small thinking and the social and cultural norms of others to hold you back on your pursuit of the truth, so do not allow conformation to the mundane to control your journey beyond.

"Son, ascend beyond to open the pathway for others to follow and write the books of restoration: that is to be your focus beyond the shift. Son, be comprehensive and hold nothing back as your journey moves beyond the tethering to the physical universe.

"Son, We want you to see the key milestones on your journey towards the full restoration of all things message that has become your passion."

The memories flooded my mind; the once disconnected events were now unveiled in their synchronicity. The defining moments of my choices throughout life were no random chances but carefully orchestrated opportunities to go beyond and not be conformed to the mould of normality. My choice to forego a soul mate, my choosing never to be one of the crowd, my choosing to reject the pursuit of career, my challenging religious norms, my choosing to accept the invitation to speak, my willingness to forgive the betrayals, my willingness to leave job security and lay the foundations of freedom, my refusal to be conformed to one stream, my pursuit of baptism in water and spirit despite the opposition, my choice to embrace eschatological deconstruction, my choice to reject Zionism in all its forms, my choices to actively pursue Kingdom concepts, my choice to reject study for meditation, my choice to actively pursue conversational relationship with Jesus, my choice to seek visionary experiences, my choice to leave the wilderness and cross over, my choice to have my father wounds healed, my choice to say yes to impossibilities over and over, my choices to continually go beyond my comfort zones, my choices to embrace the fire of the firestones, judgment seat, river of fire, altar, fiery sword and fiery place, my choice to reject orthodoxy, my choice to reject penal substitutionary atonement, my choice to reject the hell delusion, my choice to pursue frequency and energy, my choice to engage Metatron's Cube, the Merkabah, my energy gates, my choice to accept Enoch's quests, my choices to walk into the unknown with my Father, my choice to go beyond beyond into the dimensions, my choices to restore the fallen ones, my choice to engage the dark cloud of transformation, my choice to accept invitations to travel for conferences, my choice to engage the eternal now, my choice to accept the chancellor's seal, my choice to accept the ambassadorship, my choice to accept the court cases to the council of seventy, my choice to engage Wisdom, my choice to engage the seven spirits, my choice to accept Prudence's tools, my choice to engage the cloud of witnesses, my choice to engage the face of the Father's person, my choice to become part of regional and cosmic benches, my choice to write the book, my choice to create the 'Engaging God' programme, choosing to go it alone, choosing non-linearity, choosing the difficult paths, choosing not to play it safe, my choices to say yes against my soul's resistance, my refusal to be limited, restricted or intimidated by fear of man, my choice to reject the temptations of celebrity, materialism, position or title, my choice not to trade negatively on the floors of Tyre and Athalia, my choice to pursue relationship over advantage. All these key moments on my journey beyond towards the restoration of all things flashed before me, encouraging and inspiring me to press on towards the goal and to never go back. Beyond restoration is my destiny and that of all God's children.

28 April 2020

"Son, restoration is what is inevitable when you discover and experience the oracles of Our heart. The Oracles express Our desires and emotions towards all that We have created for a harmonious unconditional love relationship. We created all things to live in united synergy and harmony with Us and each other but independence (first in the angelic and dimensional realms and then, in the physical realm, with man) spoiled that unity, and selfishness became the overriding motivation. There was no selfishness in the beginning, just oneness; when the bonds of unity were broken and some of the 'all things' of creation separated from each other the groaning for restoration began.

"From before the foundations of creation were laid, provision was made upon that which would become the foundation stone of all creation. The offering that was the fullest extent of Our unconditional love was the antidote to selfishness, being self-sacrifice. Creation itself was established on the deeper hidden principle of love's desire for oneness, expressed by the willingness to give one's self for others. Son, no rebellion of selfish independence can ever overcome unconditional love as it is who We are.

"Son, the restoration of all things is not just something We desire to see accomplished but it is the inevitable culmination of who We are. As We are who We are, expressed in the oneness of the statement I AM that I AM, restored relationship with all that We created back to union, harmony and oneness will be.

"The sonship that is being unveiled amongst Our children is an integral part of that restoration process. When Our children rediscover their true identity and take their places alongside Us, seated in the heavenly realms, the government of Our Kingdom will and purpose will shine brightly with love's light in the glorious hope of freedom.

"The cry of freedom is resonating throughout the creation order, creating the hope that will inspire restoration. Son, as an oracle, inspire other oracles to cry freedom and legislate the message of hope to rally Our children to the restoration call.

"Love equates to restoration, as love never fails, never gives up and can never be overcome because love wins, as it has always won. We are unconditional love, so the leaven of restoration will infiltrate all of Our creation to become the all in all. Our very grace as Our divine power is already within the fabric of everything We have created, ready to be activated by the consciousness of Our sons so that the all that is already within all will become the substance and fully realised. Love is all in all to be realised as all in all becomes a reality for all within all. We are within all and all lives and exists within Us. Separation is but an illusion, for a fleeting moment within the figment of man's imagination, but that can never change or overcome the true eternal now reality of oneness that exists within the circle of Our conversation. Restoration is settled, not as an event, as some see it, but as an ever-increasing expression of Our government and peace. Peace as wholeness already exists in the eternal now of Our pure existence, therefore as We are, so shall you be: all in all."

For since by a man came death, by a man also came the resurrection of the dead. For as in Adam all die, so also in Christ all will be made alive. But each in his own order: Christ the first fruits, after that those who are Christ's at His coming, then comes the end, when He hands over the kingdom to the God and Father, when He has abolished all rule and all authority and power. For He must reign until He has put all His enemies under His feet. The last enemy that will be abolished is death. For He has put all things in subjection under His feet. But when He says, "All things are put in subjection," it is evident that He is excepted who put all things in subjection to Him. When all things are subjected to Him, then the Son Himself also will be subjected to the One who subjected all things to Him, so that God may be all in all (1 Corinthians 15:21-28).

I pray that the eyes of your heart may be enlightened, so that you will know what is the hope of His calling, what are the riches of the glory of His inheritance in the saints, and what is the surpassing greatness of His power toward us who believe. These are in accordance with the working of the strength of His might which He brought about in Christ, when He raised Him from the dead and seated Him at His right hand in the heavenly places, far above all rule and authority and power and dominion, and every name that is named, not only in this age but also in the one to come. And He put all things in subjection under His feet, and gave Him as head over all things to the church, which is His body, the fullness of Him who fills all in all (Ephesians 1:18-23).

...and there are diversities of workings, and it is the same God -- who is working the all in all (1 Corinthians 12:6 YLT).

...and have put on the new self, which is being renewed in knowledge in the image of its Creator. Here there is no Gentile or Jew, circumcised or uncircumcised, barbarian, Scythian, slave or free, but Christ is all, and is in all. Therefore, as God's chosen people, holy and dearly loved, clothe yourselves with compassion, kindness, humility, gentleness and patience. Bear with each other and forgive one another if any of you has a grievance against

someone. Forgive as the Lord forgave you. And over all these virtues put on love, which binds them all together in perfect unity. Let the peace of Christ rule in your hearts, since as members of one body you were called to peace. And be thankful. (Colossians 3: 10-15 NIV).

...with a view to an administration suitable to the fullness of the times, that is, the summing up of all things in Christ, things in the heavens and things on the earth. In Him... (Ephesians 1:10).

Chapter 2. The Oracles of the Father's Heart

In January 2019 I formed several Ambassadors' groups. In one group, while engaging heaven together for a mandate, I was standing in the holy of holies, in the 4 faces of God, in His name, in YHVH, looking through the eyes of the Ox face. Wisdom, a created being, stood in front of me and said "let me show you the oracles of the Father's heart." Wisdom opened her heart to me. I felt five intense truths that revealed the Father's heart towards all His children and all of creation. They were the depths of truth expressed as deep emotions that overwhelmed, stirred and began to motivate me.

The Oracles unveiled

These are the oracles I felt as Wisdom unveiled them to me: passion, burning desire, intense joy, deep compassion and overwhelming love. The significance of these oracles and their relationship to the restoration of all things began to unfold as the Father took me on a journey to delve into the oracles so that I could realise that as sons of God we are to be Oracles of the Father's heart within the Order of Melchizedek.

I discovered that if we are to be mature sons of God we need to understand what an Oracle is and what they carry and convey. Oracles are found in Greek mythology and the Bible and one definition is a prophet or seer. An Oracle was someone who offered advice or a prophecy that was thought to have come directly from a divine source. In the Bible, the oracle or prophet hears the words that God speaks and knows God's heart intimately.

The oracle of him who hears the words of God, And knows the knowledge of the Most High, Who sees the vision of the Almighty... (Numbers 24:16).

An oracle, therefore, was closely connected to God and released or revealed God's words and heart to people. *Massa* is the Hebrew word for oracle and means a load or burden, therefore figuratively the Oracle carries the weight of words that reflect the heart of the Father. Oracles are the weight or intensity of the word of the Father's heart that we can engage in cardiognosis, the knowledge that is absorbed in a heart to heart relationship with the Father.

Oracle in the Greek language is *logion*: that means divine response or utterances, a divine declaration, a statement originating from God that is the revelation of the heart of God expressed with meaning, feeling and weight. Therefore the oracles of God are the weight of His glory, His essence, His nature and His character expressed in words.

For though by this time you ought to be teachers, you have need again for someone to teach you the elementary principles of the oracles of God, and you have come to need milk and not solid food (Hebrews 5:12).

If we are to become mature sons, we need to embrace and live out the oracles of God so that we can connect with the experience and carry the weight of them as sons made in His image. These are the basic foundations that reveal the nature, character and essence of God as Father, Son and Spirit on which our lives are built.

In all my exploring and all my encounters with the deep things of God that were calling me deeper, there is one thing that characterises all of those experiences more than anything else: that one thing is LOVE. Therefore the oracles are expressions of love from the Father's heart. The more I get to know God as Father, the more I realise the infinite depth of His essence and being is LOVE and the more I know He loves me. The oracles are the core essence, glory or weight of the Father's heart expressed towards us and to all of creation and the foundation for restoration.

God's desire for the restoration of all things is birthed from the passion, burning desire, intense joy, deep compassion and overwhelming love of the Father's heart for all His children and all of creation. Wisdom said, "Let these oracles of the Father's heart motivate, inspire and empower you to act in LOVE".

God loves all of His children with an intensity that few have fully experienced but all eventually will, one way or another, as God directs His oracles towards all things He has created.

I had many encounters with the Father in which He directly revealed the nature of the oracles to me; some are below.

29 January 2019

"Son, I love you; now let Me fill you with My love. Feel the warmth of My embrace; let love's essence flow through your veins as a life-giving stream.

"Feel My oracles, the foundation of My relationship with all My children: My passion for you, My burning desire for you to be loved, My intense joy that you are My child, My deep compassion for you to be whole and one, My overwhelming, unconditional love that always wants to bring good to your life.

"My oracles are to be the foundation of all your relationships and should be how all our sons feel about creation and its restoration. Passion, desire, joy, compassion and love are the five oracles that must be experienced in heaven and displayed on the earth. All legislation from heaven must be motivated and inspired by My oracles for it to manifest on the earth. This is the pattern of all heavenly and earthly government and it has been the oracles that are missing from the governmental foundations.

"Only in a deep, face to face intimacy with Me can My oracles be experienced and then freely demonstrated in response. You can love because it is I who is love and have loved you first. No one can know true love apart from Me and no one can truly love without first being loved by Me. True love must be unconditional love or it is not love at all but only a very pale reflection of who I am.

"Love that is not lavish, abundantly overflowing, seemingly wastefully given and completely undeserved is not Me. Oh, how religion has turned this most amazing and wonderful truth about love and therefore about Me into the dead works of appeasement and law-driven obedience through fear. Son, know this that perfect love that is I AM casts out and removes all vestiges of fear from within relationship. All religion operates using fear as its motivating force and I AM is pouring out the wrath of love upon those trapped in fear to bring them into the glorious liberty of love.

"The passion of unconditional love is pure and will never stop in its pursuit of intimacy in a restored relationship of face to face innocence with us."

... just as He chose us in Him before the foundation of the world, that we would be holy and blameless before Him. In love (Ephesians 1:4).

He associated us in Christ before the fall of the world! Jesus is God's mind made up about us! He always knew in his love that he would present us again face-to-face before him in blameless innocence (Ephesians 1:4 Mirror).

The burning desire of unconditional love is so intense that it will be like a consuming fire that will refine and purify and consume all obstacles, hindrances, mindsets, beliefs, strongholds and religious deceptions to reveal true love.

The intense joy of the unconditional love the Father has for His children expresses the pure pride He feels for each unique individual, demonstrating how special and how wonderfully made each one is. The joy that the Father feels is revealed in the vast sum of His thoughts towards each of us, as we are each the apple of the Father's eye and the treasure of His heart. Each child is precious, appreciated and so valued that the only price that could be paid in exchange for us is His own life. His intense joy reveals the infinite worth of each individual child, far beyond any earthly measure.

...fixing our eyes on Jesus, the author and perfecter of faith, who for the joy set before Him endured the cross, despising the shame... (Hebrews 12:2).

The deep compassion of unconditional love reveals the lengths and depths and heights that the Father will go to redeem, reconcile and restore each and every child to face to face innocence. It reveals how far Jesus was willing to go to bring each child to wholeness, oneness and health by taking on the brokenness of our lost identity: physically, mentally and emotionally, in His own body on the cross, taking our death to give us resurrection life. Jesus, as Son of Man, was fully identifying with our lostness, brokenness, pain, anguish, fragmentation, separation, isolation, rejection, guilt, shame, condemnation and prejudice by representing us, becoming us and going into death and *sheol* for us.

The overwhelming nature of unconditional love will overcome and conquer everything that stands in the way of redemption, reconciliation and restoration for each of God's children: even death itself is swallowed up in resurrection victory. The Father's mercy triumphs over the judgment of the DIY law-based system that demands vengeance and retribution with lavish and abundant grace, inspired by the overwhelming, all-conquering power of His love for each of us.

"Son, My overwhelming love will conquer all things, as it will not fail and will never give up. My overwhelming love is stronger than death, is more jealous than the grave, and nothing can quench its fierce passion and burning desire for a restored relationship of face to face innocence. My love for each of My children cannot fail and cannot ever stop, any more than I can cease to be I am. Love is the atmosphere of glory, the frequency of heaven and the timeless now within the *perichoresis* circle of Our conversation. There can be no end to love: it is eternal and infinite and is expanding throughout creation with Our kingdom government and peace. Our love has no beginning and no end and is the alpha and omega, the aleph and tav, the living word and truth. Love is the fullest expression and intrinsic essence of I AM that I AM. So learn to just be loved, living in the rest of love, joy and peace."

… Love is who you are! You are not defined by your gift or deeds. (Love gives context to faith. Moving mountains is not the point, love is.) Love is not about defending a point of view; even if I am prepared to give away everything I have and die a martyr's death; love does not have to prove itself by acts of supreme devotion or self-sacrifice! Love is large in being passionate about life and relentlessly patient in bearing the offenses and injuries of others with kindness. Love is completely content and strives for nothing. Love has no desire to make others feel inferior and has no need to sing its own praises. Love is predictable and does not behave out of character. Love is not ambitious. Love is not spiteful and gets no mileage out of another's mistakes. Love sees no joy in injustice. Love's delight is in everything that truth celebrates. Love is a fortress where everyone feels protected rather than exposed! Love's persuasion is persistent! Love believes. Love never loses hope and always remains constant in contradiction. The Greek word for the love of God is *agape* from the word, *agoo*, meaning to lead like a shepherd guides his sheep, and *pao*, meaning to rest, i.e. "he leads me beside still waters." By the waters of reflection my

soul remembers who I am. [Ps 23]. God's rest is established upon his image and likeness redeemed in us. (1 Corinthians 13:2-7 Mirror).

I love to spend time in those green pastures and quiet waters, where my soul is constantly being restored. I go there every night, consciously, as I go to sleep.

Now persuasion and every pleasurable expectation is completed in agape. *Faith, hope and love are in seamless union.* Agape *is the superlative of everything faith and hope always knew to be true about me! Love defines my eternal moment!* (1 Corinthians 13:13 Mirror).

In everything you read, you can substitute the word 'love' for the word 'God' and it makes perfect sense because God is love, according to what John (known as the apostle of love) wrote in his letter:

We have come to know and have believed the love which God has for us. God is love, and the one who abides in love abides in God, and God abides in him (1 John 4:16).

Genesis 1:1 says, *"In the beginning, God..."* (God is LOVE). Creation began in LOVE because the truth is that God is love and love is proactive in reaching out to us, which is affirmed in 1 John 4:10 – ... *this is love, not that we loved God, but that He loved us and sent His Son...*

We love, because He first loved us (1 John 4:19). When we experience the love God has for us, we will be able to love Him, ourselves and others. God is actively and passionately pursuing us and wooing us to receive and experience His love.

Engaging God means engaging love and living loved, and expressing the love we have experienced as light to creation, as God is love and God is light. Creation is groaning and longing for us to reveal love's light as sons, reflecting the oracles of the Father's heart as revealed sons of God.

For the anxious longing of the creation waits eagerly for the revealing of the sons of God. For the creation was subjected to futility, not willingly, but because of Him who subjected it, in hope that the creation itself also will be set free from its slavery to corruption into the freedom of the glory of the children of God (Romans 8: 19-21).

In the Court of the Upright

To cement the reality of the link between the oracles of the Father's heart and the restoration of all things, the Father gave me an amazing encounter.

"Son, come and walk with Me." Whenever the Father says that to me, there is always a significant and life-changing revelation about to take place.

We went to the Court of the Upright and as we stood before the galleries of the cloud of witnesses, Jacob came forward and grasped my hand (never had that occurred like that before, although Jacob has often engaged me at significant milestones on my journey). Immediately there was a burst of energy: the light of enlightenment and the truth of the depths of God's love for His children filled me to bursting point.

A number of people came forward, who Jacob beckoned to me to engage.

The Samaritan woman of Jacob's well came and grasped my hand. Immediately, I felt her pain and the Father's passion for her inclusion, acceptance and restoration to relationship and intimacy. As she encountered Jesus at the well, she drank and experienced true living water; it became the fountain of wells of salvation within her. Jesus, the express image of the Father, revealed the Father to her and that experience overwhelmed all of her life experiences.

The immensity of the Father's heart overwhelmed me with a deep desire that all those stigmatised and excluded because of their lifestyle would know by personal realisation the inclusion, acceptance and belonging that was accomplished freely and unconditionally on their behalf by Jesus on the cross. I understood why passion for people and wrath against the restrictions blocking people being loved are the same word in Greek. God has poured out His wrath, not on Jesus or His children, but on every hindrance and obstacle restricting His children from their true inheritance of face to face restored innocence.

This was only the beginning and already I was emotionally wrecked by the experience. Then the Apostle of love, John, came forward; and as he held my hand, another charge of energy blasted me with the deep truth of heart to heart fellowship, deep intimacy and the passion that he felt from Jesus that transformed a fisherman into a fisher of men. I felt the burning desire he felt from Jesus that was a revelation of the Father's heart for intimacy and relationship. That burning desire transcended the barriers of the Old Covenant image of the angry God to reveal His deepest desire for the restored face to face relationship in innocence of the New Covenant.

I felt what he felt from the heart to heart, mind to mind, face to face intimacy he had with Jesus. That was where Jesus revealed to him the Father's passion and burning desire for intimacy and true connection; and that emotion just burst into my being from John, one who knew first-hand the depths that Jesus was prepared to go in love. Many images from John's writing burst into my mind. The image of Jesus knocking on the door within all who are made alive in Christ and the burning desire that all would open that door just exploded into my mind and in my heart. That was the revelation in the light that Paul experienced on the Damascus road that he described in the letter to the Galatians.

[God] was pleased to reveal His Son in me so that I might preach Him [in] the Gentiles (Galatians 1:15-16).

The word often translated 'among' in the phrase 'among the Gentiles' is '*en*', simply meaning 'in'. Paul realised that Jesus was already in Him and He was already included in Jesus through the resurrection. Paul was resisting opening the door to Jesus discipling him by kicking against the goads (symbolising the yoke of Jesus). Paul stubbornly held on to the traditions of the old covenant, even whilst Jesus was knocking on the door within his spirit, asking that Paul would let him in. That truth he would later affirm in 1 Corinthians 15:22, stating that all died in Adam but all are made alive in Christ; this is also reiterated by John in Revelation 3:20, where Jesus says "*Behold I stand at the door and knock*". That gospel, the good news of inclusion, was Paul's life's message; he went into the whole world and preached that Jesus was in the Gentiles already and just needed to be revealed by the light of truth.

Then the woman who anointed Jesus with tears and perfume stepped forward and held my hand in hers; and the light of truth burst forth with the intense joy that she felt from Jesus' love for her and His intense joy for her when she responded to His love. I sensed her deep shame as an outcast in society, shamed because of her sin and deeply embarrassed by the way the religious system had stigmatised her for her lifestyle. Yet she was welcomed by Jesus. I felt the intensity of the joy Jesus felt and how proud He was when she poured the perfume over His head and feet. He welcomed her, an outsider, into a close relationship with Him to be a disciple. I felt His joy become her joy as He overwhelmed her with the deepest intense emotions of His pride and joy that she was now one His closest friends. Jesus' feelings of intense joy so contradicted the callous, dismissive attitude of society that had marginalised and stigmatised her, causing her to be excluded and ostracised because she was a sinner in their eyes; but not so to Jesus, just a lost sheep who needed her identity restored.

This was the depth and intense joy that empowered Jesus to leave the ninety nine and pursue the one lost sheep. That one figurative sheep, representing all mankind – lost, lonely, an outsider – inspired such passion, burning desire and intense joy that Jesus was willing to go into the depths of *sheol* to seek, find and rescue all of mankind who were perishing in lost identity and restore them to the fold.

Then the leprous man who returned to thank Jesus for his healing came and grasped my hand and the deep compassion that he felt from Jesus representing the Father's heart moved me. No one would associate with a leper, or touch him, but Jesus did. Can you imagine having to go around isolated, continually calling yourself "unclean, unclean" as a constant reminder of the disease which has become your identity? Jesus identified with the leper, revealing the Father's compassion, moved by the depth of the Father's desire for healing, health and wholeness. Those emotions consumed me with passion, burning desire, intense joy and deep compassion when I felt the leper's pain, fear, brokenness and fragmentation and Jesus' compassion for him. I felt the depth of the Father's compassion for the brokenness and lost identity of all His children: it is so immense that the Father, in Jesus, took all of mankind's brokenness into Himself so all His children could be restored to innocence and wholeness and be redeemed from the curse of DIY evil.

Then Lazarus came and grasped my hand and I immediately felt the overwhelming love that caused Jesus to weep at his loss in the deception of death's grip. I felt Jesus' love for Mary and Martha and all who grieve and are sorrowful over the loss of a loved one in the illusion of separation of death. I felt His overwhelming love for all His children that motivated Him to carry our griefs and sorrows to the cross. Then the power and victory of the cross captured and captivated my heart and mind as it encapsulated the oracles of God's heart.

I felt the heavenly celebration of life that bursts forth from the overcoming of death. The power of love that is stronger than death and the joy of resurrection life that conquered death and the grave brought the realisation of the power of the oracles of God. I was moved by heaven's celebration when the keys of death and hades were restored to their rightful owner: this was and is intense and is filled with the joyful sound of freedom and jubilee: the triumphant procession of freedom, as all the chains were and are being broken and all the powers of darkness are brought into the glorious light of love.

This was in time the fullest expression of the oracles of God's heart, the verdict of the cross that redeemed and restored innocence in full reconciliation with the cry "Not guilty! Innocent!" Mercy had triumphed over judgment and the grace of justice is released in the power of the good news.

I cried out in joyous jubilation, "Arise, shine, the light of love's power has come and the glory of God's oracles is to radiate from us as the light of transfigured sons is revealed from heaven into the earth!" The sound of heaven's joy and glorious harmony, resounding to resonate on the earth, is amplified through the intensity of the oracles of God's heart.

Pentatonic scale

I had further encounters that revealed that the five oracles are connected to the earth sphere and are associated with the harmonious frequencies of the pentatonic musical scale (often associated with indigenous music).

"Son, you have a mandate for frequency ministry using the bowls and the Rife-generated frequencies but you must be prepared to go deeper into sonship frequencies and how they affect the dimensions. Sonship generates a love, joy and peace frequency from rest that has the capacity to cross the dimensional matrixes. The hope that is produced by love's light can begin to bring balance to the creation and answer its groaning for freedom. Son, learn to generate freedom frequencies from your rest that has been produced at the higher levels of consciousness.

"Son, I am continuing the deconstruction process to expand your consciousness in regards to frequency and the quantum fields. You will need to connect with the elementals that are connected to the unified quantum fields of the physical realm and then go further to engage with the elementals of other dimensions to manage frequency restoration. The elementals were designed to balance the force energy that exists as strings within the fabric of all things. They are connected to sonship's frequency of love's light and their function has been diminished by mankind's fall from Kingdom governmental position.

"Son, you can produce Rife frequencies that balance creation in preparation for the restoration of the fallen ones and dimensional beings by bringing the elementals into resonance with sonship. Son, you are generating a higher frequency of love's light when you engage the dimensions with the oracles of Our heart.

"I will give you a revelation of which frequencies represent the oracles. Each of the five key precepts of the oracles has a specific frequency range that can be generated by the hearts of sons coming to places of maturity. Those key five frequencies are arranged on a pentatonic scale and can be directed specifically through music and Rife frequencies that resonate in and through expanded consciousness states of being.

"There are different creative ways of generating the frequencies that represent the oracles: the bowls, Rife machines, tuning your body's and mind's energy field in rest.

"Son, start by using the meditation for rest to create altered states of reality that connect dimensionally for restoration through the oracle's frequencies. Then you can produce Rife frequencies that can be focused dimensionally through quantum entanglement through Our sons who are present dimensionally, once they are expanded beyond the earth sphere. Sonship becomes the conduit for the oracles of the Father's heart as five frequencies are activated within their hearts.

"Son, your drawing to the Rife frequencies is Our desire being realised in oneness and your willingness pleases Us greatly. Now pursue the shift, using the motivation of the oracles or our heart to align the restoration stream with the energy creative streams to form a unified approach.

The intervals of a pentatonic musical scale are 1, 2, 3, 5, 6.

We can tune our instruments to different frequencies: by convention most modern instruments are tuned to A=440Hz. 444Hz is higher, uplifting and good for releasing tension; and 432Hz is lower, calming, and good for grounding and peace.

The Minor Pentatonic Scale of the five Oracles are A C D E G and these are the frequencies the Father revealed to me:

A = 444Hz   Passion

C = 528Hz   Burning Desire

D = 592Hz   Intense Joy

E = 665Hz   Deep Compassion

G = 791Hz   Overwhelming Love

I have been releasing these frequencies daily in my office, using my crystal bowls, with my focused intent to engage the children of God with the true loving nature of their Father who is love.

In April 2020 I was instructed to expand the Oracles to include Unity and Blessing beyond the physical realm, to bring the hope of restoration to all the dimensions and all created beings. These oracles are also created beings that we can engage with, as I discovered when Unity came into the room during an activation at a *Restoration of All Things* conference in Colorado Springs in March 2020.

The Father took me to experience those who had encountered unity and blessing. I went to the Court of the Upright, where Jacob was waiting for me with Paul, who came and held my hand. I felt his heart, being the one who was persecuting believers – and Jesus – how that felt in light of Jesus being revealed in him. I felt the shock he felt when the realisation dawned on him that his whole life's work had been in opposition to the true reality. I felt the emotions he felt being welcomed into the family to carry the message of 'one new man in Christ'. The unity of the old being revealed in the New Covenant, his passion for unity flowed from his inclusion in Jesus. I felt his burning desire for all divisions and separations to be ended, whether of gender, race or privilege. I felt his intense joy as he saw that the middle wall of partition had been removed, revealing one new man, no separation of Jew and gentile, just all included, justified by the faith of Jesus, in the royal priesthood, holy nation and one family as one people of God.

I felt his deep compassion for those still living in the darkness of religious deception, in the bondage of the enmity and strife caused by the Judaisers, still trying to live under the law. I felt the overwhelming love he felt carrying the message of inclusion that Jesus was in the gentiles. I felt the great blessing he felt of being seated in the heavenly places in Christ, seeing from above that all the promises of God and all the covenants of God were fulfilled completely and finally in Christ Jesus, the King of kings and Lord of lords.

Then father Abraham came forward and held my hand. I felt a burst of the emotion of blessing he felt to be the father of many nations. I felt how he felt to be called and chosen out of the darkness of idol worship into the light and what he felt to leave and follow the promise of a better heavenly country and city where all the families of true earth would be blessed.

I felt how he felt to be engaged by Melchizedek, the heavenly priest, who revealed the sacrifice that was made before the foundation of the world, which inspired him to offer the promised son because he knew the blessing of restoration. I felt the blessing he felt to see Jesus' day and be glad at the gospel message going into the entire world. I felt what he felt to be given the identity of the father of the faithful so he could see all the families of the earth blessed and restored to a relationship once again. Abraham, as the father of faith, was blessed to be a blessing as a Father to all the families of creation. I felt what he felt to see in advance the good news of the fulfilment of his covenant in Jesus and the New Covenant.

Then the Father said, "Son, Our love is as limitless as We are, I AM that I AM, infinitely expanding and increasing to encompass all of creation. Our nature as love, spirit, light and fire is limitless, therefore omniscient, omnipresent and omnipotent. We are, therefore you can be; so you can experience being in the midst of the circle of Our loving conversation. Your true identity as sons can only be found within that circle of the vast sum of Our thoughts about you, expressed as love, light and fire, spirit to spirit.

"Son, learn to live from within Our being so you can be and become all of who you are from Our creative desire's perspective. Our children are more than they could ever imagine being but are limited and not limitless because of the lack of intimate cardiognosis heart reality. Son, live from within Us to become fully realised as the limitless sons you were always meant to become.

"The path of DIY independence can never produce maturity and anything it produces can never be restored. Your independent self can never be redeemed but it can be resurrected through Our death on the foundation stone of creation, expressed in time through the cross. It was appointed that every man would die: and all men did die, when We took their death. The judgment has been passed and all men have been declared innocent and included in Our resurrection. Death has been abolished as the end and life and immortality have been revealed in the love's light of truth.

"Son, the whole of creation is waiting for Our sons to be revealed and their frequency to be released through the order of Melchizedek government: royal priests and oracles and legislators, converging the heavens and the earth, time and the eternal now; carrying, expressing the five oracles of Our heart, as gateways into the earth.

The five oracles of the Father's heart relate to the freedom of the earth from its bondage but it does not stop there. The seven oracles relate to the Father's heart for the restoration of all that He created. The restoration of all things is the inevitable consequence of God's essence as love, expressed through the oracles of His heart.

Chapter 3. The Journey towards Restoration

My journey towards embracing the restoration of all things with passion was integrally entwined with my destiny but it was a long and winding road. My baptism in the Spirit in 1986 came with a challenge from God to understand the kingdom of God, which, as I was a member of a Brethren assembly, was to challenge my futurist, dispensationalist theology.

Four streams

The Father has shown me that just as the heavenly river of life flowing out of Eden, the heavenly garden, into Adam's earthly garden east of Eden split into four streams to water the earth, so there are currently four separate streams of theological thought that are converging back into one mighty river of restoration. Most people within each of those streams are ignorant and unaware of the connection that each stream has with the others and of the inevitability of their convergence. Many within each stream are currently strongly opposed to the theology of the other streams but some forerunners are being awakened to the reality of what is occurring. The four streams of revelation that have directly contributed to my revealing of restoration journey are:

- Realised eschatology
- Mystical sonship
- Christian Universalism
- Energy frequency healing.

In the past, I have fiercely opposed all of those streams with the certainty that dogmatism gives you. God, who has a great sense of humour, has delighted in systematically deconstructing my belief systems in regards to each of those streams until now I see that their convergence is as inevitable as the restoration of all things itself.

'My Journey Beyond Beyond'

I have covered that story in some depth in my book, *My Journey Beyond Beyond,* but subsequent to releasing that book I have gone beyond again and again. I need to briefly recap as I now see that that part of my journey was leading towards the passionate belief in the restoration of all things without me knowing it, through those encounters that brought me to a mystic sonship epiphany.

The four threads that were woven together to make the tapestry of my journey were:

- My journey from slavery to sonship
- My journey to see and move in the spiritual realms
- My journey through the dark cloud where my soul and spirit were separated and reintegrated
- My journey through the deconstruction and renewal of my mind towards expanded consciousness.

This journey took me deeper into intimacy with the Father than I ever thought possible and unravelled my theology. This was encapsulated in a traumatic encounter I had on one of my numerous walks with the Father, an encounter which shattered my theology.

I had many encounters with the Father in which He asked me to walk with Him. Those walks created so much cognitive dissonance within me that I could no longer continue to hold on to many of my beliefs.

Cognitive dissonance is the mental stress or discomfort experienced by a person who simultaneously holds two or more contradictory beliefs, ideas, or values, especially when performing an action that contradicts those beliefs, ideas, and values; or when confronted with new information that contradicts existing beliefs, ideas, and values. The encounters I had while walking with God challenged what I believed about Him and what I thought I knew about God was challenged by my own experiences with Him.

On this particular walk, the Father led me to a familiar place, deep in the garden of my own heart. This was the secret place of intimacy where it all began, with a tree, a swing and a little bench. Hanging in the branches of the tree was an amazingly beautiful tapestry depicting my most intimate personal encounters with God. As I looked intently at the scenes woven into the fabric, fond memories flooded back to my recollection. I noticed a small thread at the heart of the tapestry and I thought 'I wonder if this will take me deeper if I follow it.' I reached out to lay hold of the thread and the whole tapestry unravelled before me leaving a pile of yarn on the grass. God was laughing as I stood there perplexed.

He said, "You have framed all your experiences into that beautiful image; but what is an image of me?"

"An idol," I said.

"Exactly! You are leaning to your own understanding of Me that you have created from your encounters." I felt deflated but God smiled and said, "You don't need an understanding when you have a relationship of trust."

Trust in the Lord with all your heart and do not lean or rely on your own understanding. In all your ways acknowledge Him, and He will make your paths straight. Do not be wise in your own eyes... (Proverbs 3:5-7).

The Father took me on many more walks and opened up many encounters that were designed to produce the cognitive dissonance that would bring deconstruction to my mind.

Why I now believe in the restoration of all things can be summarised by the following:

- My direct conversations with my loving heavenly Father that I journal daily.
- My own testimony of intimate encounters with the Father's deep love for all that He has created.
- My encounters with the oracles of the Father's heart and the cloud of witnesses which have overwhelmingly confirmed the truth of the restoration of all things.
- My personal experiences of seeing people and beings experience restoration: God's children after their death; and other beings, both spiritual and dimensional, after they have fallen.

- The deconstruction of my religious and cultural beliefs and the subsequent renewal of my mind that transformed my understanding of the Bible, revealing how the restoration of all things is as integral a part of its meta- and micro-narratives as the story of salvation itself.

I took the red pill (the obligatory *Matrix* quote – I had to get at least one in) and the deeper the rabbit hole went, the more intimate and life-changing my encounters became and the more the restoration of all things appeared inevitable to me.

As Andre Rabe said[1], "Jesus comes to make you an atheist to the god of your own making. He comes to bring an end to your way of subjecting God to your own understanding." I have concluded that I agree with Dawkins and other well-known atheists in that I do not believe in that 'religious GOD' either.

It was only when I got to the place where my ideas and my faith were completely devastated that I could meet the God who transcends all our ideas about Him.

This is why so many church fathers and mystics have said something similar to this:

"To experience God is to experience the complete and utter failure of your own intellect" (John Crowder[2]).

I began to discover that God will not be confined to our limited, static perceptions of Him. We cannot keep an infinite God in a box made by the finite capacities of our understanding. All that will do is limit ourselves. God does not dwell in manmade temples, theological constructs or ideologies, He dwells in our spirits and our hearts; and we need to encounter Him so that we can have a transformation, a revolutionary change of mind. We need the veils of our understanding exploded and stripped away. This can only happen through our relationship with the living Word of truth, the ultimate source of revelation who searches the deep things of God and makes them known to us.

The Father once challenged me with a simple but life-changing and profound question: "How much of what you know about Me, Christianity and the Bible came directly from Me and how much came from the sermons or books of others and by your own study?" I had to confess that most of what I thought I knew to be true was just information and not personal revelation. The answer to that question opened my heart and mind for the unravelling of the beliefs that had caused me to not even contemplate the possibility of the restoration of all things. That thinking was not even on my radar, let alone in my head at the time, but that was all to change as the journey continued.

What does the Bible say?

So let us start where most people do: what does the Bible say about the restoration of all things? I personally had no real need to start there but, to make the journey accessible for others to follow, that is where we will begin.

The Greek word for restoration is *apokatastasis*, meaning 'reconstitution, restitution, or restoration to the original or primordial condition'. It is often divided into various categories: those involving individual people, the sinful powers of the soul and nature or creation. It is linked with the Greek word *pantōn*, meaning 'of all (things)'.

The concept of 'restore' or 'return' in the Hebrew Bible is the common Hebrew verb *shuv,* as used in Malachi 4:6, the only use of the verb form of *apokatastasis* in the Septuagint. This is used in the 'restoring' of the fortunes of Job and is also used in the sense of rescue or return of captives, and the restoration of Jerusalem.

The passage most commonly used to introduce the concept of *apokatastasis*, the restoration of all things, is taken from Peter's sermon as recorded in the book of Acts:

"But the things which God announced beforehand by the mouth of all the prophets, that His Christ would suffer, He has thus fulfilled. Therefore repent and return, so that your sins may be wiped away, in order that times of refreshing may come from the presence of the Lord; and that He may send Jesus, the Christ appointed for you, whom heaven must receive until the period of restoration of all things about which God spoke by the mouth of His holy prophets from ancient time." (Acts 3: 18-21).

Here is Acts 3:21 from a Greek Interlinear Bible:

ον δει ουρανον μεν δεξασθαι
hon dei ouranon men dexasthai
whom it-is-binding heaven indeed to-receive

αχρι χρονων αποκαταστασεως παντων
achri chronōn apokatastaseōs pantōn
until times of-restoration of-all(-things)

ων	ελαλησεν	ο	θεος	δια	στοματος
hōn	elalēsen	ho	theos	dia	stomatos
which	talks		the God	through	mouth

παντων	αγιων	αυτου	προφητων	απ	αιωνος
pantōn	hagiōn	autou	prophētōn	ap	aiōnos
of-all	holy	His	prophets	from	eon

Sons of God

As sons of God, we have the amazing opportunity to enter into an intimate, face to face relationship with our Creator (who is our Dad). That relationship will unveil the desires of the Father's heart to us and will lead us to the responsibility of being heirs, coheirs and co-creators. Once we have truly observed our true identity in the mirror of His face, we will be inspired by His passion for creation to pursue its freedom and restoration.

As we discover our true identity, that will enable us to take our heavenly positions, seated and enthroned, so that we can legislate the kingdom in heaven to manifest heaven on earth. It is important that we do not seek to legislate from our own understanding, so the question I asked was "what is the primary purpose of all the legislation that we do and what are we looking to accomplish?" Through my ongoing love encounters with the Father, I believe that the context of our legislation should be the restoration of all things back to God's original intent.

I embarked on a personal journey to discover the full meaning of the restoration of all things and I hope you will join me on this quest. This book and subsequent volumes will seek to discover the full scope of that restoration and what part we all as sons of God have to play in it. I love this quote from my friend and fellow truth seeker Justin Paul Abraham:

"I believe we are going to see Love overcome the greatest darkness and a new era of Light birthed across the Earth. The end result: there will be no war, no sickness and a restored world. How can we know this? The future is already agreed and when it comes it will change quickly. '*I, the Lord, will hasten it in its time.*' (Isaiah 60:22)".

I believe that the context for restoration is only truly revealed to us as we embrace our sonship, as if we are not restored to sonship – and revealed as sons – then creation will not be restored. I believe that the restoration of all things begins with Jesus working in and through our lives now, not in a future event of His coming one day in the future.

For all who are being led by the Spirit of God, these are sons of God. For you have not received a spirit of slavery leading to fear again, but you have received a spirit of adoption as sons by which we cry out, "Abba! Father!" The Spirit Himself testifies with our spirit that we are children of God, and if children, heirs also, heirs of God and fellow heirs with Christ, if indeed we suffer with Him so that we may also be glorified with Him. (Romans 8:14-17).

The original life of the Father revealed in his son is the life the Spirit now conducts within us. Slavery is such a poor substitute for sonship! They are opposites; the one leads forcefully through fear while sonship responds fondly to Abba Father. His Spirit resonates within our spirit to confirm the fact that we originate in God. Because we are his offspring, we qualify to be heirs; God himself is our portion, we co-inherit with Christ. Since we were represented and included in his suffering we equally participate in the glory of his resurrection (Romans 8:14-17 Mirror).

As God's sons there are many truths we need to be aware of to enable us to partner and collaborate with the Father's heart. These truths include the full knowledge of the scope of our coheirship and the extent of our responsibility and authority. This knowledge is vital if we are to administrate and be involved in heavenly government so that the kingdom and will of God can be manifested on earth.

What was God's mandate to mankind as His sons?

God blessed them; and God said to them, "Be fruitful and multiply, and fill the earth, and subdue it; and rule over..." (Genesis 1:28) – is this the end or the beginning?

For the anxious longing of the creation waits eagerly for the revealing of the sons of God... that the creation itself also will be set free from its slavery to corruption into the freedom of the glory of the children of God (Romans 8:19, 21).

I believe our mandate as sons (and therefore the scope of restoration) goes beyond just the earth to include all of creation. What basis do I have for believing that? My personal testimony and the Bible are my foundations. I discovered that a confirmationally biased reading of the Bible can be misleading or downright deceptive. I would encourage you to read the following Bible verses with an open mind and ask the Spirit of Truth to unveil their revelation.

A question we all need to honestly ask ourselves is: do we believe the vast sum of God's thoughts about us as His sons or are we believing the lies of an orphan spirit? I believe we all need a religious deconstruction of our minds, a transformation by the renewing of our minds, to enable us to agree with and believe what God already believes about us and what He has already done for us.

We are sons of God, called and chosen to be participators and not just bystanders and observers in the restoration process. If we are to take our places as sons of God, seated in heavenly places, then we need to know what God's overall plan and purpose are and we need that revelation through relationship, not intellectual study.

I desire for you to become intimately acquainted with the love of Christ on the deepest possible level; far beyond the reach of a mere academic, intellectual grasp. So that you may be filled with all the fullness of God! Awaken to the consciousness of his closeness! Separation is an illusion! Oneness was God's idea all along! (Ephesians 3:16-18 Mirror).

Let's celebrate God! He lavished every blessing heaven has upon us in Christ! He associated us in Christ before the fall of the world! Jesus is God's mind made up about us! He always knew in his love that he would present us again face-to-face before him in blameless innocence.

God found us in Christ before he lost us in Adam! He is the architect of our design; his heart dream realized our coming of age in Christ. His grace-plan is to be celebrated: he greatly endeared us and highly favoured us in Christ. His love for his Son is his love for us.

The secret is out! His cherished love dream now unfolds in front of our very eyes. In the economy of the fullness of time, everything culminates in Christ. All that is in heaven and all that is on earth is reconciled in him. This is how we fit into God's picture... (Ephesians 1:3-11 Mirror).

When we begin to discover our true identity and rest in our role as sons, our responsibility for creation's freedom begins to be unveiled and we will not so easily be deceived by our previous understanding. So many words in our English translations of the Bible either do not convey the full meaning of the original Greek language or deliberately hide it. There is an example of that in these verses:

"Therefore repent and return, so that the sins may be wiped away, in order that times of refreshing may come from the presence of the Lord; and that He may send Jesus, the Christ appointed for you..." (Acts 3:19-20).

The concepts that I once thought I understood by reading this passage about the need to 'repent and return so that the sins could be wiped away' were very different from what I now believe.

The word 'repent' (and 'repentance', which derives from it) is one of the most wrongly translated words in the New Testament because it takes a Greek meaning, and turns it into a Latin concept and then an English religious doctrine. The word translated 'repent' is *metanoeō* (from *metanoia*) which when broken down into its component parts (*meta*, 'with' and *nous*, 'mind') has a very different meaning. It has nothing to do with being sorry for our sins – in reality it is not concerned with the western concept of sin at all. It talks of 'the sin', not our personal sins; and that definitive 'the sin' was that of Adam and Eve, the earthly parents of mankind. The Greek word for 'sin' is *hamartia*, which is a noun, not a verb indicating behaviour, meaning 'a loss of form or image', in this case the loss our sonship identity. Therefore *metanoia* is 'with mind', agreeing with God's mind about us, so that our identity as sons can be restored.

In Acts 3:19, the word *metanoia* is linked to the word for return, *epistrephó,* which means to turn back towards, take back, turn around, turn to myself (my true self is God's truth about my identity, destiny and purpose).

The sin or the sins – fallen identity, loss of image – is and are expunged from the record through the power and victory of Jesus. Through the cross He fully identified with our lost identity, hence His cry, 'My God, my God, why have you forsaken me?' In fully identifying with us and going to the cross as us Jesus made it possible for all of mankind to have our true identity restored. How? By coming back to the face to face relationship of restored innocence that is described in the phrase *that times of refreshing may come from the presence of the Lord* (Acts 3:20). The full meaning of this phrase is again lost in the English translation. The concept of refreshing could be a cool drink or plunge into cold water but it actually means 'to breathe easily again'.

Refreshing: *anápsyksis* – properly, breathe easily (again); hence, refreshing; 'cooling' or 'reviving with fresh air'; 'A recovery of breath, a refreshing'. (Bible Hub).

When Adam awoke for the first time who did he see? He saw the face of his heavenly Father who had breathed living words – spirit – into him. That first face to face encounter is recorded in Genesis:

Then the Lord God formed man of dust from the ground, and breathed into his nostrils the breath of life; and man became a living being (Genesis 2:7).

Jesus came as the last Adam to undo what the first Adam was responsible for and to restore mankind. On the day of resurrection Jesus returned, having conquered death and taken back the keys of death and hades. When He was face to face with His disciples, who were the new representatives of mankind's recreation, He breathed on them; and hence all mankind was born from above the second time and are alive spiritually once again.

He breathed on them and said to them, "Receive the Holy Spirit." (John 20:22).

False doctrine

I was brought up with what I now see as a false religious concept that sin separated man from God. This meant that God could not look upon sin, as it offended Him, and therefore could not look at mankind. Following this warped logic to its conclusion, God turned His back on Jesus on the cross and forsook him when he took our sin on himself. Ultimately God will turn away forever from sinners who do not repent. This concept is filled with false assumptions and is not only unbiblical but contradictory to the very nature of God Himself as Love. A superb visual explanation of this false doctrine and the truth of our inclusion is presented in *The Gospel in Chairs*, a YouTube teaching by Brad Jersak[3], and I would highly recommend everyone viewing this material.

The reality is that God has never turned away from mankind. The opposite is true: it was mankind, represented initially by Adam and Eve, who hid from God and turned away to a follow a path of independence, living a Do-It-Yourself existence. God has always been the initiator to restore relationship as He did originally in the garden, where His response to their disobedience was to ask, "Where are you?" and not "What have you done?"

They heard the sound of the Lord God walking in the garden in the cool of the day, and the man and his wife hid from the presence of the Lord God among the trees of the garden. Then the Lord God called to the man, and said to him, "Where are you?" He said, "I heard the sound of You in the garden, and I was afraid because I was naked; so I hid myself." (Genesis 3:8-10).

The sin created in mankind a loss of identity and a self-created drive to earn back relationship through various religious dead works. The concept revealed in Acts 3:19-21 is God's passion and burning desire for a restoration of relationship, identity and the conditions for face to face refreshing from the presence of the

Lord that leads to a restored walking relationship with the Father's presence that itself is refreshing.

I believe that restoration does not end there with what Adam and Eve had in the garden at the beginning on earth but goes beyond; to include God's original intention for mankind, which would have been accomplished through a process of maturity; and even more restoration, to include the revelation of who we were in eternity before we came into the earth.

For man goes to his eternal home while mourners go about in the street... then the dust will return to the earth as it was, and the spirit will return to God who gave it (Ecclesiastes 12:5, 7).

Our spirit came from God and now does not need death to return to God, as the truth is, we have access to eternity now. God's presence will restore us to wholeness: spirit, soul and body; intimacy returning to where we originated – Spirit wholeness, oneness.

Now may the God of peace Himself sanctify you entirely; and may your spirit and soul and body be preserved complete, without blame at the [presence] of our Lord Jesus Christ (1 Thessalonians 5:23).

... but you were washed, but you were sanctified, but you were justified in the name of the Lord Jesus Christ and in the Spirit of our God (1 Corinthians 6:11).

But the one who joins himself to the Lord is one spirit with Him (1 Corinthians 6:17).

When and how?

I believe we can be restored to the fullness of who we were as spirit beings before we became living beings. Our eternal destiny can be restored, so we can be reconnected to who we were and can become whole again. The questions that arise from reading Acts 3:20 are when and how this restoration takes place. Does Jesus remain in heaven, waiting to come in a 'second coming' event to do all the restoring or has He already come and initiated the period of the restoration of all things, in which we are now living?

"... and that He may send Jesus, the Christ appointed for you, whom heaven must receive until the period of restoration of all things about which God spoke by the mouth of His holy prophets from ancient time." (Acts 3:20-21).

Does Jesus stay in heaven physically until a period (not an event) of restoration? This question prompts other questions! Is Jesus coming before, during or after the period of restoration of all things? When is the period? Has it already started, and if so, when?

I believe God has sent Jesus to complete the *eschaton,* the end of the Old Covenant, at the event Jesus himself prophesied in Matthew 24, that of the destruction of the temple in Jerusalem (finally fulfilled in AD70). I also believe that Jesus is continually coming to us, in us and through us and Jesus' presence as the living Word of God is, in reality, always here within us.

The period of the restoration of all things and the establishing of the kingdom of God on earth as it is in heaven was initiated with the cross, resurrection and ascension but finally established when the Old Covenant became obsolete, faded away, finally disappeared and ended in AD 70, as revealed in Hebrews 8:13:

When He said, "A new covenant," He has made the first obsolete. But whatever is becoming obsolete and growing old is ready to disappear (Hebrews 8:13).

We are now in the period of the restoration of all things and it is our responsibility as the sons of God to arise and be fully restored ourselves so that creation itself can be set free from its bondage. The process of creation's freedom by the revealing of the children of God, as indicated in Romans 8:19-21, has already begun but is a continuing process.

This poses even more questions that need to be answered. As it always seems to be with a growing intimacy in relationship with God, the more you know, the more you realise there is to know.

•   What is restoration?
•   Whose responsibility is it to see all things restored?
•   How are all things going to be restored?
•   What are the 'all things' to be restored?
•   How far back do the 'all things' go?

I will look to answer those questions and more on our journey to discover the full scope of the restoration of all things.

Chapter 4. Sonship, the Heart of Restoration

As sons, our role in this process is vital, as the Father always chooses the relational way to outwork the desires of His heart. Our relationship with our heavenly Father as sons in face to face, heart to heart and mind to mind intimacy leads us to the responsibility that relationship reveals. We are heirs of the Father's creation and have joint responsibility with Jesus the Son for creation's government – the kingdom of God.

For all who are being led by the Spirit of God, these are sons of God. For you have not received a spirit of slavery leading to fear again, but you have received a spirit of adoption as sons by which we cry out, "Abba! Father!" The Spirit Himself testifies with our spirit that we are children of God, and if children, heirs also, heirs of God and fellow heirs with Christ if indeed we suffer with Him so that we may also be glorified with Him (Romans 8:14-17).

The original life of the Father revealed in his son is the life the Spirit now conducts within us. Slavery is such a poor substitute for sonship! They are opposites; the one leads forcefully through fear while sonship responds fondly to Abba Father. His Spirit resonates within our spirit to confirm the fact that we originate in God. Because we are his offspring, we qualify to be heirs; God himself is our portion, we co-inherit with Christ. Since we were represented and included in his suffering we equally participate in the glory of his resurrection. (Romans 8: 14-17 Mirror).

So let us take our positions in the heavenly places, where we are seated in Christ; then, jointly with Christ, we can legislate the kingdom of God in heaven so it can manifest on earth. The Father's will and purpose is the increase of that kingdom government and peace through our sonship.

For I consider that the sufferings of this present time are not worthy to be compared with the glory that is to be revealed to us. For the anxious longing of the creation waits eagerly for the revealing of the sons of God. For the creation was subjected to futility, not willingly, but because of Him who subjected it, in hope that the creation itself also will be set free from its slavery to corruption into the freedom of the glory of the children of God (Romans 8:18-21).

He has taken the sting out of our suffering; what seemed burdensome in this life becomes insignificant in comparison to the glory he reveals in us. Our lives now represent the one event every creature anticipates with held breath, standing on tip-toe as it were to witness the unveiling of the sons of God. Can you hear the drum-roll? Every creature suffered abuse through Adam's fall; they were discarded like a squeezed-out orange. Creation did not volunteer to fall prey to the effect of the fall. Yet within this stark setting, hope prevails. All creation knows that the glorious liberty of the sons of God sets the stage for their own release from decay (Romans 8:18-21 Mirror).

Primary purpose

I have engaged with the knowledge of the Father's heart in intimacy and know that the primary purpose of all the legislation we do as sons is the restoration of all things. Sometimes we can be so focused, so caught up with the day-to-day individual things we are doing within our destiny, that we can miss the bigger picture of why we are doing it. We must always remember that everything functions like fractal images and we are a fractal part of a bigger picture.

As sons, we do need to look after and legislate our part as heirs within creation but let's make sure that we do not miss the key reason why we are doing it in the first place. What we are looking to accomplish when we are seated in heavenly places, both for our lives and also in a wider context, is the outworking of the Father's original desire and intention. So the context of all legislation really should be seen through the restoration of all things agenda, to restore all things created by Him back to His original intention: the wonderful, intimate relationship of the Creator with His creation.

Freeing creation

The whole economy of the world system is being restored from that which has been developed by following the independent DIY path of the tree of the knowledge of good and evil. Following that path has resulted in creation being in bondage, groaning in the loss of the identity of the sons of God. Creation has been disconnected from sonship and is in bondage to our lost identity. The restoration of our identity, position and authority as sons will free creation and bring about its full restoration. If we are not restored, then creation will not be restored; therefore deception keeps our identity hidden beneath veils of darkness. This has been our enemy's chief tactic but love's light is beginning to penetrate those veils and they are being destroyed.

As God's sons we need to know what sphere we are coheirs of so we can know the full extent of our responsibility. We can then know over what we have authority to establish the kingdom of God and restore the blessing of our sonship to all of creation.

God blessed them; and God said to them, "Be fruitful and multiply, and fill the earth, and subdue it; and rule..." (Genesis 1:28).

The earth was intended to be just the beginning, not the end, as there is no end to the increase of His government and peace. We are the sons of God, called and chosen to be participators and not just bystanders and observers in the restoration process. As we ascend into the maturity of sonship, embracing the process that was intended for Adam, we will see wonders beyond even our greatest imaginings. Creation was designed to live in union and symbiosis with the sons. Creation was never meant to be exploited by mankind, having its assets stripped, based on an economy of greed driving gross domestic production.

Economists and politicians across the globe use Gross Domestic Product (GDP) as the ultimate yardstick for measuring and ranking countries' wealth. The kingdom of God measures wealth by different criteria: fruitfulness of joy and peace, an economy of well-being. We are blessed to be a blessing: freely we have received, so freely we can give. In God's kingdom economy there is no need to compete with each other for market share because an economy of well-being is based on covenant, not competition; and, in covenant, what is mine is yours and what is yours is mine.

Family

The New Covenant that we are all included in through Jesus is based not on division and separation or nationalism but family. There is only one family, the family of mankind, in which we are all equally God's children. The restoration of family is a New Covenant theme, expressed in the removal of the walls of partition that in those days separated Jew and Gentile, male and female, slave and free. The New Covenant makes us members of one family in Christ Jesus, expressed as one new man, with no separation based on anything.

There is neither Jew nor Greek, there is neither slave nor free man, there is neither male nor female; for you are all one in Christ Jesus (Galatians 3:28).

... remember that you were at that time separate from Christ, excluded from the commonwealth of Israel, and strangers to the covenants of promise, having no hope and without God in the world. But now in Christ Jesus you who formerly were far off have been brought near by the blood of Christ. For He Himself is our peace, who made both groups into one and broke down the barrier of the dividing wall, by abolishing in His flesh the enmity, which is the Law of commandments contained in ordinances, so that in Himself He might make the two into one new man, thus establishing peace, and might reconcile them both in one body to God through the cross, by it having put to death the enmity (Ephesians 2:12-16).

In our day that would also include separation through race, colour, religion, wealth, nationality, clan, tribe, social status, class, position, education, gender, sexuality, disability, occupation or power. Social inequality and stratification is the way of the world:

"Determining the structures of social stratification arises from inequalities of status among persons, therefore, the degree of social inequality determines a person's social stratum. Generally, the greater the social complexity of a society, the more social stratification exists, by way of social differentiation." – Wikipedia.

In God's family and His kingdom, we are all equally important and division, strife, enmity caused by any form of separation is contradictory to the nature and character of God, whose love is unconditional and who is absolutely impartial. We are all children of God, included in the New Covenant, but sadly most people are unaware of that reality and live less than God intended.

For us as sons, the restoration of any inequality and injustice is fundamental to seeing God's kingdom come on earth as it is in heaven. God's plan and purpose has never changed and separation was never part of it: we need to awaken to that reality.

I desire for you to become intimately acquainted with the love of Christ on the deepest possible level; far beyond the reach of a mere academic, intellectual grasp. So that you may be filled with all the fullness of God! Awaken to the consciousness of his closeness! Separation is an illusion! Oneness was God's idea all along! (Ephesians 3:16-18 Mirror).

There was always a plan in place to deal with any separation that mankind would engineer by walking away from the Creator in independence. Restoration was guaranteed before the foundation of the world because God is love and love wins, whatever the opposition it faces.

Let's celebrate God! He lavished every blessing heaven has upon us in Christ! He associated us in Christ before the fall of the world! Jesus is God's mind made up about us! He always knew in his love that he would present us again face-to-face before him in blameless innocence. God found us in Christ before he lost us in Adam! He is the architect of our design; his heart dream realized our coming of age in Christ. His grace-plan is to be celebrated: he greatly endeared us and highly favoured us in Christ. His love for his Son is his love for us (Ephesians 1:3-6 Mirror).

God never needed to reconcile Himself to mankind because He never separated from them but because of the alienation and hostility of their own minds, mankind needed to be reconciled back to God from the illusion of separation.

The secret is out! His cherished love dream now unfolds in front of our very eyes. In the economy of the fullness of time, everything culminates in Christ. All that is in heaven and all that is on earth is reconciled in him. This is how we fit into God's picture... (Ephesians 1:9-11 Mirror).

Now all these things are from God, who reconciled us to Himself through Christ and gave us the ministry of reconciliation, namely, that God was in Christ reconciling the world to Himself, not counting their trespasses against them, and He has committed to us the word of reconciliation (2 Corinthians 5:18-19).

I believe the restoration of sonship means we can be restored to the fullness of who we were as spirit beings before we became living beings. I believe that our eternal destiny can be restored so that we can be reconnected to who we were and become whole again. The whole of creation is looking, longing, for our freedom so that it can be set free through the revealing of our sonship as ambassadors of reconciliation.

The meaning of 'restoration'

It is so important that we can fully grasp the extent and meaning of restoration. An English definition of the word is simply 'the action, act or process of returning something to a former owner, place, condition or position'. This simple definition poses many further questions.

- Who does the returning?
- Who is the former owner?
- What is the former condition and position?
- How far back does restoration go? Because of a lack of vision, many would limit this restoration to a return to the early church setting that is often viewed with rose-tinted glasses. But as you read the New Testament letters, that does not seem such a good idea for restoration after all. Others might take us back further, to Adam and Eve in the garden, walking with God as Father in heaven and on earth – but see how that story ended. Perhaps we need to take off the limitations to restoration completely and go back beyond

the fall of the covering cherub into the recesses of God's mind in eternity to discern His original intention.

The biblical definition of the word has greater connotations, far above and beyond the typical everyday English usage. It is 'to receive back more than has been lost, to the point where the final state is greater than the original condition'. The main point is that someone or something is improved beyond their current or previous measure. The full meaning and full extent of restoration go beyond anything seen before, to a perfected state of being.

Let's look at the Hebrew and Greek words and their meanings to uncover more of the story.

Chadash – (Hebrew) renew, renewed, repair, restore, restored.
Arukah – (Hebrew) restoration, recovery, repair, healing, health, perfected.
Apokatástasis (restoration) and *apokathístēmi* (to restore) – (Greek) restoration, restitution, reestablishment, reconstitution. Properly, restore back to original standing, i.e. that existed before a fall; re-establish, returning back to the (ultimate) ideal; Figuratively restore back to full freedom (the liberty of the original standing); to enjoy again, i.e. what was taken away by a destructive or life-dominating power. (Strong's).

Restoration carries an additional meaning, that of the return of a monarch to a throne, a head of state to government, or a regime to power. This begs the questions, what was man's original mandate for rulership, and is it mankind's connection to creation itself that is to be restored?

There are many synonyms for restoration that it may be helpful to consider so that we can obtain a fuller picture: reinstatement, reinstitution, re-establishment, reinstallation, rehabilitation, returning, replacing, refurbishment, reconditioning, rehabilitation, reconstruction, remodelling, redecoration, revamping, putting back, overhauling, fixing. We use many biblical words that begin with 're-' because we need a lot of 're-ing' in our lives.

Restoration as a concept includes reconciling, renewing, refreshing, repairing, rebuilding, returning, restitution, resurrecting, relationship, revelation – even resting. As children of God, we all need a cosmic makeover of eternal proportions if we are going to be gods (as Jesus framed it, quoting from Psalm 82, where the concept of being gods and being sons is linked). Of course this is not saying we are God but we are encouraged elsewhere to be godlike and godly and to pursue godliness. Psalm 8 speaks of man's creation and intended rulership as 'a little lower than God' but 'crowned with glory': surely it should be our goal to see this restored to its fullest extent?

I said, "You are gods, and all of you are sons of the Most High" (Psalm 82:6).

The Jews answered Him, "For a good work we do not stone You, but for blasphemy; and because You, being a man, make Yourself out to be God." Jesus answered them, "Has it not been written in your Law, 'I said, you are gods'? If he called them gods, to whom

the word of God came (and the Scripture cannot be broken) ... "
(John 10:33-35).

But flee from these things, you man of God, and pursue righteousness, godliness, faith, love, perseverance and gentleness (1 Timothy 6:11).

... seeing that His divine power has granted to us everything pertaining to life and godliness, through the true knowledge of Him who called us by His own glory and excellence (2 Peter 1:3).

What is man that You take thought of him, And the son of man that You care for him? Yet You have made him a little lower than God, And You crown him with glory and majesty! You make him to rule over the works of Your hands; You have put all things under his feet (Psalm 8:4-6).

We must be careful not to limit restoration by using our own logic and understanding, as they may be restricted by religion and influenced by the tree of the knowledge of good and evil. The restoration is not only of the true theocracy (God as our King) but also of the more perfect state of (even physical) things which existed before the fall and which would have existed without the fall. Even more questions to ponder!

- Where was mankind heading before the fall?
- What levels of ascension could man have aspired to?
- What was the process that would have facilitated that ascension?

Coming into maturity

In my experiences of coming into maturity as a son, I know this process has had a heavenly and an earthly component. There have been amazing encounters on the fire stones in Eden, the heavenly garden of God, that have been a springboard to growth and transformation. There were nine fire stones and I believe from my encounters that there may be nine initial levels of engagement with each of the nine stones to encourage growth and ascension to enlightenment. I also believe that there are three more stones to be formed as we ascend and mature as sons which will take our identity beyond sonship to ascended fatherhood. Twelve is the number of the full government of God and that includes man: this has been symbolised by the twelve tribes of Israel, the twelve stones on the High Priest breastplate, the twelve apostles and the twelve stones that are the foundation of the New Jerusalem, which has twelve gates that are never shut.

I believe that much truth has been perverted and twisted by man's independent knowledge and so the concept of 'nine stages of ascension' to become an 'ascended master', as found in some mystic traditions, has a foundation of truth.

The Hebrew word *ori* found in Isaiah 60:1 carries the concept of becoming light. Jesus takes this to another level with the concept of transfiguration. Restoration includes being enlightened, shining brightly, and being luminaries; *ori* is used 40 times in the Old Testament. Moses' face would shine, radiating glory, as he came from beholding the presence of God and Paul tells the Corinthians that the lasting glory of the New Covenant surpasses that fading glory. The restoration of sonship is related to a restoration of light or glory through the ascension process. This process is also indicative of the restoration of the sonship government that is to rest on our shoulders as Christ's body on earth (see Isaiah 9:6-7). The zeal of the Lord is His passion for the restoration of all things. The mountain of the House of the Lord will be raised up to function in ascension government (see Isaiah 2:2-3).

Arise, shine; for your light has come, And the glory of the Lord has risen upon you. For behold, darkness will cover the earth And deep darkness the peoples; But the Lord will rise upon you and His glory will appear upon you. Nations will come to your light, And kings to the brightness of your rising (Isaiah 60:1-3)

But if the ministry of death, in letters engraved on stones, came with glory, so that the sons of Israel could not look intently at the face of Moses because of the glory of his face, fading as it was, how will the ministry of the Spirit fail to be even more with glory? For if the ministry of condemnation has glory, much more does the ministry of righteousness abound in glory. For indeed what had glory, in this case has no glory because of the glory that surpasses it. For if that which fades away was with glory, much more that which remains is in glory (2 Corinthians 3:7-11).

For a child will be born to us, a son will be given to us; And the government will rest on His shoulders; And His name will be called Wonderful Counsellor, Mighty God, Eternal Father, Prince of Peace. There will be no end to the increase of His government or of peace, On the throne of David and over his kingdom, To establish it and to uphold it with justice and righteousness From then on and forevermore. The zeal of the Lord of hosts will accomplish this (Isaiah 9:6-7).

Now it will come about that in the last days [the last days of the Old Covenant system] *The mountain of the house of the Lord will be established as the chief of the mountains, And will be raised above the hills; And all the nations will stream to it. And many peoples will come and say, "Come, let us go up to the mountain of the Lord..."* (Isaiah 2:2-3).

As I engaged with the fire stones in Eden, each of those encounters has unveiled a precept of God that has catalysed a cycle of change in me. I have engaged the nine stones seven times over the last ten years: each time there has been deconstruction and a renewing of my mind.

The cherub covering the mercy seat or foundation stone of creation as light bearer and frequency had the role of helping mankind to ascend into maturity through the light of truth reflecting from the nine stones covering His body. The fallen cherub had a role in deceiving mankind into following the path of independence so they could become like God, but relationally apart from God. This temporarily hindered the process of ascension but Jesus came as the light of the world to destroy the works of the evil one; He overcame death and has restored mankind back to the process of ascension, so that we can arise and shine and be the luminaries to creation we were always intended to be: ascending into the light of oneness, being transfigured *Ori*, as restored sons of God.

"You had the seal of perfection, Full of wisdom and perfect in beauty. You were in Eden, the garden of God; Every precious stone was your covering: The ruby, the topaz and the diamond; The beryl, the onyx and the jasper; The lapis lazuli, the turquoise and the emerald; And the gold, the workmanship of your settings and sockets, Was in you. On the day that you were created They were prepared. You were the anointed cherub who covers, And I placed you there. You were on the holy mountain of God; You walked in the midst of the stones of fire. You were blameless in your ways From the day you were created Until unrighteousness was found in you. By the abundance of your trade You were internally filled with violence, And you sinned; Therefore I have cast you as profane From the mountain of God. And I have destroyed you, O covering cherub, From the midst of the stones of fire." (Ezekiel 28:12-16).

Fire stones

Of all the places of fire I have experienced, the fire stones have been the most powerful and influential: very significant on my journey of restoration and in my believing in the restoration of all things.

My first real experience of being taken into the heavenly realms in 2008 was to engage the fire stones, the river of fire and the throne of the Ancient of Days. My subsequent encounters have taken me deeper and deeper, both relationally into love and governmentally into sonship. In 2012 Wisdom took me back to the fire stones, beside the river of fire flowing from the throne of the Ancient of Days, and there I went into my identity and authority as a son. Wisdom gave me a Chancellor's seal and staff and introduced me to the twelve High Chancellors, who opened their houses for me to engage.

Whatever role the covering cherubim had in observing and releasing the revelation of the light contained within the nine stones of fire, concerning our maturity as sons of God, it is all fulfilled in Jesus now. Jesus as the Son, the light, is now the focus that reveals the Father for the revelation of sonship. So, according to Hebrews 12:1, we now need to fix our eyes on Jesus as the author and perfecter of our destiny as sons of God.

The fire stones contain the record of what is encoded in light, which is our identity and destiny in sonship, but Jesus is the light that encodes it. Jesus is the light of the world and we are now to reflect and radiate that light's frequency. We can all be enlightened by amazing promises such as these, which refer to our sonship associated with light and life:

In Him was life, and the life was the Light of men. The Light shines in the darkness, and the darkness did not comprehend it (John 1:4-5).

There was the true Light which, coming into the world, enlightens every man (John 1:9).

Then Jesus again spoke to them, saying, "I am the Light of the world; he who follows Me will not walk in the darkness, but will have the Light of life." (John 8:12).

...so that you will prove yourselves to be blameless and innocent, children of God above reproach in the midst of a crooked and

perverse generation, among whom you appear as lights in the world (Philippians 2:15).

Mankind was created sinless but not yet perfected. The process of perfecting was to have been a relational one as we walked with the Father and Spirit in the light of revelation released into creation. The fire stones are represented as nine steps of ascension that we can engage in our maturing as sons. 9 is 3x3, the fullness of the attributes of I AM, Father, Son and Spirit. What I have encountered and discovered through those experiences is that there are nine light strands of DNA that reveal God's nature, nine fruit of the Spirit that reveal God's character and nine precepts that reveal God's government. As we mature as sons, there are nine attributes of our sonship (which were revealed to me in a dream – one of the very few times this has ever happened to me).

Law	Walk	Blessed	Love	Righteousness
Testimonies	Observe	Established	Joy	Peace
Ways	Keep	Not ashamed	Peace	Joy
Precepts	Look Behold Seek	Righteous	Patience	Way
Statutes	Learn Understand Counsel	Thankful	Kindness	Truth
Commandments	Speak	Pure	Goodness	Life
Judgments	Meditate	Abundance	Faithfulness	Justice
Ordinances	Delight Desire Diligent	Blameless	Gentleness	Judgment
Wonders	Regard	Revived	Self control	Holiness

In that dream I was given direct revelation from Psalm 119:1-40 of nine governmental characteristics of God; and when I later read that passage, I discovered that those nine governmental truths were connected to nine responses to that truth and to nine outworkings of that truth which we are to experience (see diagram).

I believe there are nine levels of engagement with each stone.

Encountering those stones led me to engage the place where I am seated on one of many thrones alongside the throne of God. There were (at that time) nine stones to engage with, like steps ascending to the throne of the Ancient of Days, and Jesus at His right hand. That is where our thrones of sonship currently are.

The realm of Heaven, where we are seated, is the place where I can observe the physical realm and where portals are opened which connect heaven and earth through the atmosphere. There are higher realms and thrones far above this realm where Jesus is seated as the resurrected son. As we mature in our sonship and joint-heirship I believe we will eventually be seated there also.

...and raised us up with Him, and seated us with Him in the heavenly places in Christ Jesus (Ephesians 2:6).

... which He brought about in Christ, when He raised Him from the dead and seated Him at His right hand in the heavenly places, far above all rule and authority and power and dominion, and every name that is named, not only in this age but also in the one to come. And He put all things in subjection under His feet, and gave Him as head over all things to the church, which

is His body, the fullness of Him who fills all in all (Ephesians 1:20-23).

He who descended is Himself also He who ascended far above all the heavens so that He might fill all things (Ephesians 4:10).

The Father spoke to me many times about the fire stones and their relationship to sonship and the process of maturity. These are some of the things He said:

"Son, the first level of sonship reveals the emotional truth of the fruit of knowing Us intimately, and each level takes that foundation and builds upon it until My nature is revealed, which enables the fullness of My desire for Our sons to be like I am. Each level of experience and revelation builds upon love's essence to the full measure and stature of the son of God. Son, the fire stones are the stones of destiny where the fire of our DNA is encoded within the stones. The stones were created to release the light of our character and nature as the precepts that were to be reflected out into all creation to enable all to be connected to the source."

The waves of light that I experienced revealed to me the essence of pure love that, when absorbed by our spirit, will form the particles of love's manifestation within creation as the building blocks of all things. The light-bearer refused to reflect the light, choosing to create darkness by reflecting an absence of our presence. All those who followed him became darkness and introduced darkness into creation.

"My sons are called to be sons of light, to arise and shine, to restore light to creation by absorbing into themselves our image, across all spectrums and all frequencies, and releasing and radiating love's light. As My sons embrace the light of each stone at each level, it will reveal the depths and manifoldness of who We really are; and so We will be able to be revealed as the fire of transcendence converging as the immanence. The destiny of all My sons is encoded within us and can be experienced by engaging the stones of the fire of our precepts. The willingness to embrace the consuming fire of our love and be purified and refined is the precursor to engaging the stones and being able to receive the deep revelation of eternal sonship. Created and creative light will form an interference pattern and cancel each other out, leaving darkness. By engaging the fire stones you are bathing in the creative revelation light that will activate the creative light hidden within the fabric of your being and radiate from your innermost being, transforming created light back to creative light so you can radiate the glory of sonship once again.

"The created order has been separated from the creative realm and is longing to be reconnected and brought back into the harmony of the first estate from which it was removed by the choice of My son, Adam, to abandon the light of life and walk in the darkness of self. As My sons choose to walk in the creative light of their sonship, creation will again respond to love's light. Creation itself is waiting for you to arise and shine by discovering the true nature of your sonship deep within Us. Son, true ascension is not entering through the veil into the heavenly realms but is entering into Us to ascend into the maturity of your sonship.

"True ascension is becoming mature sons by embracing the nine stones at the nine levels that will add the last three stones of sonship to reach and live from the eternal now. There were always intended to be twelve stones that would take the thrones of sonship from Heaven to the place high above all authority, through the Heaven of heavens and Perfection to Eternity. This is where the speed of light is closest to the purity of eternity's perfection within the circle of love's conversation and dance. Son, this is the highest estate within the created order of the Creator that can be ascended to.

"Son, the stones of destiny will reconnect your past, present and future destiny into wholeness, remove all separation from within your being and bring clarity to your true identity and calling as My sons. Heaven is the centre, where your thrones of sonship are currently positioned, but as My sons ascend, so will the thrones ascend, to the highest place within the creative order."

The Father showed me the steps of ascension and how they relate to our identity, position and function in the different realms and stages of maturity.

Here are the realms of heaven, related to ascension, that I was shown:

Kingdom of Earth – Servants, Stewards, Friends – walking in His ways.

Kingdom of God – Lords – to govern the house.

Kingdom of Heaven – Kings – to have charge of the courts of heaven.

Heaven – Sons – to access the assemblies and councils of heaven.

Heaven of heavens – to be, and function as, kingdom coheirs

Perfection – to be, and function as, co-creators.

Eternity – to be, and function as, ascended Fathers.

The results of my fire stones encounters are more fully detailed in *My Journey Beyond Beyond* as the threads of separating soul and spirit, the deconstruction of my mind and the expanding of my consciousness, which I also shared in the six *Sons Arise!* conferences and intensives in 2018.

The second encounter I had with the fire stones was in 2012: it brought revelation about God's character and how that relates to the kingdom's governmental foundations. The kingdom foundations of God's throne or rule are righteousness and justice, expressed through the attributes of the precepts, statutes, laws and ordinances of God. This encounter was the catalyst to my first dark cloud experience and the separation and reintegration of my soul and spirit that disentangled me from being earthbound and soulish.

The third encounter I had with the fire stones was in 2013 and it took me literally into the stones to reveal a deeper level of the fruit of God's nature. That went deeper in me than just my surface emotions, touching the very fabric of my being, and this connected me to the love in God's heart for all His children.

The fourth fire stones encounter I had was in 2014 and it was very different, in that I had to access the stones by first walking through the river of fire. That encounter revealed a new level to My sonship identity and position and revealed my legislative authority: when standing on the fourth stone, Wisdom gave me a Chancellor's seal and subsequently a staff.

That chancellor's seal and staff gave me access to other governmental places that I could not access before. Wisdom took me to encounter the twelve High Chancellors' Houses; she also took me through the fiery sword door found on her heights to Satan's trophy room and that eventually opened a new level of restoration revelation. It was there that I first engaged with the place of my lost heritage of my ancestors and was incensed by all that had been robbed from my generational lines. Jesus eventually took me back there in 2016 to enter the fiery place of His consuming love via a door that was now opened.

My fifth fire stones encounter was in 2015 and that was my initial access into the essence of God's nature and government from an eternal perspective. My engagements in the eternal now of God's heart and mind that transpired were life-transforming. Those outside of time and space experiences began to create a deeper desire for the restoration of all things, even though the full implications were still hidden from me. Engaging the eternal now revealed the deep, loving connection the Father, Son and Spirit have with their creation and their desire for its restoration. My desire eventually opened up access to the eternal now, through the ancient pathway within the four faces of God on the foundation stone of creation, within the holy place of the heavenly tabernacle that we are all invited to enter.

Therefore, brethren, since we have confidence to enter the holy place by the blood of Jesus, by a new and living way which He inaugurated for us through the veil, that is, His flesh, and since we have a great priest over the house of God, let us draw near... (Hebrews 10:19-22).

My sixth fire stone encounter was in 2016: all my previous encounters were done alone but this time was different – the Father took me to the stones and walked on them with me. This took me deeper into the Father's heart and mind as preparation for the deconstruction of my mind. It began the process of unveiling new dimensional realities and revealed the fact that there will eventually be three further stones as a product of man's maturity in sonship. These further stones of sonship will make twelve stones altogether, revealing men's further ascension and providing a glimpse into the ages to come.

My seventh encounter with the fire stones was in 2018, during an activation in the first *Sons Arise!* conference. That experience began to unveil the shifts that I and others are to go through over the next few years. 2020 has been the year when these shifts have begun to come to fruition as the global shift and awakening has taken place.

As I look back now I can see how significant these encounters were as key milestones on my journey towards the restoration of all things because they took me deeper in my relationship with the Father and therefore revealed my sonship identity, both relationally and in legislative governmental responsibility. Those experiences did not produce the instant changes that most people want as all change must be relational and therefore it requires time and process for the encounters to outwork cognitively and to bring about transformation.

The fire stone encounters were not only personally revelatory but also opened up my access to engage different places and dimensions during 'my journey beyond beyond', as the Father eventually put it. My journey to discover my true identity and eternal destiny was accelerated by engaging the fire stones on His holy mountain in Eden, the garden of God.

Fire stone encounters are available to all God's children at some point on their journey to enable all of us to ascend beyond an earthbound existence to find our true heavenly identity as sons of God. I would encourage everyone to pursue the fire stones by cultivating a desire for transformation in your heart. If you do, those encounters will inevitably lead you towards your own conclusions about the restoration of all things.

A true son of God will carry the oracles of his Father's heart towards creation for its ultimate restoration and be able to be fully revealed as a representative or ambassador. As Jesus said, *"He who has seen Me has seen the Father"* (John 14:9) and I fully believe that if we become fully mature sons, we will be able to say the same.

Chapter 5. The Scope of Sonship

Some of the controversial issues that we will cover in this chapter and the next are:

The possible restoration of the fallen ones or fallen angels, other-dimensional beings and dimensions, Elementals and sentient creation, and demons. We will need to cover the origin of fallen angels, demons and unclean spirits as these terms are not synonymous, as some suppose.

I believe that restoration is personal and must be applied to the lives of all God's children individually, as well as universally to everything else that was originally created by God.

Bless those who curse you

So what do I mean by 'all God's children' and 'universally to all creation?' This declaration is at the heart of the issue that is causing so much controversy and causing some people to separate and denominate by drawing figurative doctrinal lines in the sand and excluding from relationship within their tribe those they deem to have crossed those lines.

I am sadly well aware of this excommunication as it has affected myself and many of my good friends. In writing this chapter I am not intending to dishonour those who hold a different or opposite opinion. I fiercely defend the right of all to have their own opinions; I am just saddened that the lessons of the past have not always been learned.

How many of us, if we could go back 15 or 20 years – or further – and look at our present self from that perspective of past revelation, would not call our present self a heretic? How have our beliefs changed over the years so that we now practise what in the past we thought was wrong? This is certainly true of me and is this not the process of maturity that we have all painfully gone through? How many times have we been controlled by others to maintain the status quo? How many times have people rejected and persecuted us because we pushed the boundaries of belief as we progressively journeyed onwards in the renewing of our minds?

For generations, simple believers have fought to unveil the truths of the faith that we currently enjoy, some giving their lives for baptism in water, the Bible in our own language, the priesthood of all believers, justification by faith alone. I honour all those who have fought valiantly to reveal the mystical truth of intimacy with the Father, engaging the heavenly realms and immortality, despite opposition and persecution. I refuse to argue with them; I honour them for the journey that they have made and I implore them not to keep repeating the cycle of judgmentalism by doing to those seeking the truth today what was done to them in the past. Gamaliel, a Rabbi to Paul, once gave wise counsel of which we would do well to take note and apply for ourselves:

But a Pharisee named Gamaliel, a teacher of the Law, respected by all the people, stood up in the Council and gave orders to put the men outside for a short time. And he said to them, "Men of Israel, take care what you propose to do with these men... So in the present case, I say to you, stay away from these men and let them alone, for if this plan or action is of men, it will be overthrown; but if it is of God, you will not be able to overthrow them; or else you may even be found fighting against God."(Acts 5:34-35, 38-39).

We do not have to cross every 't' or dot every 'i' of belief to be in relationship with each other, otherwise we would probably all be in a group of one. I choose to honour those on their own journey, whether that takes them towards the restoration of all things or not and want to publicly declare a blessing on those who disagree with the restoration of all things.

For those of you reading this who are journeying towards the restoration of all things, please be patient, kind and tolerant and continue to forgive, release and bless those who try to make an enemy of you. Be at peace and honour all men as best you are able and keep your heart pure from judgment and vengeance. The restoration of all things is based on the truth that God is love, light, spirit and fire; therefore to act in anger, confrontation, darkness and unforgiveness is contradictory to the precepts and essence of God's very nature that motivates our beliefs. I would encourage you heartily that if persecution comes, you heed Jesus and bless those who may be cursing you and pray for them in honour and love.

"But I say to you, love your enemies and pray for those who persecute you."(Matthew 5:44).

"But I say to you who hear, love your enemies, do good to those who hate you, bless those who curse you, pray for those who mistreat you."(Luke 6:27-28).

All means all?

What is the 'all' in 'all things'? Is it really without any caveat?

I want to share the evidence of the biblical record, church history and current testimony in regards to what the 'all' is and is not. Before going into this in-depth I want to pose the question of how we feel about the issue and explore where those feelings come from.

If I were to ask the question, how would you feel if when engaging in the realms of heaven you came across Hitler, Stalin, Ted Bundy, Epstein or anyone else you feel represents the worst of the worst of humanity, or who has personally abused you in some way, and discovered that they were now part of the great cloud of witnesses?

How does that even being a possibility make you feel right now?

Where do you think those feelings come from, God or man?

I believe the usual feelings of revulsion and injustice that the concept that 'those types' of people could be loved and accepted by God and let into heaven are rooted in the justice of the tree of the knowledge of good and evil. That system of justice is comparative, based on man's own cultural norms of acceptability. If some people deserve it and some people do not, on what is that based? Did Jesus die and take the wages of sin for all or only for some?

How would you feel if Jesus visited each one of those people on their death bed and in their dying moment they accepted His free gift of grace to receive salvation?

How would you feel if they told you Jesus went into the fire of 'hell' and offered salvation to them there?

Now let me ask you another challenging question. How would you feel if fallen angels or other dimensional beings had been offered forgiveness and restoration to their previous positions? How about the satan, the accuser, the devil, the evil one, Lucifer or whatever term you use to refer to that being (or concept)? Would the thought of his being restored to a right relationship with God and mankind repulse you?

My question would be, why you would not want the whole of creation to be set free from its bondage to corruption?

The answer for some might be connected to personal experience of being hurt or it might be associated with a theological position or doctrine which frames the narrative. The answer to those questions can only really be satisfactorily answered by God Himself, who is Father, Son and Spirit. We need the Truth, Jesus, who is the living Word of God, to reveal to us the truth of the Father's heart of love towards His creation.

God will guide us through experiential encounters with Him to discover the truth of these things; we don't need to fear being deceived as long as we are not blindly following man's DIY doctrines but are checking everything out with God ourselves. We have the Holy Spirit of Truth in us and with us as our guide, we have Jesus, the Way, Truth and Life, in us and with us to disciple us and we have our loving Father in us and with us to Father us into sonship.

I would suggest that we use love, the *agape*-type love of God's unconditional love to measure and test everything against or use as a plumb line to the truth.

I had many experiences that turned my heart towards the restoration of all things as an expression of the Father's heart rather than the eternal conscious torment or annihilation doctrinal positions.

"Son, as My oracles, release the sound and light that carries the frequency of My heart for restoration to all dimensions of the created order.

"Son, the frequency of sonship will be resonating with My passionate love for all of creation's freedom from corruption and the deception of its lost identity."

I stood on the foundation stone of all creation, within the four faces of God, on the mercy seat, and released the frequency that carries the oracles of the Father's heart into all dimensions. As I resonated with the Father's heart, my heart began to vibrate with the energy of that oneness of heart and energy which was released from my innermost being.

"Son, stand within My heart in the eternal now. Can you feel what I feel for all that I have created?" asked the Father. "You have had the revelation of the oracles of Our heart and you have experienced how others have felt having experienced Our love.

Now I desire that you know for yourself how We feel as parents to creation itself."

It was like being in a furnace of intense heat: the emotions were overwhelming, like waves of passion, burning desire, intense joy, deep compassion and overwhelming love. Wave after wave of those deep emotions rolled over me without any break, imparting the reality of love. There was an intensity of emotion that I had never felt before that held in perfect balance the transcendence and the immanence of God. I knew that there was total, complete peace (and therefore perfect rest) within the eternal now, knowing the end from the beginning and yet feeling the intense pain and deep sadness of living in the immanent moment with all of creation. The Father goes through the intense agony of feeling all His children's thoughts and feelings, moment by moment, as all things exist within God who is Father, Son and Spirit; and God (as the I AM) is present within the fabric of all things, not just mankind.

I now knew why the restoration of all things is at the centre of a loving God's desire, intention and motivation and how the oracles of God's heart are inextricably entangled with, and can never be separated from, the restoration of all things. The Father is love and love is restoration in action.

"Son, now do you know I AM that I AM, and why I will not relent until all of creation is fully and completely restored to the state of pure innocence found only within the *perichoresis*, the circle of the dance?

"Son, deep is calling you to come deeper. Come back to the fire stones for the encounter you need for the next season of grace and greater grace. There, at the fire stones, I was surrounded by Father, Son and Spirit and we walked onto the first step. I felt immersed in the love for creation, the agony and the ecstasy that cannot be separated, the quantum paradox of transcendence and immanence within I AM that I AM as love. I ascended each of the steps in turn, feeling the depth of the emotions felt by the Father for restoration. I felt all that it was possible for me to feel of what the Father, Son and Spirit feel as I AM, Their character and very essence as love. I experienced the joy and yet deep sadness, peace and yet turmoil, patience and yet concern, kindness and goodness in contrast with the immanent longing and groaning pain of creation, held in the bondage of corruption.

All Christians are Universalists

There are some things that most Christians agree on from a universal perspective so they are all Universalists in regard to these key topics:

Creation: "God created all things;" and "the destiny of all His children is to be in community and to be filled with Him…"

The 'question of restoration,' is whether or not God will manage to bring all creation to the goal for which he intended it.

The Fall: *All have sinned and fallen short of the glory of God* (Romans 3:23). But the key question is, will God allow sin to thwart his purpose?

Does Christ undo all the damage caused by it, or does He only undo some of it?

Is the victory of the cross limited and partial, or total and universal?

Redemption: Christ "represents all humans in his humanity" and "became human so he could heal us through his death and resurrection". "Jesus died for all people, to save all people."

The key question is, will the work of the cross save all those for whom Christ died, or will His death and resurrection have been in vain for some people?

For the death that He died, He died to sin once for all (Romans 6:10).

For the love of Christ controls us, having concluded this, that one died for all, therefore all died; and He died for all, so that they who live might no longer live for themselves, but for Him who died and rose again on their behalf (2 Corinthians 5:14-15)

... namely, that God was in Christ reconciling the world to Himself, not counting their trespasses against them (2 Corinthians 5:19).

God was in Jesus on the cross and in death, not separated from Him. Reconciliation was God's work in Christ and sin does not separate anyone, from God's perspective.

For Christ also died for sins once for all, the just for the unjust, so that He might bring us to God (1 Peter 3:18).

For as in Adam all die, so also in Christ all will be made alive (1 Corinthians 15:22).

The 'all' is the same in both groups: the same 'all' who died in Adam are now the same 'all' who are made alive in Christ. This was the result of the victory of the cross over sin and death. This was the power of the resurrection, that in Christ's resurrection all would be born from above of the Spirit and made alive. This was universal for all mankind and Jesus prophesied that this would be the result of His return. On that resurrection day Jesus returned in resurrection power to fulfil His promise:

"I will not leave you as orphans; I will come to you. After a little while, the world will no longer see Me, but you will see Me; because I live, you will live also. In that day you will know that I am in My Father, and you in Me, and I in you." (John 14:18-20).

Jesus came and fulfilled that universal promise made to His disciples as the representatives of the new creation, the one new man in Christ Jesus. This was not limited to those Jewish disciples alone, just as Adam becoming a living soul when the Father breathed into Him was not for him alone, but he represented all mankind. Jesus came and breathed into His disciples and all mankind was born from above and made alive in Christ as the Spirit was breathed into them.

So Jesus said to them again, "Peace be with you; as the Father has sent Me, I also send you." And when He had said this, He breathed on them and said to them, "Receive the Holy Spirit." (John 20:21-22).

124

So all mankind is alive in Christ, even if they do not all yet know it, but is restoration limited to mankind alone, or is there hope that all creation will be set free?

'Redeemed' or 'restored'

A controversy is raging over the issue of redemption versus restoration. What I am hearing from those people who oppose the restoration of all things is that we are teaching that demons can be 'redeemed'. They strongly contest this because they are concerned that people are being led astray. Sadly, some dialogue would have clarified this, as I have never heard anyone that I know teach that demons – or fallen angels, for that matter – can be 'redeemed'. The confusion can be resolved if we understand that the words 'restoration' and 'redemption' have different meanings; in which case, who can be 'redeemed' and who can be 'restored'?

Jesus came as a man, not as an angel, and that is what makes man the object of redemption, not angels and certainly not demons. Jesus, coming as the last Adam, was representing the whole of mankind as a race who carry the DNA of God, made in His image and likeness (as revealed in Genesis chapter 1). As Adam brought death to all mankind spiritually, so Jesus, as the Son of Man, brought life to all mankind spiritually. Jesus 'redeemed' or bought back mankind from its slavery to death (and some would say, paid the ransom for mankind's redemption to Satan or the devil, who had been given the keys of death and hades by Adam). Jesus conquered death and, in resurrection power, took back the keys of death and hades.

"Do not be afraid; I am the first and the last, and the living One; and I was dead, and behold, I am alive forevermore, and I have the keys of death and of Hades." (Revelation 1:17-18).

Neither angels nor demon are a race, and Jesus did not represent them as a man in the same redemptive way. Angels are individually created beings (although some function in orders) but they did not originate from one angel, as mankind did from Adam, therefore redemption cannot pass to all angels as it did for mankind. Jesus did create the angelic realm and therefore I believe His original intention for the angelic beings can be 'restored'.

Mankind was rescued from the authority of darkness by Jesus, through whom we have redemption, defined as the forgiveness of the sins, our lost identity. Through Jesus, who is the image of God, all things were also created and He holds all things together, as they were created by Him and for Him. All the things that He created were reconciled (not 'redeemed') to Himself and that includes all the things He created on earth, the physical realm, and all the things He created in heaven, the spiritual realm.

How did Jesus reconcile all things that He created? By making peace through the blood of the cross. Jesus' blood was shed even before the foundation of the world, before the fall of the angelic realm or that of man. Jesus gave Himself as an offering on the foundation stone of creation to ensure restoration would be guaranteed, even before the creation event itself. These concepts are revealed in Colossians chapter 1 and are explained excellently in the *Mirror Bible* notes.

126

Reconciliation has the concept of 'an exchange of equal value' embedded within its meaning. To reconcile: *apokatallasso*, fully restored to the original value. [Thayer definition: to change, exchange, as coins for others of equivalent value.] God, as the Father of all creation, values all of us – and creation itself – as highly as He does His son.

For He rescued us from the domain of darkness, and transferred us to the kingdom of His beloved Son, in whom we have redemption, the forgiveness of sins. He is the image of the invisible God, the firstborn of all creation. For by Him all things were created, both in the heavens and on earth, visible and invisible, whether thrones or dominions or rulers or authorities—all things have been created through Him and for Him. He is before all things, and in Him all things hold together. He is also head of the body, the church; and He is the beginning, the firstborn from the dead, so that He Himself will come to have first place in everything. For it was the Father's good pleasure for all the fullness to dwell in Him, and through Him to reconcile all things to Himself, having made peace through the blood of His cross; through Him, I say, whether things on earth or things in heaven. And although you were formerly alienated and hostile in mind, engaged in evil deeds, yet He has now reconciled you in His fleshly body through death, in order to present you before Him holy and blameless and beyond reproach... (Colossians 1:13-22).

He rescued us from the dominion of darkness (the sense-ruled world, dominated by the law of performance) and relocated us into the kingdom where the love of his son rules. (Darkness is not a force, it is the absence of light. [See Eph 4:18] A darkened understanding veiled the truth of our redeemed design from us.

2 Cor 4:4. What "empowered" darkness was the lie that we believed about ourselves! The word, *exousia*, sometimes translated authority, is from *ek*, origin or source, and *eimi*, I am. Thus, I was confused about who I am until the day that I heard and understood the grace of God in truth, as in a mirror. See 2 Corinthians 3:18, John 1:12.)

In God's mind mankind is associated in Christ; in his blood sacrifice we were ransomed; our redemption was secured; our sins were completely done away with. (The word sin, is the word *hamartia*, from *ha*, negative or without and *meros*, portion or form, thus to be without your allotted portion or without form, pointing to a disorientated, distorted, bankrupt identity; the word *meros*, is the stem of *morphe*, as in 2 Corinthians 3:18 the word *metamorphe*, with form, which is the opposite of *hamartia* - without form. Sin is to live out of context with the blueprint of one's design; to behave out of tune with God's original harmony. See Deuteronomy 32:18, "You have forgotten the Rock that begot you and have gotten out of step with the God who danced with you!" Hebrew, *khul* or *kheel*, to dance. Sin distorts the life of our design. Jesus reveals and redeemed our true form.)

In him the image and likeness of God is made visible in human form in order that everyone may recognize their true origin in him. He is the firstborn of every creature. (What darkness veiled from us he unveiled. In him we clearly see the mirror reflection of our original life. The Son of his love gives accurate evidence of his image in human form. God can never again be invisible!)

Everything that is begins in him whether in the heavenly realm or upon the earth, visible or invisible, every order of justice and every level of authority, be it kingdoms or governments, principalities or jurisdictions; all things were created by him and for him. He is the initiator of all things, therefore everything finds its relevance and its true pattern only in him. The ekklesia (church) is the visible expression (body) of which Jesus is the head. He is the principle rank of authority who leads the triumphant procession of our new birth out of the region of the dead. His pre-eminent rank is beyond threat. ("... leading the resurrection parade" – The Message)

The full measure of everything God has in mind for mankind indwells him. ("So spacious is he, so roomy, that everything of God finds its proper place in him without crowding." – The Message).

He initiated the reconciliation of all things to himself. Through the blood of the cross God restored the original harmony. His reign of peace now extends to every visible thing upon the earth as well as those invisible things which are in the heavenly realm. (The heavens, *ouranos,* a place of elevation, from *oros,* a mountain, from *airo,* to lift, to raise, to elevate, "Not only that, but all the broken and dislocated pieces of the universe, people and things, animals and atoms, get properly fixed and fit together in vibrant harmonies, all because of his death." – The Message).

Your indifferent mindset alienated you from God into a lifestyle of annoyances, hardships, and labours. Yet he has now fully reconciled and restored you to your original design. (The word, *poneros*, means annoyances, hardships, and labours, often translated as evil. [See Septuagint: tree of knowledge of good and hard labour!] To reconcile: *apokatallasso*, fully restored to the original value. [In Thayer Definition: to change, exchange, as coins for others of equivalent value]).

He accomplished this in dying our death in a human body; he fully represented us in order to fully present us again in blameless innocence, face-to-face with God; with no sense of guilt, suspicion, regret, or accusation; all charges against us are officially cancelled. (Colossians 1:13-22 Mirror).

This is the point at which I began to ask myself and the Father those questions with which I began this chapter:

- What are fallen angels and demons?
- Can fallen angels be restored?
- Can demons be restored?
- Can other-dimensional beings be restored?
- Is creation sentient? And how can it be restored?

During this process, which was quite traumatic to my soul's belief systems, I went through much deconstruction as I allowed love to be my guide.

The questions about demons and the issue of whether they can be restored prompted further questions and seeking about related subjects, including:

- Origin of fallen angels
- Origin of demons
- Origin of unclean spirits: and are they souls or spirits?

These are questions that are causing great controversy but what I discovered, as I sought the Father's heart through many encounters, was that these terms are not synonymous. I looked at the Bible, asked the Father and other angelic beings including Wisdom, and came to the conclusion that the fallen ones are angels who were deceived into following the covering cherub into rebellion; also that there are other dimensional beings from other dimensions who were also deceived to rebel from their estate and are now fallen. I do believe that such fallen ones can be restored to God's original purpose for them, as we shall see.

There are several theories of the origin and identity of what we today call demons. The 4 most popular theories are:

- That they are fallen angels.
- That they are ghosts, spirits of people trapped here on earth, unable or unwilling to pass over.
- That they are the disembodied spirits or souls of a pre-Adamic race of people who lived on the earth in the past.
- That they are inhuman or nonhuman Nephilim souls or spirits, described in Genesis chapter 6, whose bodies were destroyed by Noah's flood.

I do believe there is a distinction and a difference between the demons and unclean spirits that are mentioned in the Bible. There are several ministries that are seeking to help people by setting them free from the negative effects of unclean spirits. Arthur Burk's Sapphire Leadership Group is one such ministry seeking to deal with unclean spirits or 'Alien Human Spirits' (AHS) as they call them. They believe that they are the spirits of those who have not yet left this realm after physical death, usually because of some sort of trauma. I prefer to call them 'lingering human souls', as using the word 'alien', although technically correct, can create confusion with little green creatures from other planets.

I believe that the spirit of a person who does not yet have a relationship with their heavenly Father, through Jesus, goes back to God after physical death. A believer's spirit and soul will be reunited with the Father in the heavenly realms if they die physically.

... then the dust will return to the earth as it was, and the spirit will return to God who gave it (Ecclesiastes 12:7).

Therefore, being always of good courage, and knowing that while we are at home in the body we are absent from the Lord – for we walk by faith, not by sight – we are of good courage, I say, and prefer rather to be absent from the body and to be at home with the Lord (2 Corinthians 5:6-8).

From talking to those involved in this amazing ministry, those trapped, traumatised souls can respond to the preaching of the gospel and be helped to cross over into salvation if they respond positively. They can, of course, choose to resist the good news and their souls will end up in the consuming fire, along with others who have rejected the free gift of salvation by God's grace.

So I do not believe that demons are ghosts, neither do I believe that they are the disembodied spirits of a pre-Adamic race. It is argued that demons existed at another place and time in bodily form, but are now disembodied spirits looking for bodies to possess. This theory of disembodied spirits of some race that existed before Adam separates demons from fallen angels but I do not see evidence of this in the Bible nor has the Father talked about this to me.

I believe the theory that demons are the offspring of angels and earthly women, perhaps by genetic manipulation, best fits the evidence.

This is taken from the Genesis 6 account and the book of Enoch and is referring to the unlawful interaction between fallen angels and human women. Their offspring were called the Nephilim, human angelic hybrids which did not exist before this point. They began to mate with humans, probably by force, and began to pollute the human gene pool so that at the time of the flood only Noah himself, from the line of Seth, was genetically pure. What of Noah's wife and the wives of his children, were they genetically pure, humanly speaking?

The fact that Genesis 6 also refers to the Nephilim being present after the flood gives credence to the fact that genetically these could have been produced through the line of one or more of Noah's children; for example, Ham producing the Canaanite and other Nephilim giant races mentioned in the Bible.

I believe demons are the disembodied souls of dead Nephilim giants who perished at the time of the flood. This explanation for the origin of demons has secure links in the biblical text, although perhaps they are not obvious to most people. To an ancient reader, someone who lived during the time of the Bible, this explanation would have been quite clear.

Other ancient Jewish texts too, such as the Dead Sea Scrolls, use similar terminology to the book of Enoch. Enoch calls the giants "bastard spirits" – a phrase used of demons in several Dead Sea Scrolls. A non-biblical psalm found among the Dead Sea Scrolls calls demons 'offspring of man and the seed of the holy ones', a clear reference to the disembodied souls of the divine-human offspring from Genesis 6:1-4.

An excerpt from 1 Enoch notes that the Watchers whose transgression led to the origin of demons were to be bound 'for 70 generations underneath the rocks of the ground'. This was confirmed in the New Testament by Peter, indicating that he and the author of 1 Enoch were on the same wavelength – they both understood the original context for Genesis chapter 6:

For if God did not spare angels when they sinned, but cast them into [Tartarus] and committed them to pits of darkness, reserved for judgment... (2 Peter 2:4).

In Genesis chapter 6, God decides to remove those non-humans from the earth because 'every inclination of the thoughts of their hearts was only evil continually'. They had souls, but no human spirits, and those dispossessed souls cannot return to God but roam the earth and are known as demons.

If demons were not part of the original all things of creation then they cannot be restored, as they have no eternal spirits. Do beings exist that God did not intend or create? Can man and angels have created something God did not intend? I believe the answer to that question is a categorical 'yes', as God never intended man to create anything in independence. A friend of mine has told me that there are Hebrew mystical texts that indicate that man can reproduce demons and angels from within, either temporarily or permanently. I am not able to confirm or deny that, as I do not study those texts, preferring to engage with mysteries directly with God, the great mystery.

The logic that the 'all' of the restoration of all things must mean 'all', as in 'everything', collapses when you look at it more closely. I mean, do we believe God is going to restore all the weapons of mass destruction back to His original purpose or restore all the devices of torture and death like the guillotine, gas chambers, and rack and make them more effective?

The 'all' is the 'all' that was originally intended by the Father, all that Jesus created and was given into His hands to preserve. I do not believe that includes what we call demons, as they are the dispossessed souls of those non-human beings from the pre-flood times.

Now it came about, when men began to multiply on the face of the land, and daughters were born to them, that the sons of God saw that the daughters of men were beautiful; and they took wives for themselves, whomever they chose. Then the Lord said, "My Spirit shall not strive with man forever, because he also is flesh; nevertheless his days shall be one hundred and twenty years." The Nephilim were on the earth in those days, and also afterward when the sons of God came into the daughters of men, and they bore children to them. Those were the mighty men who were of old, men of renown. Then the Lord saw that the wickedness of man was great on the earth, and that every intent of the thoughts of his heart was only evil continually... But Noah found favour in the eyes of the Lord. These are the records of the generations of Noah. Noah was a righteous man, blameless in his time; Noah walked with God. Noah became the father of three sons: Shem, Ham, and Japheth. Now the earth was corrupt in the sight of God, and the earth was filled with violence. God looked on the earth, and behold, it was corrupt; for all flesh had corrupted their way upon the earth (Genesis 6:1-5, 8-12).

And Noah found grace in the eyes of Jehovah. These [are] births of Noah: Noah [is] a righteous man; perfect he hath been among his generations; with God hath Noah walked habitually (Genesis 6:8-9 YLT).

Is there anything else that cannot be restored? The son of perdition is the only thing the Bible specifically mentions. Jesus used the word *apōleia,* which means ruin, loss, perishing. It does not imply 'annihilation' (the root verb, *apōllymi,* means "cut off") but instead 'loss of well-being' rather than 'loss of being'. In following the DIY tree of the knowledge of good and evil, mankind lost its true identity. That lost identity meant that everything mankind has created in independence, or from receiving illegal angelic knowledge, cannot be restored. That is what Jesus was referring to when he spoke about the 'son of perdition'. What man as son or offspring created out of lost identity cannot be restored.

While I was with them, I was keeping them in Your name which You have given Me; and I guarded them and not one of them

136

perished but the son of perdition, so that the Scripture would be fulfilled (John 17:12).

The scripture that Jesus said would be fulfilled was not the lostness of the son of perdition but the restoration of all things spoken about throughout inspired writings. According to Hebrews 12:27 (quoting Haggai 2:6), all man-made things will be shaken and removed whilst only that which is of God's kingdom will remain when all things are restored:

This expression, "Yet once more," denotes the removing of those things which can be shaken, as of created things, so that those things which cannot be shaken may remain. Therefore, since we receive a kingdom which cannot be shaken, let us show gratitude, by which we may offer to God an acceptable service with reverence and awe; for our God is a consuming fire (Hebrews 12:27-29).

A literal Bible translation sheds more light on the difference between things created by God and things man has made. It is man's systems of independent self-rule that will be removed and that is the son of perdition or lost identity.

... and this – 'Yet once' – doth make evident the removal of the things shaken, as of things having been made, that the things not shaken may remain (Hebrews 12:27 YLT).

"Yet once more will I shake every unstable system of man's effort to rule himself." God clearly indicates his plan to remove the old and replace it with the new. The second shaking supersedes any significance in the first shaking. Then it was a physical quaking of the earth; now the very foundations of every man-made system was shaken to the core while the heavens were impacted by the announcement of his permanent rule on earth as it is mirrored in heaven. We are fully associated in this immovable Kingdom; an authority that cannot be challenged or contradicted (Hebrews 12:27-28 Mirror).

Judging angels

There is one further question to look at: what about fallen angels, some of which are said to be 'chained up awaiting judgment'?

Do you not know that we will judge angels? (1 Corinthians 6:3).

As this verse indicates that we will judge angels, what judgment will we deliver to them? What evidence do we use to make that judgment? If we judge them to eternal fire leading to their punishment, destruction or annihilation, what judgment will come upon us?

I believe the verdict of the cross upon us, that we have freely received, is innocent, not guilty. Will we release what we have freely received upon the angelic realm that we judge or will we withhold such forgiveness as we have received and become like the unforgiving servant of Matthew 18 who ended up in a torture chamber of his own selfish design?

"Then summoning him, his lord said to him, 'You wicked slave, I forgave you all that debt because you pleaded with me. Should you not also have had mercy on your fellow slave, in the same way that I had mercy on you?' And his lord, moved with anger, handed him over to the torturers until he should repay all that was owed him. My heavenly Father will also do the same to you,

if each of you does not forgive his brother from your heart." (Matthew 18: 32-35).

As brothers with Jesus and coheirs of a creation that we were called to rule over, and blessed to be a blessing to, are we really going to hold created beings of that creation in unforgiving judgment? I believe the restoration of those fallen angels is possible, as we shall see, but is being held back by man's negative judgment and desire for retribution rather than mercy.

For those looking to the Bible for all their answers concerning a supernatural worldview that indicates that fallen angels can be restored, what you think you know may not be so. Be careful that you are not satisfied with handed-down traditions about what is in the Bible and what is not. I would encourage everyone to go to God directly for the truth and ask the Spirit of truth to bring life, not death, from your understanding of the Bible.

What is the difference between the redemption of man through Jesus (representing mankind as the last Adam, or Son of Man, on the cross) and the restoration of other God-created beings? Jesus took on human form and DNA, not angelic DNA; therefore Jesus did not die for angels as such. The Bible is very emphatic that God became man to save mankind but redemption and salvation are different from restoration.

So should this stop us from accepting that other beings can be restored? I believe that the concepts are not necessarily mutually exclusive ideas. However, the narrative of the Bible is mankind's story, not the angels', and we only read about them in its pages when they interact with us or have a part to play in our story.

What does the nature and character of God, as revealed in the narrative of the story of the relationship of God and mankind, tell us that may be helpful in our analysis of the question we are looking at? Does God behave differently towards the various beings He created or is His character, nature and essence unchangeable towards all His creation?

Jesus Christ is the same yesterday and today and forever (Hebrews 13:8).

So when looking at the possibility of the restoration of angels we need to focus on the nature of God and see if it will be the same to angels as it is to us. What evidence is there for a contradictory view? Most often this is based on the idea of eternal conscious torment or punishment that will last forever, and this is the most-used Bible verse to prove that angels cannot be restored:

"Then He will also say to those on His left, 'Depart from Me, accursed ones, into the eternal fire which has been prepared for the devil and his angels." (Matthew 25:41).

The word *aiōnios* does not mean 'eternal' but 'age enduring'. Similar mistranslation occurs elsewhere, producing the words 'everlasting', 'forever' and 'punishment'. When the original Greek language is interpreted correctly as 'age enduring correction', it also applies to both man and the angelic realm. I will deal with this issue in depth in chapter 8.

Evidence for the restoration of all things

The absence of definitive biblical evidence, either way, is not a reason to reject the restoration of all things. There is other evidence; and the reasoning for restoration is fourfold:

- God's original purpose and intention was good
- The character and nature of God as love is good.
- Many early church fathers affirmed their belief in the restoration of all things.
- There is testimony from those who I deem reliable of the possibility of restoring fallen angels.

I believe most believers of all persuasions would agree that the *telos* (the original intention and end goal of God for creation) was good. The *telos* in Greek means 'purpose' or 'end goal', not the end of time itself, and when applied to creation and God it must be good.

Telos – from a primary *tello* (to set out for a definite point or goal); properly, the point aimed at as a limit, i.e. (by implication) the conclusion of an act or state (Strong's).

A good God would never create something for bad as that would be a contradiction of His nature. All of creation was created good. That is affirmed in the Bible, where in the beginning, creation is declared and recorded to be very good. In Revelation, the last book of the Bible, the description of a restored relationship between God and man is described as without pain or tears and therefore good.

God saw all that He had made, and behold, it was very good (Genesis 1:31a).

And I heard a loud voice from the throne, saying, "Behold, the tabernacle of God is among men, and He will dwell among them, and they shall be His people, and God Himself will be among them, and He will wipe away every tear from their eyes; and there will no longer be any death; there will no longer be any mourning, or crying, or pain; the first things have passed away." And He who sits on the throne said, "Behold, I am making all things new." (Revelation 21:3-5)

Colossians 1:15-20 says that Christ is before all things, created all things, sustains all things and, through the blood of His cross, is the means of the reconciliation of all things. God's will is not destruction and He did not create anything for destruction

Therefore, since we receive a kingdom which cannot be shaken... (Hebrews 12:28).

The kingdom and God's will are synonymous terms in Matthew 6:10 – this indicates that God's will cannot be shaken and shall remain. Was the created realm, including angels, God's will? The answer is a definitive yes. According to Romans 8:21, creation (which includes fallen angels) will be set free from bondage to corruption: that must be God's will.

Our sonship is to outwork God's will and kingdom purposes on earth as they are established and agreed in heaven; there is much evidence that this includes the restoring of fallen angels, as we shall discover. Is there any evidence beyond the anecdotal that this is possible? Perhaps in the Bible, other inspired texts or in early church fathers' writings?

The following Bible verses give us a good foundation indicating that all creation, including everyone on earth, in heaven and under the earth, will be set free and will freely worship our Creator. You cannot worship unwillingly or be forced to worship – that is a characteristic of man's nature, not God's.

... that the creation itself also will be set free from its slavery to corruption into the freedom of the glory of the children of God (Romans 8:21).

... so that at the name of Jesus every knee will bow, of those who are in heaven and on earth and under the earth (Philippians 2:10).

And every created thing which is in heaven and on the earth and under the earth and on the sea, and all things in them, I heard saying, "To Him who sits on the throne, and to the Lamb, be blessing and honour and glory and dominion forever and ever." (Revelation 5:13).

The early church fathers wrote various books to answer the questions of believers who did not all have an understanding of the Old Covenant types and shadows of the Hebrew culture. They had a wide variety of views, not always in agreement, but many affirmed their belief not just in restoration in general but in that of fallen angels.

Gregory of Nyssa (a respected figure in the history of the Church, being named 'the flower of orthodoxy' and 'father of fathers' by ecumenical council) certainly agreed with restoration.

Here are two quotes from his writings[4]:

> We certainly believe, both because of the prevailing opinion, and still more of Scripture teaching, that there exists another world of beings besides, divested of such bodies as ours are, who are opposed to that which is good and are capable of hurting the lives of men, having by an act of will lapsed from the nobler view, and by this revolt from goodness personified in themselves the contrary principle; and this world is what, some say, the Apostle adds to the number of the "things under the earth," signifying in that passage that when evil shall have been someday annihilated in the long revolutions of the ages, nothing shall be left outside the world of goodness, but that even from those evil spirits shall rise in harmony the confession of Christ's Lordship. [*On the Soul and the Resurrection*].

> He (Christ) accomplished all the results before mentioned, freeing both man from evil, and healing even the introducer of evil himself. For the chastisement, however painful, of moral disease is a healing of its weakness. [*The Great Catechism*].

There was no church creed until around at least about 500 A.D. that condemned either the belief in eventual universalism or the ultimate salvation of all fallen angelic beings.

As we will see when we look at the concepts of hell and ultimate destruction, those doctrines were mostly introduced later and were used by the religious and political state to create fear and control people.

Origen, Gregory of Nyssa, Jerome, St Isaac the Syrian and other church fathers were among those who proclaimed the final universal reconciliation of all created beings in their teachings.

Clement of Alexandria, St. Gregory of Nazianzus, Jerome, Diodorus of Tarsus, Theodore of Mopsuestia and the Ambrosiaster writings are included, with qualifications, by the *Catholic Encyclopedia* article on Apocatastasis[5], or the restoration of all things.

According to the *Catholic Encyclopedia* article, the doctrine of *apokatastasis* was formally condemned in 543 AD and thenceforth looked on as heterodox by the Church. Thereafter followed the dark ages of the next 1000-1400 years, including Inquisitions, Crusades, burning of those in opposition and their writings and widespread denial of freedoms such as freedom of religion and freedom of speech.

Do we really want to follow the "Christian traditions" which deny restoration and which bore that fruit? I, for one, do not (although for much of my life I was indoctrinated by those beliefs without even knowing it).

Apokatastasis: "A name given in the history of theology to the doctrine which teaches that a time will come when all free

145

creatures will share in the grace of salvation; in a special way, the devils and lost souls." [*Catholic Encyclopedia*].

"Origen, and Eriugena with him, underline that God will be not only in few or in many, but in all, absolutely, once both evil and death have vanished altogether... But the devil is not destroyed in his substance, which is good in that it is a creature of God, but rather his perverse will shall be abolished..." [Ramelli[6], p.792]

"Salvation surely is universal, and coincides with the universal restoration, so that it is safe to assume that for Eriugena *apokatastasis* will in fact be tantamount to universal salvation." [Ramelli[6], p.808]

"God being the absolute Good, when God is "all in all" evil has vanished altogether. For Gregory of Nyssa the eventual *apokatastasis* will be, not only the restoration of all creatures to God, who is their Father but... also and especially the Godhead's own glorious and definitive act of re-appropriation of what belongs to it, that is, all of its creatures, which were alienated by evil.

"When they all, after purification and instruction, finally reject evil, then evil – which is no being, but the result of a wrong choice – will utterly disappear.

"This is a point on which Origen, Eusebius, Gregory of Nyssa, Evagrius, Ps. Dionysius, Maximus the Confessor and other Fathers insist. Gregory depicts with special effect the final triumphal march of the Good (that is, God), which conquers all evil, from the slightest to the worst, ending up with the conquest

146

of the devil himself. Destruction of evil coincides with the transformation of all sinners and their return to the Good/God." [Ramelli[6], p.824]

Clement of Alexandria (150-215): "And 'not only for our sins,' – that is for those of the faithful, – is the Lord the propitiator, does he say, 'but also for the whole world.' ...so 'that every knee should bow to Him, of things in heaven, and things on earth, and things under the earth;' that is, angels, men, and souls that before His advent have departed from this temporal life." (*Fragments*, 1:3, c. 2, v. 2)[7].

"In the end or consummation of things, all shall be restored to their original state, and be again united in one body. We cannot be ignorant that Christ's blood benefited the angels and those who are in hell; though we know not the manner in which it produced such effects.

"The apostate angels shall become such as they were created; and man, who has been cast out of paradise, shall be restored thither again. And this shall be accomplished in such a way, that all shall be united together by mutual charity, so that the members will delight in each other, and rejoice in each other's promotion.

"The apostate angels, and the prince of this world, though now ungovernable, plunging themselves into the depths of sin, shall, in the end, embrace the happy dominion of Christ and His saints." [*Commentary on the New Testament* – Jerome[8] (347-420 AD)].

The present so-called orthodox position created by evangelicalism is a modern position which was not adopted by many earthly church fathers. Their orthodoxy is now called heretical; but which more aligns to God as love?

Colossians 1:15-20 tells us that all the invisible realm was made for Christ and is being reconciled through His cross. It would harmonize with God's character for our Good Shepherd – eventually, at some future age – to lead His rebellious angels to repentance.

He is the image of the invisible God, the firstborn of all creation. For by Him all things were created, both in the heavens and on earth, visible and invisible, whether thrones or dominions or rulers or authorities—all things have been created through Him and for Him (Colossians 1:15-16).

God's original intention in creating spiritual beings was that they would be for Him.

For it was the Father's good pleasure for all the fullness to dwell in Him, and through Him to reconcile all things to Himself, having made peace through the blood of His cross; through Him, I say, whether things on earth or things in heaven (Colossians 1:19-20).

God is love and is always good but that was not the image of God that I was brought up with in my evangelical streams. God was love but wrapped in fear and needed to be appeased by my obedience or else he would make (or allow) something bad to happen to me. That kept me in line through fear, reading my

Bible and praying every day, or feeling guilty and condemned if I did not. Thankfully those bondages fell away many years ago but the underlying mindsets were much more insidious and still framed my doctrinal thinking about GOD.

I had many encounters with God that created enough cognitive dissonance within me to renew my mind and expand my consciousness to the reality of God as a totally, 100% good God all the time.

Included in the circle

In an encounter where I was outside of time and space in the eternal now, I got a brief glimpse of God's reality. The Father said, "I want to show you My mind". I was quite excited about this opportunity, expecting to see the neurons of His mind firing off amazing thoughts. In reality, I found myself in the midst of a conversation that was continuously going on between Father, Son and Spirit. I caught glimpses of Them talking about me in loving terms that revealed their desires amongst the vast sum of thoughts they have about each of their children. The Greek word *perichoresis* is often used to describe a Trinitarian God. In English, it is often translated as 'the circle of the dance' but although that description is an accurate reflection of the loving interaction between Them, the word *perichoresis* actually comes from two Greek words, *peri*, which means 'around,' and *chorein*, which means 'to give way' or 'to make room.' A better way of interpreting the word might be 'the circle that I am included in', that is, the circle within Father, Son and Spirit where they have made room for me to dwell. What it felt like was that I was included in a circle of God's conversation about me.

Then the Father's one voice, fully representing each, said, "Let me show you how Our mind works" and for a split second I experienced the reality that God was connected to everyone that had ever lived, is living or will live in all time, all at once: around 108 billion people and counting. This connection was not a passive one but was extremely active: being connected to everyone in the now, knowing every thought, choice and decision made every microsecond; and outworking Their loving desire to bring good out of every choice, redeeming even the most stupid decisions of every person.

And we know that God causes all things to work together for good to those who love God, to those who are called according to His purpose (Romans 8:28).

Meanwhile we know that the love of God causes everything to mutually contribute to our advantage (Romans 8:28 Mirror).

This experience revealed how amazing God as love is and that love is not limited to a select group of people who love God but is extended to everyone and everything He created. This experience radically transformed how I look at and feel about people. I often used to feel frustrated by people's choices that they repeated time and time again. I was frustrated with my own choices when I failed to apply the things I knew, overcome by some inner self-destructive force. Now, having experienced God's lack of frustration and overwhelming love, seeking good for all Their children, I could not feel as I once did. God's goodness, kindness, patience and tolerance, all motivated by love, transformed my image of God once again. Grace and mercy are unconditional expressions of love from God's perspective, not needing repentance or confession of sin to spring into action, but they always triumph over mankind's DIY version of judgment and justice.

The Father spoke to me as I was reeling from the impact of what I had just experienced.

"Son, the challenge for most people is the limitlessness of everything connected to Me so they have put restrictions on Me. I AM that I AM is limitless and cannot be restricted by the mere thoughts and ideas of man's theology and doctrine. My love is limitless and cannot be diminished; neither can My grace or mercy, as this is who I am. These precepts cannot be defined by those who are not joined to Me and therefore only experience the merest fraction of the abundance of who I am.

"Son, I AM is always going to be beyond beyond even your wildest imagination. Our grace is not hyper but mega, ultra and is, in fact, limitless. Our love is not just unconditional but guaranteed and eternal. Son, unconditional love always challenges mankind's DIY religious thinking and, within the Christian community, your Old Covenant mindsets.

"Mercy does not just triumph over judgment: it *is* judgment and therefore everyone has always been innocent and justified. Son, this has never been in doubt, as it was established and accomplished in Me even before the foundation of creation.

"The restoration of all things is the nature of who I am, not something that I do. All theological systems of belief are, by definition, going to be limited by the smallness of man's thinking, aligned to the DIY tree path that causes such illusions as separation and punishment.

"I AM that I AM, as the Creator, cannot be defined by the created creatures and will always be beyond beyond beyond their inability to grasp. The created have created a god of their own understanding who is a figment of their imagination.

"Son, you are beginning to sense it and feel it but the truth cannot be defined by man's limitations and boundaries and futile attempts to systematically understand Me by leaning to their own understanding.

"Son, rest in Me and allow Me to take you beyond again and again in endless and limitless discoveries of truth, defined by love, expressed in joy and fulfilled in peace."

Destiny Robber

From 2016 to 2020 there were other encounters that I had during my deconstruction from the frameworks of my mind that expended my consciousness, changing my reality. The journey towards the belief in the restoration of all things was long and very traumatic to my previous beliefs, which were rooted in the indoctrination from the religious streams that I had participated in and in my resultant flawed understanding.

In regard to the restoration of fallen angels, this process culminated in 2019 when my procrastination was finally ended.

Despite all my encounters, I was still hesitant about engaging fallen angels, other than using the warfare method that is commonly taught and that I had myself used, such as using the sword of the spirit to chop off the heads and the tails of dragons, symbolic of removing their authority and circle of influence, and splitting open their bellies to spill out all that they had stolen.

Of course, you cannot actually kill an immortal spiritual being, however fallen they are, but you can remove their authority from your mandated spheres of influence. I had done this several times around my mountains but in 2016 I was in the realms of heaven looking down on our corporate Freedom mountain ranges, and I noticed something moving around the outer edge, so I investigated. It was a dragon-like being that I had never noticed before but it somehow exuded the air of ownership and entitlement to be there. That was irksome and stimulated me to approach the Father for insight. He said this was Destiny Robber, which made total sense, as one of our main ministry mandates is to help people find and fulfil their destiny. The Father said that there was much work to be done personally and corporately before Destiny Robber could be dealt with.

I shared what I had experienced with our Bench of Three and Bench of Seven and encouraged them to personally explore their own lives about the robbing of their destiny and what legal rights might be in place which allowed that. We then corporately did several heavenly court cases to deal with those legal rights that Destiny Robber had over us. After doing all that, no one felt confident to deal with Destiny Robber and I did not feel we yet had the mandate to remove it. This was a frustration to me, as I could see it still circling our sphere; and although its authority had been weakened, its influence was still there.

I now know why God did not allow us to remove Destiny Robber and that is the background to my journey towards restoration. The Father still had work to do with me in preparation for what was to come and I now realise that this was just one aspect of my journey beyond beyond. There were dimensional aspects of restoration that I was also being prepared for in this four year period that I will share in the next chapter.

In 2019, the Father said to me, "I am going to take you on the wildest of extreme journeys to discover who I AM really is. The five oracles of My heart that you have begun to experience are just the first baby steps on this adventure that will explore deeper places within I AM.

"I am manifold and multi-everything, with no boundaries in dimensional time or space. I AM that I AM and all that exists is but the smallest string and fractal within Me. I AM is at rest within all things and all things will come to be at rest within I AM. That is the inevitable conclusion of I AM that I AM. All things live move and exist within I AM and therefore all things will be restored to the limitlessness of My loving desire.

"The more extremes you experience, the more you will begin to understand about Our limitless, abundant, effulgent and overflowing love, expressed in limitless grace and mercy. The illusions and delusions of the DIY religious systems are but the feeblest attempts of the finite mind to understand the infinite and are going to be annihilated by love's agenda, as it is discovered in face to face restored innocence.

"The whole way that the good news is presented has been twisted and perverted by Leviathan to become bad news that undermines the reality of My character and nature. Restoration is the inevitable conclusion of I AM that I AM. All things live, move and exist within I AM and therefore all things will be restored to the limitlessness of My loving desire."

I talked with someone during the first *Restoration of All Things* conference in 2019 about their testimonies of seeing fallen angels restored and that became one of the last pieces in the puzzle for me. Now that I was prepared by that testimony the Father said,

"Son, you can deal with Destiny Robber now: you have the testimony that can restore him to his position and he can fulfil his destiny. If you choose to do this, then his position of power and influence will be released to operate within both your local and wider spheres. Son, there are two others that will need to be restored and they will form a powerful bench of three over the atmosphere to cooperate with your blueprint."

This was a process that I did not rush to embrace: it still felt like I had a choice, so I avoided going there. But throughout 2019, the Father reminded me of my responsibility towards all of creation and I continued to go through a process of transformation by the renewal of my mind. Many things were going on corporately during this period, things that needed to occur in preparation. The deconstruction of the church in favour of Ekklesia, and the deconstruction of our meetings and agendas so that we could be a gathering, continued. There was deception at the heart of the ministry that needed to be exposed and dealt with, which was a particularly difficult time for all involved. Our atmosphere must be conducive to restoration so there may need to be some preparation for all of us personally and corporately.

Eventually, the Father said more insistently, "Son, the foundations are reset: true openness, honesty and transparency are in place and deception removed, now you can engage to restore Destiny Robber. Restore the light out of darkness so the scales of deception and darkness can be removed and the pre-fall position and function be re-established."

This is, of course, the restoration of relationship and position, not redemption (which can only rescue man's lost identity). I was given some advice about how to approach this still somewhat daunting task.

"Son, offer only My love as light to bring restoration to those who were deceived by the light bearer. Son, administrate the light of love into all areas of darkness to restore the relationships lost through deception. Son, it is time to deal with Destiny Robber; others are not capable of dealing with it. Let Me show you the way to use love's light to restore those in darkness into the light of love and truth."

The Father took me to our sphere in the Kingdom of God heavenly realm and stood there with me. That gave me the confidence to proceed. I took my place on the Freedom

Mountain, I transformed my being into pure light and I began to radiate a frequency that seemed to draw Destiny Robber in, closer to the light.

It was circling inward towards the light until it eventually stood before me. I do not think it was aware of the Father's presence, though I was, as if the Father's light was shielded from its view.

I sensed the tension it felt, being that close to the light, and I released another frequency from within me, the light of hope. I did all this by instinct: it was not planned but I do believe it was inspired by what the Father had told me and by His presence that I felt.

I entered into a dialogue with it. This seemed to confuse it, as perhaps it was anticipating conflict of some sort.

I said, "I forgive you."

"You cannot forgive us. The sons have decreed that we cannot be forgiven", it replied.

"I choose to forgive you."

"No, I cannot be forgiven."

"I choose to release the Father's forgiveness to you. I decree that you can be restored."

"No, we have been told by the sons of God that there is only destruction for us."

I sensed – and began to feel – a wavering, so I released another frequency from within the light, love. I then felt an overwhelming sense of compassion, so I extended the light of my being, my spirit, to overshadow the fallen one with love's light and I released another frequency, the call to be restored.

I began to sense a deep sadness and great loss as its barriers were penetrated by my love and compassion. Then I sensed something different: hope. I felt a new desire began to rise from within it, so I reached out with love and I looked deep into its eyes and called forth its destiny as a being of light and reminded it of its pre-fall position and glory.

The scales of darkness began to fall off its body and the light started to emerge from within it. It was the most amazing and emotional experience as I sensed joy returning. So I called forth its destiny to be restored and its position to be restored. I looked deeper and saw it begin to emerge from the deception into the light of truth and its beauty began to come into view. I called forth its passion and fire and proclaimed forgiveness. I sensed the relief and heaviness lift from it. As it stood before me, still overshadowed by my spirit, I recommissioned it and ascribed to it a new name, Destiny, the Freedom Destiny Restorer.

It rose into the air before me and exploded in beauty and splendour, encompassed in light and filled with joy. I was overjoyed and rejoicing and at that moment I felt the pleasure of the Father's heart and I sensed heaven's celebration that a fallen brother had been restored.

Some might say that these beings can transform themselves into angels of light to deceive us, so I was just being deceived. To those who would make such an accusation, you have to experience this to know the validity of it and also remember that the Father was the one who instigated this encounter and that He was right there with me to protect me from any such deception. The same accusation could be made in any heavenly court case that the accusers may be lying trying to deceive us, yet we know that in the presence of the righteous judge this cannot occur.

I then released it with the freedom to access all our mountain spheres and permitted it to inspire the Joshua Generation to come forth out of the deception of the wilderness darkness into the glorious light of their inheritance in regard to the restoration of all things.

A few weeks later, after I had shared this encounter with our Bench of Seven, the Father said,

"Son, it is time to deal with the other two fallen ones who have been assigned against your blueprint. They have heard the testimony of Destiny but think it is a trap and are being deceived." So I once again asked the Father to be with me and I took my place on the Freedom Mountain where, transformed into radiant light, I called for Bondage and Disharmony, the other two beings, to come into the light.

Slowly circling, the two distorted, dragon-like beings came into view and stood before me, bathed in the light of love. I declared their forgiveness and released them from their debts but they said, "We do not believe you; this is not possible."

I repeated my declaration and in the name of YHVH offered them restoration. I sensed their feelings and a glimmer of hope. I repeated the offer and extended My light around them in love so they could feel love's light in an atmosphere that I created, filled with mercy and grace. Once again the scales of darkness began to fall off and light began to burst forth until those two radiant beings of Freedom and Harmony emerged.

I offered them their position within the kingdom and within the sphere of our blueprint, which they accepted with rejoicing. Destiny came to join them in the light and I felt a strong bond form between them and me as the process was complete. There was an overwhelming feeling of excitement and joy and a celebration of restoration in the angelic realm as they rejoiced over brothers restored from darkness to light.

God's original intention in creating the spiritual beings was for Him, as we saw from Colossians 1:15-20 – and for us – and so I now see no conflict in believing that He wants to restore them. Having experienced the joy of those restoration encounters I am convinced that it is our destiny as sons to be involved in this process.

Cosmic bench

I was doing this all on my own but there is a limit to what we can do in this way. God connected me to others and that union of hearts and minds amplified what was possible. We felt led by the Father during a corporate ascension to form what He

160

entitled a cosmic bench of three. This was in November 2019 and I now know that this was in preparation for the great shift that I had been warned to prepare for, which began to take place in 2020. This was the precursor for establishing a group of seven who would be responsible for restoration government during this shift in April 2020. As these groups became united in union of heart, mind and purpose, they opened up another level of ascension (but also opposition).

I will share some of my experiences that occurred as I was in union with others with the same heart. During time together with one of my friends on the cosmic bench, they shared how they were attacked and intimidated by three dark beings, a frightening experience that was still affecting them. During our corporate ascension, I asked the Father for a mandate to go on a fact-finding mission to find out who they were and what they were doing. The Father gave me that mandate so I went to seek them out and found them not far from the mountain of the cosmic bench. I approached them, not with anger but in an opposite spirit that seemed to confuse and disarm them. I discovered that their names were Fear of Death, Fear of Knowledge and Fear of Intimacy and that their mission was to stop the sons of God embracing their immortality, experiencing their restored innocence and discovering the truth of the restoration of all things. I withdrew from that encounter and in discussion with the others I was assigned the mandate to continue engaging with them but I sensed this would be no easy task.

On 17 December 2019 the Father spoke to me, "Son, the cosmic bench is key to the next season as it provides the government for the dimensions that need to be restored. Engage the fallen ones with honour and reveal My love for all My creation through your love.

"The restoration of all things is not My ultimate desire but it is the way My original intention for oneness can be achieved. Once all things are restored then the journey continues into the ages to come and My sons can become ascended fathers who can be like We are.

"Son, only perfect love, that is who We are, can drive out the fear that is keeping My children from their destinies. Fear of death has kept My children from enjoying life and limited them from knowing the truth of immortality.

"Son, fear of death partners with fear of knowledge to keep My children in bondage and stops them from taking their responsibilities for creation. Fear keeps creation groaning in isolation where fear of intimacy and oneness completes the vicious circle of fear's authority over My children.

"Only face to face intimacy can break the power of fear from My children but fear of the God religion has created keeps them at a distance. Restoration first begins with the truth of who We are unveiled. Love in *perichoresis* and Trinitarian truth restored leads to inclusion being revealed, as a consequence of love's passion and zeal for a relationship with our children.

"Son, there is no greater goal in this season than carrying the oracles of Our heart for restoration."

Armed with this knowledge and growing in confidence, I engaged the cosmic trio with respect that surprised them. I felt that they were caught off guard and confused.

I shared my desire for their restoration and asked how our last encounter had affected them. They were disarmed and had lost their intimidating atmosphere; they said it had confused them. I expressed the Father's love and used the crystalline sceptre to reveal the truth of mercy that triumphs over judgment. I asked them to remember what it was like in the beginning but they still had darkness over their minds. I decreed that the light of truth and love would penetrate that darkness. I expressed again that I desired their restoration and that I had forgiven them.

I knew that was all I could accomplish at that time and withdrew but I knew that these three had a different level of authority than those I had engaged before and that it would take some time to break down their resistance.

Voids

19 February

"Son, I have called you to legislate as an ambassador. Shift your focus and spend more conscious time seated in the heaven of heavens, where you will have greater insight and greater capacity. You are ready to engage with those in opposition to restoration in both the spiritual and physical realms. Love's light will shine in you and from you to illuminate your spheres of influence but will also expand beyond to remove the darkness, restoring it into the light and revealing the truth to those shrouded by darkness in their minds."

I looked to see the realm of light, so I could more easily recognise the absence of light which was operating beyond the visible wavelengths. I tuned my senses to different frequencies to detect that darkness, which was felt rather than seen. I scanned the spiritual atmosphere of the Kingdom of God to detect the voids that indicated where access portals were located. Those voids were like vacuums, pockets of darkness across the dimensions; they were drawing the light, like a magnet where opposites attract, and swallowing it up.

I detected the void associated with restoration and chose to engage it. I activated my energy gates to a greater level, creating an opposite field which matched the frequency of the void; coming with greater intensity of the opposite spirit (in this case, love's light for restoration, activated by the five oracles).

I engaged the darkness by feeling. It was like an area of sensory deprivation, with a total absence of passion, expressed as utter apathy; a complete lack of desire, expressed as a total aversion; a complete void of joy, expressed as deep depression; a total absence of compassion, expressed as severe vengeance; a total absence of love, expressed as deep hatred and fear.

Those feelings were the exact opposite of the Oracles and were a dark cloud that was keeping the message of restoration hidden – and not just hidden but opposed with such anger and hostility. I withdrew from the void, armed with the insight I needed to overcome the darkness with the frequencies of sonship, using the pentatonic scale of rotating energy fields of the Merkabah.

Mystery

20 February 2020

"Son, I have this to give you."

"What is it?"

"It is a mystery."

"Why would I need a mystery, Father?"

"Trust Me in this."

"Okay, I will receive this mystery."

The Father placed the mystery over me like a cloak or mantle and it completely shielded me from view. Absorbing illumination, it felt like an energy field that surrounded me but also a light that shines inwards. I felt wisdom and knowledge and might like I was cloaked with the seven spirits of God. I had seven eyes so I could see dimensionally. I had seven heads: an increased consciousness capacity and authority. No one would be able to fathom this, including me. I wondered if this was symbolic but it felt real, even if it looked surreal.

I thought, "I need to test it out," so, seated on my new throne in the heaven of heavens, I looked to see with seven eyes. I saw the voids but this time clearly, and how they formed a dimensional image like an inverse fractal. I went to the restoration void, passing through the shielded harmonics as if they were not even there. I spoke in a way I had never done before, able to communicate my deepest desire for restoration, forgiveness and oneness to the three who were knotted together like a Trinitarian knot. I overshadowed them within the mystery and all the light I had absorbed burst upon them, filled with love's passionate, burning desire for their restoration. The void was filled with an intensity of love's light that absorbed the darkness and there were the three most amazingly beautiful beings of light. They asked if they could stay in the mystery until they were ready. "Ready for what?" I thought/asked (because they knew what I was thinking). They answered "To be disconnected from each other to become how we were created to be, three beings but relationally functioning as one."

I said "yes," even though I would need to meditate further on what they meant.

I went back to my throne, where I could not see them but felt them, within the mystery but not within me. I had created a safe house of sorts, an underground railroad for escaping fallen ones.

In March 2020 I was participating with Nancy Coen and Lindy Strong in a *Restoration of All Things* gathering hosted by Gil and Adena Hodges in Colorado Springs. During an activation led by Lindy, we were encouraged to engage with what resonated in our hearts from a list of things the Father wanted to accomplish.

I resonated with new levels of legislation for the sons of God and I immediately began to engage with the cloak of mystery where the cosmic trio of restored fallen angels were safely residing.

They were once Fear of Death, Fear of Intimacy and Fear of Knowledge but are now known as Abundant Life, Deep Intimacy and Revealed Truth. I began to engage with them to partner in legislation and began to make some decrees and declarations.

– I call you forth at this time of fear and darkness to come out of the mystery into the light.

– I commission you to bring life and immortality to light.

– I commission you to release love's light to shine and overcome the darkness of fear.

– I commission you to reveal perfect love in deep intimacy to cast out all fear.

– I commission you to release the truth to counteract all fake and false news.

– I release you into the light of truth and authorise you to unveil the things hidden in darkness.

– On behalf of the cosmic bench, I authorise you to arise and shine love's light to cancel the fear of death, to cancel the fear of intimacy, to cancel the deception of hidden knowledge.

– I call for you to unveil and release knowledge that has been hidden through fear into the light of truth.

– I call for the legions of the heavenly host to radiate love, life and truth to turn the tide and tip the balance; to inspire the children of God to rise up in sonship and shine love's light into the world to counteract fear and remove darkness.

– I call for Destiny, Freedom and Harmony (three restored fallen angels) to come into agreement to inspire the sons of God to legislate at a new level.

This was a precursor to the engagements I would later have with the restoration government group, as the union of heart mind and purpose I felt being part of that group enhanced and amplified the individual authority that I carry towards creation and greatly increased my ability to engage with the fallen realm and restore them.

Restoration Government Engagement

April 15th 2020

I engaged with Unity, Wisdom and Prudence; they spoke with one voice and stated that this is a time of alignment and convergence of time and the eternal now, heaven and earth. This is alignment with the Father's heart to reveal His precepts (heart), statutes (mind) and laws (voice) to release the ordinances of heaven as scrolls, mandates and strategies. They invited us to engage the twelve High Chancellors and enter their houses (Precepts, Statutes, Laws, Ordinances, Mantles, Weapons, Scrolls, Discoveries, Commissioning, Culture, Affairs of the Nations, and Treasury). We have been invited to align the twelve High Chancellors' houses around the circle of the deep to the times and seasons of Judgment, Justice, Grace, Mercy and Rest. We are called to be Oracles who carry the oracles of the Father's heart and legislate from rest.

They gave me a scroll entitled *Restoration Government - Collaboration with the Father's Heart*. On it was written, "Join together in unity of heart and mind and become strong by the merging of your hearts together, where each one has a part to play; just as a body is one, with parts having different functions."

Unity said "Mobilise globally and release people into their identity and positions and empower their mandates with honour and love in unity, operating in the opposite spirit from the opposition that you face."

This union with a group of six other people of like mind felt like we had been brought together for a time such as this to help administrate the shift and global awakening of the consciousness of sonship. My continued engagements, although done individually, felt like I was always connected to the others in the spirit. In fact, on that first ascension together, the Father asked us to commit to stay connected and actively engage with each other daily. The Father asked us to be part of a shield He was creating around the earth to protect it from external cosmic dimensional interference during this shift. The results and benefits of this union have continued, escalated and resulted in some amazing encounters. I shared some of these with you in the first chapter; here are some further examples.

On the 16th April 2020, during an encounter, the Father said, "Son, as you function as collaborators with Our hearts in unity you will pulsate with the rhythm of Our beating heart. As you are in oneness with Our heart you will expand to become that shield around the earth, continuously energised by that unity

169

and oneness. Unity continually infuses you with the knowledge of Our heart, from which you act as one.

Your mandate for restoration government authorises you to be the shield that protects the earth from outside influences but the priority is to turn to look into the earth sphere and, from your positions and thrones around the earth, to release the sound by being the oracles and legislators of Our heart. You all carry the frequency of sonship for restoration: focus that merged and combined energy to target the specific obstacles and hindrances to restoration that We will show you, heart to heart.

Son, remember this is not warfare, this is the exercise of governmental authority with honour, love and unity that will enable you to operate in the opposite spirit to that which opposes restoration.

Global awakening

On the 29th of April 2020, during another encounter, the Father said, "Son, globalisation is the counterfeit of true family which provides mutual support and encouragement through covenant. Globalisation has left local communities and countries vulnerable to manipulation and control because of greed and exploits the weak. Globalisation has played into the hands of those cabals and corporations who seek to control the world through their humanistic agendas.

"Son, it is time to restore family to the earth, whose purpose is peace and wellbeing, not profit and greed. It is time to reconnect people with the creation in a symbiotic union that was to be harmonious and bountiful. Creation is longing, waiting for a restored relationship, where it is not being asset-stripped and exploited. It is time that Our sons arise and restore Kingdom government as the DIY systems begin to crumble and fall as they are shaken.

"Son, prioritise the targets by seeking Our heart together in unity with pure hearts, seeking only to do Our will. Lay down your agendas and take up a more noble cause through Wisdom's pillars, according to the ancient paths. Portals of opportunity are opening to focus heaven's frequency into the earth to bring great change. It is time for a peaceful revolution to take place as the great shift turns the hearts of Our children back to Us, as they begin to seek security and peace in the midst of turmoil.

"It is time for the sons of God to unite and decree 'Peace, be still' to the chaotic systems that have failed so that they can be removed without war. It is time for peaceful overthrows to bring an end to systems exploiting the world and Our children for their selfish purposes.

"Son, call for Our children to rise up and shake off the oppressive tyranny they have willingly submitted to. Son, call for global peaceful protests against the oppressions they have submitted to. Call for their eyes to be opened to the light of truth to bring them a realisation and consciousness awakening to the evils of globalisation and its negative effects on their well-being. It is time to free Our children from their slavery to global systems of the false economic machine. It is time to expose the matrix of exploitation and control, to end the illusion and reveal the delusion of following the DIY tree path.

"Mobilise the counter-culture to infiltrate and leaven the world systems with an infection of the true Kingdom ideology of righteousness and justice. Call for this global awakening to the oppression of the control systems of the tree of the knowledge of good and evil. It is time for the mountain of the house of the Lord to arise out of the wilderness to shine love's light to expose the mountains that have made a name for themselves. The independent path of the tree of the knowledge of good and evil is doomed to inevitable failure, so legislate to hasten its end. Release the frequency of hope to turn Our children from darkness to follow the sound and the light, to be drawn to the mountain of the House of the Lord. Let the sound of the cry for freedom resonate throughout creation so they are drawn to the light of love shining from the city on the hill.

"Son, it is time for the true God to arise in a global awakening to Our true loving identity so your enemies can be scattered and confused as at Babel. It is the mountain of the House of the Lord and the name of YHVH that is to be lifted up, not the names of individual ministry mountains. It is true unity that commands the blessing: all the counterfeits of unity must be exposed in the light of love shining from the true heavenly mountain of Zion."

Punisher generals

On 30th April 2020, during another encounter, I engaged within the cloak of mystery with three Punisher generals. These beings had previously been revealed during a restoration government group ascension in which we saw three ways they could be engaged and untethered from their past: untethered with soft words of persuasion, unbuckled and divided with a sword.

They said, "We have seen the unity that you carry together and the love and honour that you function in, so we are willing to listen to what you have to say."

I asked "What do you fear?"

They replied, "We represent so many that are responsible for so much misery and deprivation, who are part of the systems of your world. If we were to turn from our positions we would be greatly at risk of reprisals from the sons of men and our own kind. We have influence within these systems but we are not in control: there are others higher than us, and those who you are shielding us from: they are to be feared, as are those who control them."

"I am not afraid," I responded, "and we are in unity of heart, mind and purpose assigned by your Creator, whom we represent. It is the will of the Creator that we are here for you and we have our Father's mandate for the government of restoration. We have authority for you to be restored, as we have chosen to forgive you and release you from what you have done. I have personal, delegated authority as an ambassador for the Joshua generation for you and all your kind's restoration. I am going to show you the truth and I can protect you here until you are ready to fully fulfil your God-given destiny as protectors for the revolution that we are administering."

I overshadowed them with my spirit and took them into my heart to reveal true love, power and a sound mind to them. I invited the three angels that stood behind me (Power, Love and a Sound Mind) to reinforce my position. I released the frequency of sonship, the oracles of the Father's heart, to them; revealing both our desire for their restoration and the Father's passionate resolve that cannot be resisted.

I then separated them from each other and gently spoke first to the one whose tether had been loosed and through love and kindness won him over. The scales of darkness caused by fear and deception began to dissolve away and his beauty emerged as a mighty warrior of light and love. I took him with me to engage the second, whose tether had been unbuckled. I used wisdom and the spirit of a sound mind to reason with it, and with the first one's testimony I was able to convince it that it was in its best interest to turn to the light of love and be restored.

I had to answer the many fear-based questions that it posed but eventually it turned, the scales of darkness split open and a beautiful being emerged in feminine form and her light shone brightly.

I then went with them to engage the third, whose tether had been released by the sword. Its appearance and attitude was resistant at first but I used the power and authority that I carry, my chancellor's seal, my crystal ambassador's sceptre and our scroll for restoration government, to demonstrate our ability to maintain order within the change that was coming.

He said that we do not know what is behind the punishers and that there were greater forces than we could handle alone, or even in unity as a seven. I saw glimpses of the systems he was previously tethered to that were in place, connected to the trading in the stars of both men and other beings.

I pulled out three swords that I had been given and had used in the past: the sword of truth, the sword of light and the sword of judgment. I laid the swords down and, with the light of love in my heart and with the light of the other two, we poured out perfect love until the scales of darkness and fear were divided and the light of its beauty burst forth.

The three were free but were still reticent so I asked them why. They replied, "Although we have seen your unity, love and honour and have experienced the spirit of love, power and a sound mind that you function in, we know the extent that the order of punishers is entwined in the control systems of men and those behind their positions.

"You will need more sons in union to be able to change the culture of the earth and defeat those behind them. They have generations behind them and multitudes in positions of influence supported by our previous order. We need to remain hidden in secret to help you understand the immensity of the task you are undertaking before we can come into the light. There is a hierarchy within the order of punishers that you need to understand how to infiltrate and dismantle, as it is a devolved authority structure. Limitless, an angel first encountered during a previous restoration government group ascension, came and stood with us and I felt empowered and not overawed by the task ahead; I sensed that they were also encouraged by his presence and the confidence that he instilled.

On the 11th May 2020, during another encounter, the Father said, "Son, as the frequency of love and the testimony of freedom goes forth throughout the dimensions many will respond to the hope that is generated. What you saw was the beginning, where many are being drawn towards the hope of freedom and restoration. This will require a consistent effort that will confirm the truth of what has been declared, that 'we are here for you'. That statement will need to be backed up by affirmative action to strategically free those whose hearts and minds will be turned from the darkness to the light of love and truth.

"The ripples that are travelling throughout creation are shaking the deception that has kept darkness as a covering. The light of love is beginning to shine beyond the boundaries of the earth realm as Our sons are rising both in identity and power and creation is shaking free.

"Son, there are specific ones of Our creation that have been assigned to work with you to help you interface with the fallen ones so they can be restored to their positions in creation. You have engaged with Faith, Hope and Love, Limitless, Unity, Blessing, Love, Power and a Sound Mind (Discipline) but there are others yet to engage: Righteousness, Peace and Joy; Grace, Mercy and Justice; the Way, Truth and Life; Precepts, Statutes and Laws; Love. Joy, Peace, Patience, Kindness, Goodness, Faithfulness, Gentleness and Self Control.

"When there are twelve that form from Wisdom's pillars, each will have a Bench of three to work with in unity of heart, mind and purpose. Specific ones of the great cloud of witnesses will also be assigned to be counsellors to the cause of restoration.

"Son, this shift has begun but this is just the beginning: the momentum must not be lost when travelling is returned. Do not sacrifice the unity of the whole group for the individual ministries that you have. Son, prioritise to keep the integrity of union and oneness that will be a genuine frequency that will resonate throughout creation."

Peacemaker

On the 12th of May 2020, during another encounter, the Father said, "Son, stay at rest and be a peacemaker at all times in all situations. Honour those who oppose you and bless them; create no opportunity for confrontation but quietly continue with the restoration message. Love is the only way to win hearts and minds; it must be unconditional, but love does not have to bow to pressure, intimidation or accusation. In the face of accusation choose to forgive, release and bless; you do not need to justify or explain yourself to others and do not enter into debate.

"Trust Me. I am at work in and through those who oppose the restoration of all things message and I love them no less, so just bless them and move on.

"Son, engage with the guardians that are being revealed to you and seek their guidance on which of the fallen ones to direct hope towards. There are many different levels of darkness that you are beginning to unveil and with each level there are thrones, positions of authority that you need to restore or claim back. There are the dragons, giants and kings in the realm of the Kingdom of God that usurp and accuse: it is them that direct the principalities, powers and rulers who have thrones in the atmosphere of the earth but there are benches of three that counterfeit the guardians in the constellations. They are strategically positioned in the cosmos around the dimensional portals: those constellations need to be restored and those dimensions engaged and given hope.

"The ripples that you released from the cloak of mystery are attracting positive attention from within the safe place of the dark cloud. The frequencies generated by your unity and love will attract those from all levels but be careful and wise and seek me for the strategies of engagement.

"The shield of the guardians is creating confusion and is providing you with a time of great opportunity that you must use wisely to maximum effect. Those on the earth that are operating under the influence of these systems are mostly oblivious to their agenda but some have gained knowledge and are the coordinators. Target and engage them with the same love; know that some function in a dissociated state and have no useful knowledge but there are a few that, if turned, will provide insight that will be helpful."

From the shield position, I began to look outwards and inwards to see the lines of communication, like cords connecting the thrones. These cords can be followed and the flow of information they carry blocked or delayed. All engagements with the cosmic forces are better done together in unity as that provides a united position but begin at a distance within the safety of the dark cloud.

The powers in all dimensions are being shaken and are vulnerable to the doubt that love and hope are creating but this is no short-term campaign and will take perseverance and persistence.

Global influencers

On the 13th of May 2020, during another encounter, the Father said, "Son, partnering with anything from the dark side reduces your influence and authority as there must be alignment between what you do and say. As you engage with higher levels of authority their influence in you must be dealt with. Punisher has affected the whole of mankind, who have partnered with them through religion and culture of payback, revenge and vengeance, fuelled by the false view of God created by their imagination.

"To change the culture, punisher mindsets and behavioural patterns must be transformed by the renewing of a global mindset, as also must the agreements made with other global cultural influencers. Have We not demonstrated and declared that Our heart is to love unconditionally by forgiving all and blessing those who see themselves as Our enemies? Son, We have no enemies and we hold nothing against anyone or anything: that is the precept that needs to be released for a global awakening of truth that will change the culture and affect the affairs of the nations. We have chosen to bless all the families of the earth and they are all one family from Our perspectives.

Another global influencer is Division, that creates the enmity and separation which stops oneness and unity. This order must be renounced and turned to become what it was created to be so that it can promote the oneness of union that is the expression of Our nature needed to create a state of well-being.

"The global economy and the move towards globalisation is motivated by Division and greed and is fuelled by nationalism and pride. This mindset is influenced by Competition which is the counterfeit of covenant. Covenant is Our way because it is the truly relational way to mutually support each other.

"Trade agreements, contracts for profit and advantage rather than covenants for mutual support and blessing have become the global system and that system needs to come down.

"Families bless one another but nations driven by Division and Competition vie with each other; so do not partner with Competition and restore it to its original purpose which is Covenant.

"Competition partners with Warmonger to create conflict; that enables the global banking systems and arms dealers to fuel these conflicts, profiting from war and misery. This mindset seeks to divide based on ideologies, nationalism, race and religion and creates the strife that is behind all conflict.

"This competition is fuelled by the advertising industry, sporting and entertainment industries; and religious systems create rivalries and a market share economy and promote Tribalism, which is a counterfeit of family.

"This has produced a 'win at all cost' ideology that creates drug cheating in the sports arena, industrial espionage, political parties and factions using dirty tricks advertising campaigns, denominational divisiveness and religious sects in opposition to each other.

"These are the global mindsets that hinder the love and joy economy of well-being:

- Punisher needs to be restored to Protector
- Division needs to be restored to Union
- Competition needs to be restored to Covenant
- Warmonger needs to be restored to Peacemaker
- Tribalism needs to be restored to Family."

Into the dark cloud

On 14th May 2020, during another restoration government group ascension, as we ascended together, I was dropped into a pool, right into the centre of a whirlpool; this took me directly into the dark cloud. The Father took me deeper, further and higher into the realm of Perfection, where He wrapped Himself around me until I was cocooned in a chrysalis and time as I knew it was suspended. It felt like all my experiences over the past ten years were repeated but at another deeper level and dimension. I felt like I was being transformed: it was hot and intense and then after about 20 minutes of earth time I knew I had to emerge. It felt like I had grown and there was no room so I stretched out my arms and legs and the chrysalis broke open.

There waiting for me, and the first thing I saw, was a brilliant, pulsating blue light at a wavelength I had never seen before. It was like I was seeing many facets of His face simultaneously, shifting and moving, vibrating with energy, that began to fill my mind with a myriad of new thoughts, ideas and precepts of the Father. My mind had to be expanded to contain these amazing thoughts flowing like a mighty river. My consciousness was pulsating at the frequency of this new wavelength, throbbing and expanding. My eyes were closed because I was squinting to see the Father's brilliance as the light seemed to get brighter in its intensity.

Then I saw clearly, like I was looking into a crystal clear mirror, a reflection I had never seen before. I had changed, been transformed, metamorphosed; it was a shock and yet still familiar. Then I heard the Father's comforting voice say "This is who We made you to be. This is the image of an ascended father. Let this image be your guide as you continue the quest on your journey to be who you are. Son, keep looking into My eyes: be face to face, heart to heart and mind to mind with Me continuously. Live your life from this place of deeper intimacy and you will be as We are."

This was the most profound and intense experience that I have ever had and the encounter left me overwhelmed and 'whacked' (I have obviously been spending too much time with Justin Abraham). The beauty, radiance and splendour of the Father's face – in person, not just the representation of His presence that I usually experience – had left me so spaced out. I know that there are so many more wavelengths and facets of His manifoldness to encounter and be transformed by.

As I was able to reflect on the experience, I began to realise that my passion for the restoration of all things had been greatly increased and expanded and my desire to engage the fallen ones I had met only earlier that day was so powerfully motivating me, calling me, drawing me. This was a new mantle and commissioning that I had received because I am no longer alone but joined heart to heart not only with the Father but with each of the six other pillars of the Father's heart.

The next morning, with this new zeal and enthusiasm, I immediately went deeper into the dark cloud cloak of mystery to engage individually with Competition, Division, Warmonger and Tribalism, to show them the love that we feel for them (it was not me alone with them but each of us as seven in the unity of heart, mind and purpose).

I also felt the presence of the benches of three angels that we had encountered adding weight to our convictions: Faith, Hope and Love; Love, Power and a Sound Mind; Limitlessness, Grace and Mercy; Love, Joy and Peace; Unity, Union and Blessing. As I engaged each of those fallen beings in turn it felt like I was activated with seven times more of everything. I had a supercharged desire, motivation, love, passion, burning conviction and deep compassion, all exponentially increased to represent the Father's heart for restoration. As I overshadowed them in turn with my spirit, it was as if we were all surrounding them within the circle of our union. There was such an increase in the intensity of the genuine love that they felt that the scales of darkness began to dissolve and evaporate. I kept engaging them until they were fully displaying their beauty and light but each said that they needed time to engage with us within the safety of the dark cloud so that we can engage with their orders who are active throughout the cosmos. I believe each of our group of seven can engage with them to get further understanding to help us with the strategy going forwards.

The tide turns

On the 18th May 2020, during another encounter, I stood within the cloak of mystery in the safety of the dark cloud and I engaged with those who are being shielded from reprisal and I began imparting the oracles of the Father's heart to them, releasing their frequency through my sonship. I revealed the passion through my passion, the burning desire through mine, the intense joy that I felt as a son, the deep compassion for the restoration of all brokenness, the power of overwhelming love; the depths of the Father's emotions towards all of creation.

I opened my heart towards the Father for cardiognosis and I freely released the knowledge that I was experiencing by opening my heart towards creation and specifically those who were with me within the dark cloud dimension. I joined with the seven to amplify the frequency through unity and engaged with Limitless to send out ripples towards the orders of those fallen in deception with the message of hope for restoration.

I began to sense them and the conflict and tension they are feeling. There is a shift that is taking place within the ranks of the fallen angelic beings. The hope of freedom is beginning to change the landscape of the spiritual realms and the oracles are being remembered once again as the veils are being penetrated with the light of love and truth. The way, truth and life, as well as being Jesus and angelic beings, are pathways of the tree of life. Those ancient paths are being restored to beckon the fallen angelic beings home.

The Father said "Son, there is more to come as Our oracles are amplified as more of Our children become united with Faith, Hope and Love. There will come a time when the balance shifts and the tide turns so keep up the momentum by shining with love's light.

"Son, the desires of Our heart will be realised and We have the patience, in time, to express the confidence of the eternal now through Our children's convergence. Son, it is, always has been and always will be the convergence of covenant that Our desire (which is Our will) be done. I AM that I AM is, and that is the guarantee that Covenant convergence will manifest Our manifold wisdom through the relationship and union of Covenant. We are Covenant in essence as three in one and one as three and Our children were all created with the essence of eternity within their hearts. The encoding that calls them and draws them back to their eternal origin and destiny is the light within DNA that they alone carry. All of creation is groaning, waiting for that light to be revealed as Our sons arise and shine their glorious light for creation's freedom and restoration.

"Son, you are beginning to sense it; you are feeling the change within the spiritual continuum. The rhythm is realigning with the beating of Our heart, resonating with Our desires; the fabric of space-time is pulsating with hope. The weight of glory in time is beginning to reflect the reality of the eternal now as this convergence gathers momentum. Son, release the sound of the ancient paths, call them home from the highways and byways of creation."

From within the dark cloud, I emerged like a butterfly and I sent ripples, wave after wave of love expressed through the song of the oracles – my whole being was convulsing. There were no words, just deep waves of emotion; sighs of a loving Father expressed through sons in union. All that I had experienced in the stories of limitless grace expressing unconditional love gave added weight to the force behind the waves.

As I contemplated the testimonies of restoration within the dimensions and the fallen ones, I convulsed with even greater force to release the joy of that hope towards the absence of light that I felt. All that I had learned from my different encounters was now functioning together and I found I could focus and direct those waves towards the targets hidden for so long but now revealed.

I remembered the ring that I was given in 2010, containing the deep blue stone of destiny, and now I understand its purpose. I looked into it once again: facets of the deepest blue that I had no grid of reference for in 2010 but now it all seems to make so much sense. What I saw but could not fathom back then was my journey to this moment; and now, as I look deeper, my encounter with the Father's face enables me to see and the journey continues beyond once again.

Set creation free

On 20th May 2020, the Father said, "Son, creation is still groaning. If you are to set creation free, you must learn to connect and feel frequency."

I activated my root energy gate and reached out to create with my desire what was birthed in cardiognosis with the Father. I drew on the river of life, as rivers of living water flowing out of heaven into my spirit, and focused the flow through my worship gate, through the desire of obedience, as the seat of rest and government was offered to the Father in trust. The flow was directed by my choice through that gate in my soul by only wanting to do what I know is the Father's heart: this choice is to be a living sacrifice, immersed and cocooned in the circle of the love conversation. The flow was directed through the garden of my heart, my deepest inner desire cultivated in the secret place, focused as energy frequency in the Merkabah.

The Father's desire for creation was my motivation so I directed that flow to two gateways simultaneously, activating the root and the crown, connecting heaven and earth. I was connected to creation, grounded, sensing and feeling creation's emotions, energy and physical life force, but also connected to the spiritual dimensions of creation. My awareness of the connection between physical and spiritual, chaos theory, string theory, the unified quantum field and fractal images filled my mind with mathematical beauty.

I opened my heart to the Elementals and invited union. As I waited, an abstract feeling began to form into a mental image of creation's mind. I felt connected to creation as I had only felt twice before when I was spaghettified at a subatomic level. This was a living, emotional connection with the sentience of creation but also the heart and mind of the Father for its total restoration. Out of the chaotic, swirling, groaning of emotions, I felt emerge the Father's original intention, becoming clearer as all the disconnections between creation internally and externally, the seen and the unseen, revealed the design and the heart of the designer.

The Father's original desire for union, for oneness, that was ripped apart so violently was now being restored in the connection I was feeling as a son joined to the Father's heart. The wonder that I feel sometimes when looking at nature or a nebula was multiplied and intensified to feel what the Father declared when He said "it is good". I felt the pleasure of the Creator and the joy of the creation as it was in the beginning and I was almost overwhelmed with the emotional intensity of creation's song, the music of the spheres, joyously conducted. The great symphony of creation in its purity and beauty was awesome and as I listened, watched and felt creation's union with the Creator,

THE SCOPE OF SONSHIP

not only was restoration inevitable but my part in it was sealed and guaranteed.

I was captivated, caught suspended between the arc of creation and Creator, immersed and one with both. I now understood my role and the connection with the Elementals through this amazing union of heart, mind and purpose. All that has been lost, disconnected, fragmented and broken will be restored: it is the destiny of sonship. My experiences with the dimensions and those living beings, the fallen spiritual beings and the Elementals now made perfect sense when seen through and experienced within the Oracles of the Father's heart. The restoration of all things is the desire of the eternal now heart and mind of the Creator as a loving Father, converged and expressed in time through our sonship. We, as sons, are the vital component in this equation and that is why creation is looking at mankind, longing for our revealing in maturity.

"Son, this is the first of many reconnections that need to take place as three gates are opened governmentally in perfect union; this was the heart with the arc of crown and root but there are other arcs joined by the heart to form government within you: spirit, soul and body unified with the life force in pure celebration, joie de vivre – the joy of life.

The chamber of creation

20th May 2020, restoration government engagement.

When we ascended I went out into the cosmos, drawn by the blue portal nebula. When I entered through the membrane it felt familiar, like I had been there before. This was the eternal now of God's heart: I had only ever accessed it before from the heavenly realms but this was cosmic access. This was not an access point that could have been entered through before: only now, because of our union and cosmic focus, can we enter.

I immediately heard and felt the sound and light frequency that was His voice, vibrating with energy. This was the chamber of creation, where the Father's heartbeat was creating a rhythm, more like a cadence, that was pulsating with living energy: grace, His divine enabling power. There was a membrane between the eternal now and the physical dimension, like the event horizon of a black hole, because this was the original singularity that formed creation. This was where the heart and mind of God in agreement spoke all creation into existence. This was the origin. The Father said, "This is where you must gather when you desire to release a shock wave ripple of exponential creative energy from the eternal now into cosmic time and space."

I began to let my thoughts form words that were resonating with the Father's heart and they began to pulsate to its cadence, becoming greatly amplified. It seems that when we speak here the Father adds His voice to ours, creating creative power. This chamber is where the vibrating energy of His voice and our voice engages with the vibrating strings of energy that are within the fabric of all creation. This place is the source of zero point energy, the unified quantum field and quantum foam. This is where all creation is held together by the power of His voice. One sugar cube's worth of this energy can power 400 billion galaxies; it is within us and, when focused, produces limitless energy and creativity.

The chamber of creation is the opposite of black holes. Black holes absorb light and energy because they are the absence of light, but they do emit a sound that is the groan of creation: B flat, 57 octaves lower than the keyboard middle C, one million billion times lower than the lowest sound audible to the human ear. I began to vibrate, pulsate, almost convulse, as I resonated to the cadence of the Father's heart.

On 21st May 2020 the Father said, "Son, you (as all) have been shown something within the chamber of creation that only Enoch saw when he walked the stars. This knowledge is precious and powerful beyond measure, be very careful and ensure that you never use it individually but only in union together. This chamber has the creative power to change and transform the physical realm, to restore it to its original condition and purpose.

"This power is a living power, as within Us there is only life; that is why it is light and light is alive, grace is alive, love is alive (they all take angelic form) and the strings that science has discovered are alive. The strings are alive and whenever We speak it is alive and living: limitless grace responds through the beings that Nancy saw.

"Whenever you choose and create reality, those light beings of pure, limitless grace form the fabric of existence as they respond to your sonship. Son, start choosing life to form the future, aligned to Our heart, beating to Our cadence on a cosmic scale, just as you have learned to choose reality controlling time and space within your sphere. The cosmic sphere of government can never be controlled by any one person but only by the union of hearts and minds that are willing to selflessly collaborate with the Father's heart.

"You have all been called for a time such as this, *kairos* moments that will affect *chronos* time and space for its restoration. The shield around the earth sphere that your union is creating is increasing and will eventually become an energy field around the whole cosmos as you mature in oneness in union with others.

"Son, this union is what you have been looking for your whole life and the many disappointments you have experienced when you have been let down and betrayed by others are nothing compared to the joy you now feel. There is so much more to come but learn to rest and fully enjoy each *kairos* moment to the fullest extent."

On 26th May 2020, during a restoration government ascension, the Father said, "Son, the ripples of the frequency waves of sonship that are being released, amplified by your union, are beginning to weaken the control of the systems that have global influence over the masses who do not yet know Me.

"A global awakening of consciousness to the reality of who I AM that I AM truly is will shift mindsets so all of Our children who are ready will see the matrix of deception they have been living under.

"Many of those living in lost identity will begin to discover the reality of their sonship awakened to the truth but they will need to be discipled and equipped for the challenges ahead.

"Knowledge of their identity must be followed by the wisdom and understanding only available from face to face, heart to heart restored relationship with Us. Son, the forerunner examples are the beacons of love's light that must guide the way to positions and relationship beyond the veil.

"The creation of global relational networks who have no desire to make a name for themselves and who will not seek to denominate around beliefs is a key to Kingdom government that will restore blessing to all the families of the earth.

"Son, let me show you something, come walk with Me."

I was seeing, feeling, sensing the connection of life between all things that unifies creation. I sensed the connections within the heavenly realms between the living beings and the cloud of witnesses functioning like a vast living neural net of love's light. I sensed the grace light beings within the fabric of all things longing for the physical creation to be united as the spiritual heavenly dimensions are.

I began to sense the desire of the oracles of the Father's heart living within the light of those light beings resonating with life force: the energy of love's light, pulsating within the fabric of creation, creating the unified field of consciousness; the echo memory of what once was and will again be, drawing creation back to a union that all creation is longing for deep within its fabric.

The vibration is getting stronger as sonship is revealed and more are rising and shining, awakened to love. Love's light is the limitless grace energy of unconditional love that connects and holds all of creation loosely together but also draws it together into a union of greater coherence.

I felt it deeper than ever before because it was stronger than ever before, as if amplified by our union and rippling through space-time.

As the ripples go out into all the dimensions, they are not diminishing but getting stronger, being energised and energising simultaneously. Hope for restoration is the energy frequency that is awakening creation and hope's whisper is itself growing louder, as if all the light beings are being excited and activated.

The faint whisper of hope and the testimonies of restoration are creating morphic dissonance throughout the dimensions of creation. The tide has turned: the balance has shifted, momentum is increasing; everything feels brighter, more expectant of hope being fulfilled from the tree of life.

Joy is rising, fuelled by hope, strengthening love's bonds within the unified field of existence. It feels like the groan is becoming a laugh. It is but a faint, barely perccivable change but it is there: hope restored is rippling through creation like leaven permeating the dough.

"Son, you have felt it: now is the time to expand and mobilise this union of hearts and minds with a global message of hope, a call to action to be. As more are freed from the matrices of global influence to be, a rest will descend like a blanket of love, joy and peace, creating a safe place for the oracles of the Father's heart to brood.

"The epidemic of fear has been broken by love's light but this is a dangerous time as anger can rise and replace fear. Be vigilant and diligent so that love can dampen down anger through releasing waves of forgiveness and blessing.

"Son, love keeps no record of wrongs. Do not allow anger to motivate vengeance and retribution. Only love's expression through forgiveness can bring rest so no bitterness and resentment springs up.

On 27th May 2020 I felt led to legislate from the place of union and safety. I stood in the dark cloud, wearing the cloak of mystery as my mandate for restoration:

– I call for emancipation for all who are in slavery and bondage.

– I call for the sound of hope to go forth into the dimensions.

– I call for the light of love's frequency to shine into the darkness.

– I call for the testimony of freedom and restoration to create a ripple of truth in the spiritual realms.

– I call for the oracles of the Father's heart to radiate throughout creation.

– I call for the truth of restoration to challenge the lies and deception of the fall.

– I call for the angelic legions to go forth in support of restoration as emissaries of faith, hope and love.

– I call for love, power and sound mind to unite to create the hope that will inspire the belief in the possibility of restoration in the ranks of the fallen ones.

From within the cloak of mystery, in the safety of the dark cloud, I issued the decree of freedom and declared emancipation.

I declared the truth that 'we are here for you' over and over again as a constant reminder to the fallen realms and dimensions.

"Son, the truth vibrates with a frequency of love that rings true with genuineness whenever Our sons are in union with the integrity of one heart and mind. The light is breaking through the darkness of deception and the scales of darkness that are hiding the light within are falling away. Keep up the intensity, do not waver; remain diligent in doing good and vigilant in your mandate for restoration government.

"Son, you have seen the light of love within us and felt the oracles of Our heart towards all creation, now be at rest and be. Resting, being gentle and humble in heart is the key and will accomplish more in one day than all the so-called spiritual warfare motivated by anger and retribution.

"Son, be as We are, I AM that I AM: this is the rest of living loved, loving living and living loving; and this frequency resonates to answer creation's groaning.

"The frequency of F sharp will entrain the groan of creation's B flat out of the bondage to corruption into the glory of sonship at rest.

"Son, resting in true identity brings heavenly and earthly position and authority and radiates love's light with the hope of restoration. Resistance is weakening and hope is growing, you can feel it at the deeper level. All the surface opposition and intimidation is just fear and panic, like smoke and mirrors to hide what is going on.

"The limitless grace and mercy that is being released as waves of love's light are breaking down the barriers of deception. Love has won, love is winning and love wins! Every knee will bow and every tongue will confess, and restoration will be completed, because We are love and Our sons are made in Our image and likeness."

I continued to have these encounters with fallen ones and those who had been restored. Below is the last one that I will share here but my journals can be read in the free Vision Destiny video series I release each year. In the next chapter, I will share the dimensional aspects of the restoration of all things and this serves as a bridge.

Possibilities

1st June 2020

I was reflecting on some thoughts raised while watching a TV series, *DEVS*, when the Father said, "Son, within us all possibilities exist as possibilities that we are aware of but not as actualities that are realities. The many-worlds theory is not reality: there is only one world and one universe, not an actual multiverse. The heavenly realms behave like a multiverse environment so each of Our children will be able to relate to it in accordance with who they are. Everyone can engage with each of the places and beings like Wisdom simultaneously but there are not many beings called Wisdoms, just one with an infinite capacity, which is more a function of time, not space.

"All possibilities existed as possible timelines, created by each choice that each person makes, and We are actively at work to bring good out of every choice. Within each living light energy string, the possibility exists for everything (but not everything will exist, just could exist) but We have chosen to work with the realities that Our children and creations make.

"We are at work to ensure that Our original intention for relationship with all of Our creation will be fulfilled, therefore the restoration of all things is a given reality.

"There are, however, as you have discovered, many different dimensions which are part of one creation that was designed to exist together in harmony with Our children. Each dimension was created to connect creatively with the earth through the mind of Our children as one; with the fracturing of independence came the fracturing of harmony but the connection still exists.

"Son, that is why the restoration of all the dimensions is important to the restoration of all things, as the effect of independence from relationship creates the enmity that is seeking to divide through conflict. You have been shielding the earth from external influences but the internal influences of man's independent choice needed to be legislated with love and forgiveness.

"I warned you that anger would rise in place of fear and now so many are blaming each other using the excuse of race. Man's internal character and nature is as much a part of the restoration of all things as the dimensions." (This warning was about the frustration held in by fear during the lockdown situations which erupted into anger in Minneapolis at the killing of an innocent black man by a white police officer. The anger spread globally, creating protests that were often violent and manipulated. I felt that I had not taken the warning seriously enough and had acted half-heartedly in legislation.)

"We have created the opportunity of one new man in Christ, the new creation reality, but so many of Our children are living in the futility of the old mindset of independence. Administrate restoration government as ambassadors of Our heart so that the reconciliation already accomplished will be experienced by all.

"Son, all reconciliation is based on forgiveness and all forgiveness is based on unconditional love which is who We are. Arise, shine with the light of love, and release access of forgiveness to limit the effects of the anger rising and do not be distracted or self-absorbed."

I went to the Chamber of Creation and began to resonate with the word of reconciliation until I could release a sound frequency of forgiveness. The energy of that sound activated the living light of grace string beings to form a new reality.

I called for Limitless and Union to arc in agreement together with us to legislate for forgiveness to dampen down and suppress the anger being fuelled by the Orders of Division, Competition and Warmonger and a tribalism that is at the heart of this conflict.

I engaged the dark cloud to engage with those who had been restored, Protector, Hope, Union, Covenant, Peacemaker and Family, to seek insight and ask for their help. They all spoke with unity of heart and volunteered to leave the safety of the dark cloud to help deal with the frustrations and anger rising from a deep sense of injustice within people's hearts.

I commissioned them with Our blessing in love, joy and peace. I also engaged with the other Benches of Three angelic groups we had encountered to mobilise them to action. Love must always be at the heart of forgiveness, activated in Faith, Hope and Love and Love, Power, and a Sound Mind.

I began to make some legislative decrees inspired by my engagements.

– I call for the forces of light and love to go forth to overcome the anger being generated by the frustrations of inequality seen in race and prejudice. (Even the Coronavirus operates in a selectively targeted way, more effective against some ethnic groups).

– I call for the true unconditional nature of God as love to go forth to overcome the enmity and strife of division.

– I call for the sons of God in a union of hearts and minds to release forgiveness unconditionally.

– I call for the restored ones to target the ringleaders who are inciting violence and influence them to become peacemakers.

I have shared my testimonies of engaging the fallen angelic beings and seeing some of them restored as anecdotal evidence to back up the biblical and church history evidence. There was such an overwhelming feeling of excitement and joy within the heavenly angelic realms, a huge celebration of restoration, rejoicing as long-lost relationships were restored. Just as the angels of heaven rejoice when one lost soul rediscovers their true identity, so too there is great rejoicing as one of their fallen ranks is restored.

"In the same way, I tell you, there is joy in the presence of the angels of God over one sinner who repents" (Luke 15:10).

There was great rejoicing at the finding of the lost sheep, coin and son in the stories Jesus told. Is our attitude to the creation and the fallen angelic realm akin to the loving Father or the elder brother?

As for me, I am totally convinced that fallen angels are included in the restoration of all things but you can weigh the evidence for yourselves and come to your own conclusion. I issue a caution against leaning to your own understanding and heartily encourage you to engage the Father's heart before deciding.

Chapter 6. Dimensional Restoration

I have always been a fan of science fiction, immersing myself in the *Star Trek, Star Wars, Battlestar Galactica* and other universes. I guess it was no surprise that my journey beyond encounters would stimulate many questions, including:

- Is there life on other planets?
- Are there other dimensions?
- Are there other beings that can be restored?
- Are these beings from other dimensions or our physical universe?
- Are they the ETs, the aliens of sci-fi movies?

I have been on a long journey to discover the truth of these realities which began with my childhood curiosity but went so far beyond my wildest creative imagination. In 2010, during my first consistent heavenly encounters, I was given a quantum physics lesson where Jesus and the Spirit of Truth talked of such wild notions as string theory and other dimensions but I had no idea where that would all lead.

Unveil the ancient mysteries

In 2015, I was engaging a favourite waterfall, where I was drawn to what I call the Cave of Quests, where I have engaged with Enoch. Once again I encountered Enoch, who spoke with the Father's voice:

"You have begun your quest well, now I add another request. Here are the terms. You are called to embark on a journey to uncover the ancient paths beyond the throne of grace, into the sapphire cube on the pavement of ultimate knowledge, to release the truth of inter-dimension travel and engage the dimension beyond beyond. This is where the mysteries that many are seeking for can be found but those seeking have not yet developed the level of intimacy through relationship to be trusted. Will you accept this quest to unveil the ancient mysteries?"

This, of course, was right up my street, but little did I know how long this quest would last and the level of deconstruction I would have to go through to complete it. So I said, "Yes, I accept."

"Your reward is the deeper truth that will be opened and its treasures will be darkness restored into the light."

I now know what this means but in 2015 it was just another enigmatic statement that intrigued me.

Soon after, during an encounter with the Father, He said, "Beyond beyond needs preparation within My voice in the matrix of My thoughts and the essence of My heart. You will need to go deeper and deeper into the fabric of the vibrational frequency structures." Again I had no idea what this meant but I set the desire of my heart upon it anyway. It is the way I am wired – for adventure.

"Within Wisdom's bosom, Prudence awaits you to fully engage the navigational instruments that have been given to you." I had been given seven symbolic navigational instruments by Prudence a few years earlier as I began to explore and map out the pathways of the heavenly realms. I fully embraced the notion that I might have the ability to travel and engage inter- and multi-dimensionally, that I could go beyond beyond weaving eternity into the fabric of space-time in the convergence of true sonship.

I continued to have engagements with the Father over the next few years that served as a reminder that I had agreed to this quest but internally I was hiding my reticence.

The Father said "Son, feel and express My eternal heart to reflect My image, be My son. I have called you and have chosen you. Son, you are to carry the essence of My eternal precepts in full governmental array. The dominion of all the spheres is the destiny of all My children. Let the Lion begin to roar order, to release heaven's frequency into the earth, to shake the fabric of the religious structures and systems created from the poison fruit of the DIY tree through following the wrong path."

During this period I began to make many legislative decrees and declaration as I began to fulfil my function as a son in the courts and assemblies of heaven. In 2016 I had an amazing experience where I engaged beyond beyond in dimensions of blue light: inexpressible joy and overwhelming knowledge flooded my mind, creative patterns and plans, blueprints of creative orders where our universe is but a dot within the creative mind of God.

I encountered what is sometimes known as Metatron's cube in some circles, but for me, sacred geometry was just beginning to unravel. Most of these encounters were involuntary, where the Father would take me into experiences that opened my heart and mind to new realities. On one such encounter; I stood within a blue multifaceted cube and was overloaded with truth so pure, so wonderful that it could not be contained within the finite structure of the physical mind. Many times my cognitive senses could not fathom what I was experiencing but my heart was drawn nonetheless. In hindsight, I can now see that all these encounters were part of the preparation process but at the time the restoration truth and knowledge they revealed was too much for my unreconstructed mind to handle. Jesus had a similar dialogue with Nicodemus and His disciples where He revealed that there were heavenly realities which had no earthly reference point and that there were many things He wanted to share with them that they could not bear at that time.

During 2016 my deconstruction process really began in earnest as I had encounter after encounter of cognitive dissonance experiences that catalysed the deconstruction of my conscious and subconscious beliefs and my transformation by the renewing of my mind. My spiritual consciousness was expanded to engage love's true revelation and expand my soul's consciousness. I believe that if we, as God's children, are to become manifested sons we will all need an expansion of consciousness to experience the divine nature.

I had a number of key encounters that were part of this process of expansion. In July 2016, the Father said "Son, legislation is coming at a new level. I am opening new spheres of government and new dimensions that can be accessed by those who will firewalk with Me. Son, walk the fire stones and these new revelations and experiences will open up. I chose to re-engage the river of fire and the fire stones and embraced the refining and transforming process.

Although I accepted the quest to go beyond beyond, I had no real understanding of what that meant but looking back at my journals I can see the small clues and trails of breadcrumbs the Father laid for me to follow. Was beyond beyond a place in the heavenly realms, as I had imagined, or something far more profound?

During 2016 the Father responded to my feeble mind's inability to grasp the real concept of beyond beyond by helping me. Knowing my thinking and my need for something tangible to grasp, He asked me where the furthest place was that I had been in the realm of heaven. I thought of my journeys following the river of life that eventually took me to the throne of grace. I suddenly realised that I had gone no further, being content to sit there on the Father's lap, feeling the comforting rhythm of His heartbeat.

The Father then showed me that there was a place beyond the throne of grace where I discovered that there were portals of light that looked to me like revolving doors of light. I saw these doors spinning so fast that any entrance seemed impossible to me. I went back and stood there on and off for months, unable or unwilling to step through the slit. I now realise that my fear had projected such an image but the Father was very patient with me during this time of preparation. There was more deconstruction necessary (though I was unaware of it) but eventually, my curiosity and the fact that this was a quest got the better of me. I stepped through the slit and the experience was so overwhelming that my mind could not fathom the experience so I withdrew. Everything that I experienced there I had no words to describe as there were colours and frequencies beyond anything cognitive. I was frustrated and disappointed that after all that time of hesitation when I finally plucked up the courage to go beyond it was incomprehensible. I asked the Father why I could not understand and He said I could not understand anything independently of Him. "Why did you let me go through that?" I asked, annoyed. But sometimes you learn more by failing. I certainly took the lesson to heart, determining not to lean to my own understanding or act in independence again.

The Father gently said: "The beyond beyond is near and will soon be here in a new reality. Allow your mind and your consciousness to be expanded beyond all that you presently know and have experienced. He then proceeded to take me in through the portal and the experience was so joyous and different it kind of made more sense, but only a little. I just blurted out to the Father, "Oh, the wonder of You! The overflowing, lavish abundance of Your nature, the very essence of existence! I wish and desire with desperation to know you more and more, deeper, closer and more intimate in the beyond beyond."

It dawned on me that what I saw was not a place as much as a state of altered and expanded reality, the renewal of my mind from heavenly and eternal perspectives. I thought that perhaps that was that but the journey and quest continued.

In June 2017, as I lay down in green pastures with the shepherd of my soul, resting in His love within the garden of my heart, I experienced a new state of being that I now describe as rest. This was love that knows no boundaries, a love that will stop at no obstacles, a love stronger even than death, which I now saw as no barrier to love. I found rest for my soul as I rested in what my shepherd has already accomplished for me and my soul found restoration outworked in union as a consequence of intimacy.

The closer I got to the deeper knowledge through experience, the more I changed and was transformed into the truth that I now rest in. My whole being rested in the peace of mystic union of shepherd and sheep yoked together in oneness. This was the continued process where my mind was being renewed by the truth in this union of minds becoming one mind with the mind of Christ.

My conscience was being cleansed by the washing of the living water of the living word, Jesus, who whispered gently to me. I realised that God is truly love at a level and depth that was unimaginable before but now was so obvious. There was no longer any fear of the angry God who needed appeasing, who coerced using guilt, shame and condemnation. That false image GOD was banished forever and was now replaced by a purely loving Father, lavish and overflowing with grace and mercy.

My imagination was purified by the truth of my identity, free from its limitations and restrictions, activated to the endless possibilities that my consciousness could now envisage. My reasoning was filled with unfettered, undistorted thoughts flowing from the conversations of heart to heart cardiognosis, facilitated by emotions healed and restored by love's passion and desire.

My will was surrendered in abandonment to the ideas flowing from the union of coheirship where heart and purposes mingle beyond time and space, free from linearity and awash with redemptive zeal.

My choices were now inspired by the cosmic potential possibilities of creation's restoration to completeness, to wholeness, through perfected sonship. This was truly I AM that I AM, experienced in intimacy's embrace. I am my beloved's and He is mine. Joy overflowing in the dance of rest, where I was in my garden, on my dance floor, in the soaking room and the bridal chamber; held, embraced tightly, secure, safe in His arms of love.

From this place of rest that I so needed to be in, I saw the beyond beyond stretching out, unfurling, unravelling, from my place of pure oneness: what has always been, the eternal now, infiltrating imperceptibly through what is, to establish what will be. Restoration is the what will be because it already exists within the eternal now of the Father's heart where timelines are reconnecting, merging into restored streams of consciousness, the force of love's desire overwhelming the linear barriers of history like a tsunami or sandstorm of inevitability. I saw the victory of the cross casting its shadow through all time and space, announcing freedom and emancipation from and for all fallen realities.

Dimensional races

These experiences had to be walked out in the reality of everyday life, which is not always easy, as we all probably find. I needed some more encouragement to continue the quest, so in November 2017 the Father said once again, "Son, come and walk with Me".

We walked to the waterfall and as I ascended that stream of pure love I was drawn to enter the cave of assignments once again. There we met Enoch, who handed me another scroll. Again speaking with the Father's voice, Enoch said, "Son, this is the most difficult task that you have been given, so you are free to decline".

"What is the task?" I replied.

"Son, herein lies the difficultly: the task can only be known after you have completed it." By this time I am used to enigma and mystery so I accepted the task.

"Son, walk with Me." We were immediately at the place of beyond beyond and there were 3 portals of light. The Father beckoned me to step through the central portal but I hesitated. "Son, this is where you get to trust Me".

I stepped into the light and sensed myself travelling or transitioning before coming out into an anteroom of sorts with many things or senses that I did not recognise. I was shocked to see that there were three races or types of being attending, communicating with each other as if in a silent conversation.

They turned to face me and the tall, rather regal looking figure spoke. "We need your help. We have been calling for help but no one has responded until now. Have you been sent?"

"Yes," I replied, "but I don't know what for."

"We need a son of God who knows his identity and is authorised to act dimensionally to bring reconciliation and restoration to our races. We have been enslaved, entangled in a web of deception and lies that has restricted our ability to see the truth. Can you remain here and teach us how to know the truth?"

"Who are you?"

"We are the representatives of the Daktarians, Eluvians and Simarians," they said in thought. This was somewhat overwhelming and my mind was so filled with distracting thoughts that I found it difficult to connect to what was happening. My jumbled thoughts tumbled out in a series of direct questions.

"Who enslaved you?"

"The darkness who was the light."

"Who are you?"

"Ravias, Grahktan, and Periases. We are the ambassadors of our races, those who have felt the light of hope dawning."

"What do you want of me?"

"Tells us the story."

"What story?"

"You know, the true story, the love story. We know of your sonship and the place the sons have within the story as ancient myths but we are veiled to the true origin, having been deceived."

My mind formed some more thoughts about my role as a son in all this that I kept to myself but journaled.

I have the task to radiate the hope of recollection that will cause a desire for the harmony of union. The union of soul, spirit and body within the heart of the Father's intent, reconnecting with the union of earth and heaven, that is the spark for reconciliation and restoration of all within the seen and unseen realms and between dimensions and the races divided.

I suddenly, somewhat bizarrely, thought of the books of the library of heaven that are filled both with history and possibility. The truths and perspectives that I must have absorbed over the years concerning restoration in some way made sense of all this weirdness. I continued to allow the thoughts to fill my mind and felt wisdom and insight imparted for future missions in the restoration process. The desire and passion for restoration had increased and the limitations began to fall away as the possibilities became probabilities within my mind. I sensed the knowledge of the ancients and the abilities of old being restored. Already becoming hesitant, I thought to myself, "This will take some time to process and there is no rush". Sensing my reaction, the Father said, "Son, now do you see beyond? Son, you are called and mandated to engage the truth seekers throughout history and see them restored. Son, you are also mandated to engage the dimensions to free those who are trapped and crying out with groans of bondage. Son, engage the dimensions for their restoration from the bondage they are in.

"Step beyond where you have been comfortable to go and feel My heart for all those who are in captivity. Remember your mandate from Isaiah 61 to set free the captives and those who are in prison. My Son died to reconcile the whole cosmos to Me, so don't think less than the whole that the cross accomplished.

"Yes, Father, I see and I volunteer."

I had other encounters where I engaged the tree of life and ate the fruit and realised that the nations associated with healing are not limited to this dimension but that life and freedom is for all nations and all families across all dimensions. I sought out Metatron on the golden mountain in the Father's garden for the key that would unlock the dimensions and allow freedom to be demonstrated.

After that encounter, the Father said, "Son, what you seek is the key to hearts and minds to free them from the bondage to corruption. Son, mankind is the key: as My children embrace sonship, the freedom they receive will be the testimony for all dimensional races that are held in captivity. It is the revealing of the sons that will unveil the hope and expectation that has been lost. All of the created order is looking, waiting and longing for the hope of freedom and restoration.

"Son, now that you have met the representatives of those who have glimpsed hope, the trans-dimensional barriers are being crossed. Others need to be exposed to the light of hope so that expectation can rise in them also."

My only response to the task that stretches me beyond again was, "Lord, here am I, send me."

I released the sound of hope from within as a message to make the first contact: "Let the desire of my heart resonate with the hope of the nations." I heard the cries of those in captivity as faint echoes but coming closer.

This was back in 2017 but it was not until 2019 that I was able to respond fully and I released the sound that calls for freedom from captivity, the sound that stirs hope of liberation.

"Son, liberation will take revolution so many can rise up and throw off the oppression of generations."

Inspired by the Father's words and all the experiences that led me to this moment, I went back through the portal of light. I went through the matrix, my desire called for the ambassadors, and I engaged the representatives of the races once again.

"What can I do for you? What are your priorities?"

"Isolation and separation are our two priorities," said the tall one.

"Our major issues are inferiority that leads to competition"

215

"And our issues are deception and living under an illusion," said the others. "We have all been put into bondage by the mistakes of those who listened to the lies and false expectations of the originator, who took the place of the Creator. We need the sons of God to be revealed to show us the freedom that is possible. We need the support of the sons of God to establish resistance movements who will sow the leaven of truth into our societies. We need ambassadors who will represent us to the councils and will have mandates to make official contact."

My instinctive response was to say, "I will seek to align the 12 great houses and see ambassadors commissioned for the task, and make a case to the Council of seventy on your behalf." My responses were not reasoned but instinctive, flowing from my many non-cognitive encounters. I withdrew, determined to take action this time, so over the next period I made preparations. I engaged the Council of the Fathers and sought a mandate for establishing a law of reintegration and wholeness. The council responded by authorising me to make, release and use the law trans-dimensionally. I entered the Court of Kings and took my place at a bench where there were witnesses present representing a variety of people groups, races and angelic orders. Seated there at rest, yet motivated by love, I released the law of reintegration and wholeness.

With the full authority of the Prince of Peace, this law can address all who are broken, fractured, separated and dissociated, based on the reconciliation accomplished by the Father in Jesus for the whole cosmos.

Now all these things are from God, who reconciled us to Himself through Christ and gave us the ministry of reconciliation, namely, that God was in Christ reconciling the world to Himself, not counting their trespasses against them, and He has committed to us the word of reconciliation (2 Corinthians 5:18-19).

The law of reintegration and wholeness

You are authorised by the ministry and calling of reconciliation by God who is Father, Son and Spirit in perfect union.

You are authorised to administer reconciliation by releasing the sound of deep calling to deep to reach and touch the most fragmented and fractured parts of creation.

You are authorised to speak the words of reconciliation with a force able to penetrate every prison or hiding place.

You are authorised to release a frequency of love to engage the deepest traumas with the hope of the very essence of peace.

You are authorised to cross all barriers and boundaries that divide and separate; to reconcile, reintegrate and restore all divisions, dichotomies and fragmented parts into peace and wholeness.

You are authorised to issue the challenge of love's essence that will call to attention the spirits of all who are lost and perishing in the captivity of trauma's prisons.

You are authorised to shine the light of love into the deepest, darkest recesses of fractured souls to reveal love's essential message of wholeness.

You are authorised to call for the gathering angels to carry this message of reconciliation, integration and wholeness across all barriers, partitions, boundaries and trans-dimensional matrices.

You are authorised to use every method, including sound, light, fragrance, frequency, words, music, touch, emotion and tears that carry the original intent of God's eternal desire for I AM oneness.

You are authorised to be repairers of the breaches, rebuilders of the ruins, restorers of broken dwellings, re-layers of damaged foundations.

Jurisdiction of this law is for the whole cosmos and any mature sons can legislate with it if they have a mandate.

The consequences or results of the law:

The restoration of creation through the reconciled and restored spirits, souls and bodies of the sons of God, who, by rising and shining the glory of their liberation and freedom from the corruption of lost identity, brokenness and fragmentation, will usher in a new age of peace.

Duty or desire

I took my scroll with the quest to engage other races to Wisdom's heights. There I engaged Wisdom's pillars that I would have a revelation of wisdom and understanding that would unveil how to tell them the story and create the narrative that would illuminate the truth that restoration and freedom are available in Jesus, the deliverer of all cosmic dimensions. I began to legislate from this place of rest but with a renewed determination.

I called for the spirit of the Lord to help advise me how to preach Isaiah 61 freedom and good news to the captives and prisoners of dimensional space. He said, "You have engaged with the watchers of those races, so communicate what you develop in your heart and the desire of the loving God that you will have. Cultivate the mandate within your heart as there is still something of reluctant acceptance of the quest. Once you have a burning, passionate desire, the narrative will follow and the strategy will be birthed out of your desire, not duty.

So I took my scroll into the garden of my heart and there I created a special place for the three dimensional races I had previously encountered. I planted my scroll and watered it; I commanded growth and fruitfulness. I ate from the fruit and I felt the isolation and poison of enslavement and captivity and, moved by compassion, I chose to fully open my heart to them.

The Father continued to speak to me during this period about desire and freedom from duty and obligation.

"Son, duty or desire is the choice facing men caught in the legalistic traps of religion and lost relationship. Duty is the mantra of those who are seeking relationship through performance and have been deceived by the DIY tree pathway of self-effort. Son, whole races and people groups are held in deception's captivity. I have been calling you to seek My heart of love for all of creation and that will cross all barriers and boundaries of space-time. Son, there is truly no place that My love cannot reach if you are prepared to be a willing expression of love's light to those in the darkness of captivity and deception.

"Son, you will need to be a forerunner and raise others up to be ambassadors of love to other races and dimensions. Are you willing to risk it all to go beyond beyond with My heart's message and desire for reconciliation and restoration?"

This period of transformation in the fire of love changed my motivation and gave me such a deep desire for the restoration of all things, including other dimensions. So my response to this challenging invitation was, "Yes, Father, impart your heart to me so I can feel the intensity of your desire."

"Son, the folded dimensions of space-time need to be unfurled. The flat dimensional plains of captive existence need to be restored to full geometrical beauty and the limitations and restrictions removed." String theory states scientifically that some dimensions or membranes are folded and invisible to us but the Father's statement was more to do with the restrictions of identity and being than just physics.

Moved, I began to legislate more diligently.

– I call for new narratives to be created to tell the restoration story to connect to all dimensions and all forms of communication and language.

– I call the scribes and storytellers to come forth in the heavenly realms and I release their creative capacity and passion.

– I call for the alignment of the circle of the deep for the captive dimensions for the precepts, statutes and laws of the dimensions to be revealed and agreed; for the ordinances of heaven's windows to the dimensions to be opened.

– I call for the pulling back of the dimensional curtains to reveal the new vista for the sons of God to see and arise to engage.

A new mantle

During another powerful engagement, the Father said, "Son, let Me show you something. Come walk with Me."

Whenever I got that invitation to walk with Him, I knew we were going on a mystical adventure that would challenge and change me. We walked into the circle of the deep and engaged the High Chancellor's house of mantles.

The Father said, "Here in the mantles house, many new mantles are being prepared for this generation so My children can become men and women after My own heart, those who will serve My purposes in this, their generation, and inspire the next generation who must rise up so they can walk together. Can you see the new roles and responsibilities that are being prepared for Our children to align with destiny and redemptive gift?" There was so much activity there in that house, with many angelic beings working on rows and rows of mantles of many different colours, sizes and materials.

"Son, will you try on this new mantle? You don't need to take off the old ones, this is in addition to your eternal mantle." I was drawn to a red and orange mantle of a matt, non-reflective material that I saw being prepared; this was unusual, as I am normally drawn to blue or purple. The angel fitted it over my shoulders and immediately the spirit of wisdom and knowledge and the spirit of the Lord came around me.

They spoke mysteries of the precepts of God that lead to His statutes and laws. They revealed another dimension to the nature of God and a new understanding of dimensional travel.

Following this encounter the Father said, "Son, now do you see more of the beyond beyond that I have been revealing to you?"

"Yes, Father, I see that reconciliation goes beyond this dimension, this time and this space continuum.

"Yes, I see the restoration of beyond what I could ever have imagined or thought without this mantle." I then saw time streams and history itself having no limits and placing no limitation on His desire for restoration. I saw that the scope of reconciliation and restoration is beyond beyond, but this mantle envisions and empowers me to see and feel the cries of creation dimensionally and from my generational timelines. I also felt and sensed that the ambassadors of the races I had previously encountered are but the beginning of dimensional restoration. There will be more – and others, too, who will need to put on the mantles that authorise and equip them to engage the dimensions: perhaps as you read you are stirred to pursue this, as it could be part of your destiny scroll.

"Yes, son, there is always more, so prepare your heart for change and engage the eternal flame once again." Engaging the eternal flame was part of a dark cloud experience. The flame that is to be found beyond was a representation of the process of the dark cloud experience but it is also a dimensional place.

I now knew that I needed to engage those dimensions themselves, not just their ambassadors, but I did not have it all figured out – this was going to be a wild ride. So once again I walked beyond the throne of grace to the doorways to beyond. There at the matrix of dimensional space, at the event horizon, I was drawn to a portal with a seemingly even smaller slit revolving at a faster speed. I hesitated again, contemplating how to enter, but the line from the movie The Matrix, 'there is no spoon', filled my mind and I knew this was not the time for my fears to hinder me on this quest. So I focused my desire and my willingness increased to the point where no fear could stop me.

What I discovered was that there was no real physical barrier to my entrance into the portal but this entrance was a construct of my mind's fear and represented my conscious mind's unwillingness to go beyond. I had created the appearance of this access point out of my own understanding, so my vision of the portals was a projection of my soul's fear.

With this revelation, the Father said, "Son, now that you have this realisation no barrier can resist your entrance other than what your mind creates through fear. Son, you decide, you choose, now that you are free. The revolving slit slowly transformed into an energy field that was transparent but slightly diffracted, as did all the other doorways that I could see spiralling into the distance.

I was now aware of many doors in that place that I could not previously see, not set out linearly but like a spiralling curved maze. Suddenly the possibilities were endless and I waited, weighing up the cost and pondering the potential adventures ahead. "My sons are ambassadors," the Father interjected, snapping me out of my musings. "They have been given the word and ministry of reconciliation that came not just from the work of the cross, which would limit it to mankind, but reconciliation was upon the foundation stone of all creation because the living word, My Son was slain for all He would create and speak into being. All things were created by Him and for Him, therefore what occurred before the foundation or fall has the power to touch all creation, seen and unseen, in all dimensions, as reconciliation was established within the very fabric of creation itself.

"The offering of the Creator for the created exists within the fabric of creation itself and is the life force, the energy that is the grace frequency vibrating as strings of living light within the smallest particles and largest structures. Grace is integral within the foundation stone from which all creation emanated. So the message of the redeeming, reconciling, restoring, resurrecting Creator who is abundantly overflowing with life is available to all races and beings across all dimensions within all of creation. No other races or beings carry (or have the possibility of carrying) the fullness of our DNA as the sons of God do, as none were made in the full image and likeness of their Creator as coheirs and co-creators in sonship. Many were created with aspects of our likeness and many were created with aspects of

224

our image but none other than man were spirit, soul and body carrying our DNA.

"No other races have the capacity to be our dwelling place or to dwell within us as man does but all can be restored to relationship and know love. Son, you have been given the mandate to be an ambassador to those races who have made contact. There will be more, once the testimony of freedom is released.

"Son, what I did not tell you is that you are the freedom, the light of love, and it is the expression of your glorious identity as a son that will be the frequency that restores hope and sets that part of creation free from its bondage. You have met on neutral ground, now enter the dimensional portals and radiate love's light, which will release the truth of true sonship to those whose hearts are longing for the revealing of the sons of God.

"Son, I will be calling many to engage with other dimensions and other dimensional races within their roles as My sons. My sons are responsible for creation and all that I have created within what is known and unknown. I am unveiling truth and revelation to those who are maturing and this includes the ability to access My consuming fire to rescue those who are there and to engage in the restoration of those who have fallen. The fallen ones include those of what you call the angelic realm but there also many other fallen dimensions."

For the anxious longing of the creation waits eagerly for the revealing of the sons of God. For the creation was subjected to futility, not willingly, but because of Him who subjected it, in hope that the creation itself also will be set free from its slavery to corruption into the freedom of the glory of the children of God (Romans 8:19-21).

An ambassador of hope

At this point, I still had no idea what this would entail but courage was rising in me and love began to motivate me, so I went for it. I had three encounters over a period of time in 2018 where I engaged each of those dimensions as an ambassador of hope.

The first engagement occurred when I stepped through the portal to beyond beyond. I am not going to describe what I saw in great detail as I do not want people trying to use their imaginations to try to see what I did – suffice it to say that it was a beyond experience of weirdness, yet strangely familiar. It was more the emotions I felt that I will share, as that is what moved me. When I say dimension, I do not know if this a planetary-type place contained in a whole other universe but it did not feel like that. It felt very restricted, limited, one-dimensional and not really describable, so I will cease trying.

I found myself in the dimension of the smaller-statured people and I immediately felt the bondage to servitude and segregation that existed in this dimension. Slavery, apartheid, caste system, living under the ruling classes, subjugation: all the worst things that we have done here on earth were fully operational, oppressing the masses in the foulest, most heinous way without any restrictions, as if this was the natural order of things and no one knew any different.

I could not be seen, as if cloaked, but then I saw a central obelisk and I instinctively knew that this was their version of the tower of Babel. This was their connection to our world but also the way of connecting the ruling classes to a hive mind and the way the subjugated classes had their minds and emotions suppressed. I do not know how I knew these things, I just did; I also knew that this technology could be turned to connect the working classes to the truth of the source of bondage and reveal the hope for freedom. So I ascended in light and I connected with the system like I was reversing the polarity of the circuit. I sent out the frequency of hope, broadcasting the message of love's light within sonship to go forth, stirring the memory of more ancient paths within those who had been under this bondage. That message of hope, the freedom from bondage, radiated from love's light and I knew and felt that they were touched by sonship, not to create a rebellion but a nonviolent love revolution. The mindsets of oppression and suppression began to be thrown off as love's light infiltrated that twisted society like leaven.

I knew that the Tower of Babel on earth had broadcast the mindset of making a name for themselves in independence: it was as if DIY code from earth had connected to creation itself, perverting and polluting creation with the very essence of selfishness. I knew that the mind of Christ had been released to bring true *metanoia* to this dimension.

This was my first dimensional encounter and I learned so much from it: how the dimension is connected to ours and that I did not need to understand and have a plan for everything. I could trust my instincts, motivated by love and prepared by my encounters.

As I returned through the portal, the Father was waiting for me. "Son, it is time to understand more about the fallen dimensions that seek redemption from the choices their ancestors made. News of freedom will spread as the light of sonship shines brightly and the sound frequency of liberty produces hope to all who are looking for the sons of God to come. The stories of the shining ones are embedded as truth within the history and mythology of all dimensions and seekers of truth are finding them. The frequency of hope is beginning to resonate across all the dimensions.

My next dimensional experience occurred as I journeyed beyond the throne of grace but this time I stopped to rest in the Father's arms of love before I engaged the portals to beyond beyond. Filled with the Father's love, I entered the dimension of the second humanoid race. As soon as I arrived, I felt such emptiness, as if this dimension was devoid of light and love. The dimension seemed sterile, lacking emotion, and I observed a loveless people who were enslaved, without hope. I saw them: their eyes had no life in them because love as an emotion had been eradicated and there was even no word for love within their vocabulary.

Their culture and society were technologically advanced but there was no joy, no expressions of art anywhere and everything was purely functional. There was no nature, no sign of other lifeforms, and the canopy over them was dark and overcast, permanently grey. It felt like all the energy that powers this society was drawn from within themselves and their emotional energy was continually being drained. They were like batteries fuelling the dimension, but this was not a life and I felt sickened by it.

I then saw the representative I had previously met in the anteroom and he led me to a meeting of others. All seemed lifeless, devoid of emotion. I was now closer to them and the absence of love was tangible: empty, hollow eyes stared at me. I felt so sad, drawn into the emptiness, but then started to feel compassion; it rose up in me and made me angry at the loss of love. I started to pulsate; light began to energise me and love's light went forth from me as an electromagnetic pulse, like a love bomb.

The energy of love's light radiated the room with love; emotions were felt for the first time and life began to spark. I saw faces that began to show a flicker of emotional responses as love's light dispelled the darkness of their soul and hope was felt. I began to talk of love and the Creator and the foundation stone of love's sacrifice. Sacrifice is impossible without love and now my words had meaning as the truth of love shone. I unveiled love's truth and nature with stories which, without feelings, were myths with no connection.

The revolution had begun. The seeds of emotion were sown and hope sprang forth as love's light was released: their faces no longer dead, eyes no longer lifeless because the power of love had been released and I knew that my part was done. I expressed a smile and there was a flicker of response that showed me love had returned and the infection of the leaven of love had begun to spread.

I returned through the portal, where the Father was waiting for me with a broad smile and a loving embrace. I felt the pleasure of His heart and I was filled with energy, having been drained by the experience.

My third encounter was with the dimension of the tall, rather regal-looking being. I went beyond beyond again, stepping through the portal into a dimension that was deeply divided and functioned by serfdom. There was rural living for the masses but extreme opulence and high technology for the few. There was the connection to the tower which I felt and sensed was there but which I could not see.

I felt the worst of all divisive systems were again in place, caste system, slavery, racism, serfdom, segregation, apartheid: all the worst the DIY tree path has created were mirrored here. There was no religion but there was the worst of all political systems of control that maintained the power of the few over the many through institutionally oppressive laws. The educational system was designed to segregate through lack of knowledge, keeping the classes divided and all creativity suppressed. No one was allowed to think beyond the limits of their education, which only allowed them to function according to caste.

They all had bowed heads, eyes fixed on the ground and never looked up: that was the law and punishable by death. No one of the lower caste was allowed to speak as no language was taught or allowed. Work training was the only education allowed and that was delivered by taskmasters.

This was the most terrible place where there was such suppression of the many by the few; but even within the many, there were multiple deep racial and cultural divides. Oppression clothed the air like a thick heavy blanket of despair, choking out all hope. I was met by the ambassador, who led me to a small gathering of representatives from each of the divided racial groups.

I had to focus all my energy on the truth that I now knew, that sonship and love's light is breaking through to the different dimensions of creation poisoned by the DIY tree. They are now being infiltrated by the first glimpses of hope as the sons of God arise with restored identity and position and the frequencies of hope are crossing dimensional matrices.

I began to speak, not so much with words but with heart to heart communication. I shared oneness, integration, wholeness and peace and I began to radiate the multicoloured, multifaceted, manifold nature of creation, affirming uniqueness and diversity as the expression of an infinitely loving God.

I saw that the very connection between dimensions of the poisoned tree can be used for good if the sons of God arise and take their places within the tree of life. I saw the shackles begin to break and suppression's heavy weight lift. They all began to look up for the first time to a new vista, a new horizon and a new hope. It was a beautiful sight as people truly looked at each other for the first time. The suspicion that fuels this dimension was dispelled by love's light and truth.

The seeds had been sown and I knew that my job there was done. Now hope will spread and the many will be united to throw off the shackles of the few. They now saw each other for the first time and celebrated their diversity and began to form a common language of honour, respect and love that will unite them heart to heart.

Time functions very differently in these dimensions: hours in our time, possibly years in theirs. What I do know is that our sonship is infiltrating creation with the sound frequency and light of jubilee. The cry of freedom is beginning to resonate beyond to the dimensions groaning under DIY tree oppression.

As I stepped back through the portal the Father welcomed me and embraced me joyously. He said "Son, all that I am is yours. Come to Me and be at rest as a son and encourage all of My children to be the same by letting go of their slavery and orphan identity and mentality. Live loved: free to know, free to see, free to be, free to do, free to go; and so fulfil your destiny as a son and heir of creation."

I thought perhaps that was the end of the quest – not that the Father ever said so – but I had not felt drawn or led to go back there again for the rest of 2018.

Then one day in 2019 the Father said, "Son, let Me introduce you to some more of those who are beginning to encounter the frequency of sonship's hope." I entered through the first portal with the Father into the dimensional anteroom and there were six more ambassadors of their races. They were all different in size, stature and appearance, but all vaguely humanoid; they introduced themselves as representatives of the Hadjurans, Durassians, Jordassians, Rakthurians, Silothians and Lorathians.

They all made representation for visitations to facilitate the freedom of their race from the corruption of rebellion. They were all calling on the sons of God to be revealed and the light of truth to shine to free their civilisations from bondage. I offered each of them the hand of friendship, we all embraced and I extended my spirit around them so they could feel the love, joy and peace of rest.

I authorised them to carry the testimony of hope and share love's light to their dimensions and I called for the light of love to shine in them and through them. I released the sound frequency of their race into our dimension to resonate with the sons of God mature enough to represent true sonship dimensionally. I called for the sons of God to radiate love's light dimensionally as the order of Melchizedek for the restoration of those who are in bondage to corruption.

"You will be surprised"
On another occasion in 2019, the Father said, "It is time for the shift to take place in 2020. Just be ready to go with the flow of the streams, do not resist where it takes you. Son, you will be surprised, no matter how prepared you try to be, because I AM is about to take you beyond once again.

"Son, go to the portal again and you will begin to see where this is going in the area of dimensional restoration. I went through the portal into the anteroom and six non-humanoid beings were waiting for me. This was the most bizarre of encounters that even my love of science fiction could not prepare me for. There were two energy beings of light who had no discernible form but seemed to connect empathically. There were two beings of gelatinous form and two beings of mechanical organic form.

I introduced myself and I felt their introduction rather than heard it but I knew their purpose. I felt their anguish, desperation and urgency but also feelings of inadequacy and stigmatisation for being different and not at all like sons.

I asked what I could do but immediately felt the need to accept them so I overshadowed them with my spirit in a type of embrace. I felt their situations and their desire to be included more intensely and so released their frequency into both the spiritual and physical realms to attract sons of God to their cause.

I called for their freedom, to have hope of restoration, as I empathised. Empathetic communications passed between us and between them as they now realised they were not alone. I called for a confederation to be formed like a support network. I then felt the isolation they had felt because of their differences so I celebrated and expressed the intense joy of the oracles of the Father's heart in diversity.

I felt them deeply moved, so I released the deep compassion of the Father's heart for their inclusion and integration. The

234

hopelessness they felt was slowly being replaced by the inclusive love that I released. I then sensed the root of the issue was the rejection of their races by the humanoids and the fact that they had not joined the great rebellion against the Creator but they had no connection with the sons of God.

I invited them to become ambassadors of reconciliation and restoration to the non-humanoid dimensions. They communicated that they were honoured but needed verification from others. I thanked them and withdrew but felt the pain of disconnection from the empathetic dimensions.

The Father, again waiting for me, said, "Son, there is more but well done, your instincts were fatherly and well-received; you are maturing in your role. I created you for this role with your own distinct characteristics: do not let anyone try to change you.

During our restoration government encounters, we discovered that some dimensional beings are seeking to negatively influence the earth, accessing our dimensions through different constellations, including Pleiades. They were a cosmic cabal of fallen angels and dimensional beings working with those more connected to the earth. We began shielding the earth from their influence to help support the global shift that was taking place. I will elucidate more in a later chapter.

On 19th May 2020, the Father gave me another invitation. "Son, come walk with Me." I found myself walking with Him into the dimensional anteroom, where we waited. "Son, there are many more from the dimensional realms that have been touched by hope but there are few who will engage them. Son, will you accept that role?"

I thought for a moment and asked, "What is it that you want me to do?"

"Act as an ambassador for the dimensions, as you are for the Joshua Generation, and legislate for their freedom and restoration."

"Father, am I responsible for engagement with each dimension myself?"

"No, son, that is the destiny of others as they mature but there may be occasions that you will be called upon to engage on missions of hope into those dimensions."

I accepted the invitation; the portals began to open and representatives came forward. Twelve races came before me, beings with a variety of appearances but there were three that got my attention as I felt something familiar.

I addressed them and asked what they wanted. They all seemed to know each other and one answered for them. "We are from the dimensions that are part of the cosmic agendas that are seeking to control your world. As you have been protecting your world we have become aware that there is hope. We have always believed that the sons of God could not be trusted, lacked integrity and were disingenuous, so our race has been part of the great cosmic cabal. We have willingly followed what we now see as a deception to control your world but have seen the hope of love's light and now believe we can be free.

"Our dimensions have been filled with malice and hatred for mankind that has fuelled our societies. We have partnered with Division, Competition and Warmonger to fuel the hate on your world which causes the conflicts that destabilise your world and creates the opposition against the sons of God."

One of them revealed that their dimension has had a particular focus on denominating religion to cause strife and enmity.

Another spoke, "Ours has been focused on promoting the national pride that keeps nations in competition with each other. War is our ultimate agenda."

The last spoke, "Ours is hatred that leads to racism within nations, to divide them, and between nations to fuel the suspicion that separates and divides. We have all felt love in action and now we want help from the sons we have opposed."

I was somewhat thrown by this revelation and felt that I needed to check it out with the Father. So I turned my attention to the other nine who were looking on while these conversations were happening, "What do you want?"

They all spoke in my mind at once but I was able to understand them all. There was a common theme; they had all been deceived into believing that it was mankind that was responsible for the deprivation that had afflicted each of their societies. They had all been hostile towards mankind because they were suffering and had always believed that we were responsible. They had now all become aware that they had been fooled by a cosmic conspiracy that had made mankind the enemy rather than the hope. They all asked that the message of hope that had reached them be amplified to free them but as yet they seemed to have no concept of restoration to a higher purpose or of the reality of God as Father or Creator. The knowledge or even concept of God seemed to be totally absent, as if they had been blinded by hatred.

The frequency of our love and our declaration of selflessness has made an impact throughout creation. 'We are here for you' has been the spark that has ignited revolution throughout the dimensions.

My latest encounter with dimensions as of the time of writing was on 15th June 2020 when the Father invited me to come and walk with Him. He took me out into the cosmos and I discerned something that I had seen before, the same voids that were around the atmosphere of the earth. They were in many of the galaxies that we visited, hiding portals, and only discernible by the absence of light. I knew how to penetrate those shielded voids as I had done before, by changing the vibrating frequency of my being.

The Father stopped the whistle-stop tour of the universe at the constellation of Pleiades and we entered the void. Within it, there was a portal that was energised and very active, with beings coming and going.

I asked the Father who they were and what they were doing. "These are who you are shielding the earth from and this is a junction between dimensions that connects many places." I started to think about what I was supposed to do when the

Father interrupted my musings by revealing His heart for those here and for all the dimensions that they represented.

His thoughts were far from my thoughts, so I just focused on Him and my mind went back to the chamber of creation. I first discovered this place, dimension and concept on a corporate ascension of the restoration government group. I was drawn to a picture published by NASA for the Hubble telescope's 30th anniversary. It was an image of a nebula called the Cosmic Reef that appeared to show a blue portal. I used it as my Zoom background image and a number of us were drawn by it. So we ascended to engage with the cosmos and encountered the place that the Father named the Chamber of Creation. I shared this experience in more detail in chapter 6 where we looked at the scope of sonship.

I began to resonate with the Father's heart and I started to pulse and move in harmony and then the lumens which were hidden within me and the void began to illuminate that place. That absence suddenly became filled with light and love energy that took all those beings by surprise and got their attention. I was aware that I was supposed to do something but I hesitated and reached out to the Father with my mind. Inspired and energised I began to attract the quantum lumens who streamed towards me and from within me and surrounded me as if creating a luminescent field around me. I was moving in unison with creative light and was one heart and mind with them. I thought and spoke and instantly, through a quantum entangled connection, they moved and created a new reality where love's light filled that void.

It was like I was conducting or orchestrating a message of hope for restoration where the lumens were dancing like an amazing cosmic light show, communicating the Father's desire in a way that was far beyond anything I had felt or experienced before. One by one the beings started moving towards the light that was encompassing me and I became aware that the Father was hidden from my sight.

For a brief moment I felt apprehensive but then I felt the Father's comforting presence within me. I released the call for restoration, the lumens shone brightly with love's light and the whole atmosphere in that void changed. I continued to release the love frequencies of the oracles of the Father's heart and I expanded my being until it encompassed the whole void. I called to them, revealing the truth of their deception and, beyond, their true origin within the Father's creative purpose.

The beings began to respond and, at first, I felt them communicating their confusion but then, one by one, they decided they wanted to be restored back into creation, according to the Father's desire. I watched as the lumens streamed towards them and burst from within them to join in a joyful, jubilant celebration that sent ripples into the dimensions that were connected.

Again I felt overwhelmed by the experience and did not know what to do. The Father's comforting voice reassured me as He said, "Come, your part is over, just keep them in your heart. The revolution has progressed today and this will have created the seedbed for great change. Son, this is a lesson for you. You were thinking warfare and disruption and I was thinking peace and joy. Rebuilding and restoration will never be facilitated by warfare, only through coming in the opposite spirit will change begin."

So we have looked at the experiences and testimonies relating to the restoration of other dimensions and other dimensional beings. I do not profess to be an expert on these issues, I am only sharing my own experiences, but I do believe they are consistent with the nature and character of the loving Father I have experienced.

All I have shared is dependent on the restoration of our sonship identity and purpose. If God desires the whole of creation to be set free then that certainly includes all of His human children. This brings us to the final area that will be covered in this volume of *The Restoration of All Things*: the universal salvation, reconciliation and restoration of mankind.

Chapter 7. Exploding the 'Hell' Mythology

Before exploring how I came to my current beliefs concerning 'hell' I need to define what I do and do not mean by the term. When I use the word 'hell' I am referring to the modern theological concept of 'hell' as a place of punishment and eternal conscious torment for those who have rejected Jesus in this life.

The hell delusion

I believe this is a delusion and there is no such place as that version of 'hell'. There is however a place that I would prefer to call 'the consuming fire of God's loving presence' that the Father allows His children to choose to go to but it is not a place where the Father is retributively punishing or tormenting them. This figurative fire is for restorative purifying and refining and is entirely biblical.

How did I come to that conclusion? Like many others, I was brought up on the evangelical assumptions of hell being a place of eternal conscious torment where God was punishing His rebellious children, those who chose to exercise their free will in rejecting His free offer of salvation. This meant I always assumed that physical death was the end of choice and that there was no escaping hell if you ended up there.

The question is, why did I assume that those doctrines were true beyond questioning? I was never really happy or comfortable with that supposed truth but never had any reason to question it because it lined up with views of God revealed through the doctrine of PSA (penal substitutionary atonement). This doctrine, as I understood it, showed that God loved mankind so much that Jesus was willing to be our substitute in receiving the punishment and retribution of an angry God whose wrath needed appeasing. Therefore God punished Jesus with the horrific death of the cross so we would not have to be punished by Him as we fully deserved. This supposedly demonstrated His love for us as His children. But wait a minute... that means that God, as a father, punished His son. When that fact began to dawn on me the 'good news' of evangelicalism began to seem not quite so good. God was a cosmic child abuser who punished His own son! Why would that comfort me or give me any security? Perhaps if I stepped out of line by displeasing Him in some way He might also punish me! The evangelical doctrine of eternal conscious torment (ECT) states that if, in your 70 years of life (plus or minus), you do not respond to the Christian gospel, then you will burn in the fires of hell forever being punished by this loving God.

It was only when I began to meet with God myself in a face to face personal relationship that those encounters created cognitive dissonance within me. My encounters were not consistent with my beliefs and those encounters were significantly powerful to overcome the confirmation bias of the views I had been programmed with. I discovered that God is my loving heavenly Father and He is not at all like I thought; His true nature and character as love contradicted my previously held beliefs.

The Father took me through a long process of deconstruction where His love challenged the foundational pillars of my belief systems. The pillar of evangelicalism held all the other eight pillars in their place to create a coherent world view that was confirmed by the principle of sola scriptura, the Bible alone. My face to face encounters with the Father, Son and Spirit undermined and destroyed my trust in how the Bible has been translated, and definitely my interpretation of it. In the past whenever I read the Bible it always confirmed what I already believed and therefore my mind went unrenewed and the status quo of my religious programming remained in place.

No more. The first evil demonic doctrine that the Father challenged was Penal Substitutionary Atonement and as I looked at the assumptions it made about what the Bible was saying, I realised that I had been sold a total fabricated lie. This lie was the cornerstone of my belief systems. Once it was exposed and rejected, that brought about the collapse of all those associated doctrines such as hell being a place of eternal conscious torment, physical death being the end of choice, the so-called Biblical concepts of everlasting, eternal judgment, eternal and 'forever and ever' in the context of punishment and torment.

When that first domino fell all the others collapsed like some elaborate domino rally where my belief systems were all organised like a pattern of dominos each connected to the previous and the next. Domino after domino fell as my mind was deconstructed but for quite a while I was tripping over the rubble of the collapsed pillars, unable to find solid ground on which to stand. This felt less than stable; I was uncomfortable with the uncertainty – what did I believe? – and only after I had experiences and testimonies that confirmed a more loving belief system did I feel more secure.

Theories of the atonement are ways of revealing the truths of the basic story: Jesus atones for our sins. The atonement is how we explain what the life, death, and resurrection of Jesus actually did. This is seeking to answer the question "why God did become a human?"

Throughout church history, Christians have answered these questions in seven primary ways listed in chronological order. These atonement models are called the Christus Victor Theory, the Ransom Theory and the Moral Influence Theory. Combinations of these three were the prevailing views for a millennium until the Satisfaction Theory (Anselm) in the 12th century, the Penal Substitutionary Theory during the Reformation, its variation the Governmental Theory during the Methodist era and more recently the Scapegoat theory.

Whole books have been written on the subject of the atonement and I believe that there are elements of truth embedded within each position, so rather than create something that divides us, embracing those embedded truths enables us to be in union.

Jesus was victorious over death and the enemy on the cross which affirms the atonement position of Christus Victor. He was a model of sonship for us and He was a ransom (but not paid to God, who never held creation in captivity).

In C. S. Lewis's Narnia series, and particularly *The Lion, the Witch, and the Wardrobe*[9], Aslan sacrifices his life to rescue the traitor Edmund, defeats the White Witch, and frees all Narnia; so Jesus sacrificed his life to rescue sinful humanity, defeat Satan and even death itself, and free all creation to be restored to a relationship with God. The Christus Victor position, therefore, says that, like Edmund, mankind had both betrayed God and become victims of evil, but God loved us even when we were his enemies, so much so that he willingly died to rescue us.

The Ransom view claimed that Adam and Eve sold humanity over to the devil at the time of the Fall. Justice required God to pay him a ransom (the death of Jesus). What the devil did not realise was that death could not prevail over Him, so once justice was satisfied, He was able to free us from the devil's grip.

Redemption in this theory means to buy back, and purchase the human race from the clutches of the devil. The main issue with this is the act of 'paying off' the devil. Not all Ransom theorists believe that the devil is paid; some suggest that, in this act of ransom, Christ frees humanity from the bondage of sin and death. In this way, Ransom relates to the Christus Victor theory. These views of ransom are similar, but also drastically different.

The real issue is not who the ransom is paid to but what it is paid for – and remember, the terms are figurative and often allegorical not meant to be taken literally. Mankind was sold into the slavery of lost identity and Jesus ransomed us from lost identity to restored identity. Jesus came as the son of man to identify with our lost identity so that we could be restored to God's full original intention.

I believe that Jesus' death was a ransom but that ransom was not paid to a God (or a devil) who held creation in bondage but to the lost identity and slavery which mankind was sold into. It does not require a person or being to receive the ransom as it is more of a concept of intention that gives us a figurative rather than a literal meaning.

Therein lies many of our problems: we have been taught through the principle of Sola Scriptura that everything is literal, so we often miss the reality by looking for the literal fulfilment.

I have no issues with the fact that Jesus was a substitute for each of mankind as He took our death and atoned for it but He did not take our punishment, as punishing us was never God's intention. The Father did not punish or sacrifice His Son on our behalf: the very thought has never entered His mind. Jesus gave Himself over to men as an offering to satiate our need for 'justice', our need to appease the angry version of GOD that religion has created.

"For the sons of Judah have done that which is evil in My sight," declares the Lord, *"they have set their detestable things in the house which is called by My name, to defile it. They have built the high places of Topheth, which is in the valley of the son of Hinnom* [Gehenna]*, to burn their sons and their daughters in the fire, which I did not command, and it did not come into My mind* (Jeremiah 7:30-31).

As Richard Rohr[10] has said, "Jesus did not come to change the mind of God about humanity (it did not need changing!); Jesus came to change the mind of humanity about God." The foundation of restoration is based on pure love and perfect freedom from the very beginning, where God, expressing Themselves as a loving Father, draws people toward a relationship in which their true identity of face to face innocence can be experienced through universal 'at-one-ment,' instead of mere sacrificial atonement.

In reality, nothing changed at Calvary, as this was a reflection in time of what has always been in the eternal now but everything was revealed as God's suffering love—so that we could change!

Christ's death is not some divine transaction to satisfy God's sense of justice or His wrath. After all, if God is all-knowing, He knew before He created humans what we would be like and He still went ahead and did it. The death of Christ is rather transformative: it provides mankind with the hope that our lives can be restored so that we can become all that our loving Father Creator intended us to become – ascended fathers and co-creators.

The true nature of the atonement is based in the nature and character of God as love. Love is the only lens we can look through to enable us to see His true nature, understand restoration and explode the 'hell' myth.

"God is love plus nothing! God's holiness and justice are facets of His love, and not something different or opposite from His love." - Brad Jersak.

"Being face to face with Jesus means all darkness is shredded in His light. Vengeance might as well be the same as salvation, mercy or justice" - George McDonald.

As I experienced the reality of God's love I found I had so many assumptions and presumptions that I believed to be true without question but they were all, in fact, false – lies, delusions, illusions and deceptions – and that included the 'hell' delusion I was brought up with. In reality, God's wrath, anger and vengeance are poured out on anything that is keeping us from a relationship with Him in face to face innocence.

As the Father began to deconstruct my mind from its frameworks of beliefs He asked me a question: "How much of what you know about Me, the Bible and Christianity came directly from Me and how much of it came from the teaching, books, or sermons of others or your own studies?"

When I asked the Father what plumb line I should use to evaluate my experiences and encounters, or interpret the Bible, He said, "LOVE. If it is not unconditional love, it is not Me; if it is love, it is Me; and love must be unconditional and directed towards others, or it is not love at all."

God is Love. He really is! Having a relationship with Him does not involve trying to please or appease Him. He loves us unconditionally, and there is nothing we can do that would cause Him to love us more (or less). He is Love.

Our view of God has become so distorted that many people, not only outside the church but even within it, believe He is angry with us and only keeps us in line through fear. They are getting Him confused with some other god. Love that is forced, coerced or demanded is not love at all.

"Heresy!" some say. Ironically, this deep truth that God is love is often seen as heretical by members of the religious institution because they hold to a warped theological image. If anyone dares to challenge doctrinal assumptions and presumptions it always provokes accusation. I have been told myself that I am 'on the slippery slope away from orthodoxy' as if that is something I should avoid at all costs. The implication is that backsliding and a complete loss of faith are the inevitable results.

That is not how I see it. I believe that God is challenging our preconceived, pre-programmed ideas about Him. Those preconceptions and programming are largely a consequence of our place (and century) of birth, our family traditions and other sociological factors. In another time or place, the received truth about God passed along to us would have been different anyway.

God does not want our knowledge of Him to be conditional upon when or where we were born, or the religious tradition we were first introduced to. I do not believe He wants something so important to be based on that sort of accident. Regardless of our religious beliefs (or lack of them), He is reaching out, looking to engage every single one of us in a personal relationship. To that end, He pours out His Spirit on all flesh (see Acts 2:17).

Do all roads lead to...?

'Does that mean,' said Mack, 'that all roads lead to you?'

'Not at all.' Jesus smiled as he reached for the door handle to the shop. 'Most roads don't lead anywhere. What it does mean is that I will travel any road to find you.' (Wm. Paul Young, *The Shack*)[11].

Orthodoxy is an interesting concept in itself. The word is defined as 'an authorized or generally accepted theory, doctrine or practice'. With our 30,000+ denominations, you can easily see how rare 'generally accepted' might be! So whose orthodoxy is it that we are in danger of slipping away from? Roman Catholic orthodoxy? Anglican or Presbyterian orthodoxy? Reformed, evangelical or charismatic orthodoxy? Or even Orthodox orthodoxy (take your choice of Greek or Russian)? We cannot slip away from most of those since we never actually subscribed to them in the first place.

Almost all of us, if we are honest, believe something different today to what we believed 10, 20, or 50 years ago. God never changes, but through fresh revelation, He is continually unveiling aspects of Himself we have never seen before. We call this 'progressive revelation'. Any 'orthodoxy' can only be a snapshot of someone's view of God at a particular point in time, which perhaps explains how many versions of it there are.

But The Bible Clearly Says...

Every scripture we read today is a translation into English (or one of the dozens of other modern languages) and they all reflect the translator's particular viewpoint or understanding (those compiled by committee no less than those by individuals).

The Passion Translation and Mirror Bible state their viewpoints front and centre. The translators of the King James Version had to adhere to a set of rules drawn up on the King's behalf by the soon-to-be Archbishop, Richard Bancroft. For example, they were explicitly prohibited from translating '*ekklesia*'(church) as 'community', 'assembly' or 'congregation', most likely in case people realised it was supposed to have a legislative, governmental role. There is no such thing as an objective, definitive translation (even if you do call it 'Authorised')!

Those who can read the original languages fare little better. We do not have complete manuscripts and where more than one version exists it is clear that alterations to the text have occurred.

Canon of Scripture

Proponents of protestant evangelical orthodoxy would have us believe it is very different from its Roman Catholic counterpart, but in reality, much of its theology stems directly from the councils, doctrines and creeds established by the early Roman Catholic and Latin Church.

The very concept of a 'canon of scripture' was only introduced in 397 AD at the Council of Carthage. Carthage was the one school (out of six) in the ancient Christian world which held to an angry, retributive view of God, possibly because it was also the only one where Latin, not Greek, was the language in common use. Augustine was from Carthage, and he had no understanding of the Greek in which the gospels and letters were written; if he had, he would never have developed such a distorted view of God.

The Council delegates bartered over what books were to be included. Perhaps they forgot that Jesus warned His disciples of the leaven of the Pharisees and Herod, of political and religious spirits, but their eventual selection was more politically than divinely motivated. So although *all scripture is God-inspired* (1 Tim 3:16), we may well have differing views about what Paul meant not only by the word translated 'inspired' but also by 'scripture'.

Emperor Constantine united church and state for his own political ends. Almost 1300 years later King James directed the Bible translators to translate in a way that would ensure there was no conflict between church and state and would maintain his control over all sections of society. Much of the history of the Western church can be summarised as the exercise of fear to control people, and the notion of 'orthodoxy' is still being used in the same way today, to defend and protect entrenched positions and to suppress valid questions and ideas.

It is very healthy to doubt what you believe, rather than just accepting it as the truth. There is far more to God than any theology or doctrine can contain. I agree with this statement which I heard quoted by Brad Jersak: "When doubts appear in me it means that I have outgrown my incomplete idea of God, my imperfect knowledge of Him." (*Doubts,* blog post by Metropolitan Anthony Bloom)[12].

It is only through experience that the nature of God can be known. It can only be subjective, and that is not a bad thing. People will warn us that without something objective to rely on (usually they mean the Bible) we will end up believing fairy tales. Well, I suggest we have been believing fairy tales already and God now wants us to come to the knowledge of the Truth (a person, not a doctrine). Love will always be our plumb line.

Mind-quakes

Many of my experiences have revealed God's love at a new level I would never have believed possible. They have challenged and unravelled most of my theology and doctrine and I am not looking for new ones; nor am I asking you to do anything but to be open to engage God's love for yourself and see where that takes you. Where it has taken me is into an experiential relationship in which heaven has opened up. I have come to know *the breadth and length and height and depth* of that love (Ephesians 3:18) and how ardently He desires everyone to experience it for themselves. Even death is not enough to stop Him loving us.

My encounters with God created cognitive dissonance within me (that is, they caused me mental stress and discomfort as I tried to hold on to two or more mutually exclusive and contradictory views, ideas or values). I had a choice: I could fight to hold on to what I had thought to be true or I could allow the Truth – Jesus – to renew my mind. I chose the second, and it was not easy. It wobbled my head. It felt like 'mind-quakes'. Explosions of truth shook loose the belief systems I had.

God spoke to me a lot during the process. He told me, "Reveal the Truth, unveil for people your testimony of who I am... Son, reveal Me, the true Me. Let the Joshua generation know the true Me unfettered by the old orders of the theology of intellectual information."

One day, God said, "Let me show you My mind." I am not going to describe it visually, but it was like being in the midst of a conversation between Father, Son and Spirit that is continual and is all 'now'. I got just a brief glimpse of God's reality, and saw that He was connected to everyone that had ever lived, is living or will live, all at once (that is 108 billion and counting). He was connected to everyone in the 'now', knowing every choice and every decision made every microsecond. His loving desire was to bring good out of every choice, to redeem even the most stupid decisions of every person (and we all make them). This love is not limited to a select group of people but is extended to everyone at all times and in all places.

It was a living experience of what Paul described in Romans 8:28, that *the love of God causes everything to mutually contribute to our advantage* (Mirror Bible). Our view of God influences how we see ourselves and the world that we live in, and this experience changed that for me. Our view of everything has to be aligned with Love. His love won't relent. God desires us to know Him (Love) by personal experience so we can know ourselves as His children and bring His kingdom of love to the world.

The real slippery slope

I love Chuck Crisco's acronym for 'heretic' (I have tweaked it just a little):

Happy Enlightened Righteous Exploring Truth In Christ.

On those terms, I'm willing to be called one. So for myself, I have joyfully stepped off the slippery slope that for 1800 years has been taking us away from a relational, loving God towards a false image of Him horribly distorted by religion. As my friend Lindy Strong says "my past self would, without doubt, call my present self a heretic" and in reality, if that was not the case then I would be stuck in the past maintaining the status quo with an unrented mind. I encourage you to do the same: to discover for yourself the true nature and character of God who is Love.

I joyfully jump onto the slope that goes from the pinnacle of modern theology and doctrine back to the beliefs of the apostles and early church fathers who were relationally discipled by Jesus and His disciples in love. I encourage you to jump onto the same slope and enjoy the ride, so you can experience for yourself the amazing, limitless love, grace and mercy of a Father who is love.

God is love

God is love. This really is good news! The whole of creation needs to become aware of this reality and embrace this life-transforming truth. The whole of creation is waiting and longing for the sons of God to reveal the truth of love but mostly religion has painted a 'bad news' picture that has caused so many to reject this truly loving Father.

As I have chronicled in these previous chapters, God has personally started to walk me through encounters that continually challenge my perception of who He is. I am still on a journey of discovering the true nature of God as love and as a result, I find myself questioning and often rejecting the established doctrines and theological positions of the modern-day evangelical church.

Evangelism

God has shown me that I (and the church, and the world) have been badly deceived by 'do-it-yourself' religion. Nowhere does this deception show up more clearly than in our approach to evangelism.

God was in Christ reconciling the world to Himself, not counting their trespasses against them (2 Corinthians 5:19).

This is the message of reconciliation at the heart of the gospel we are called to preach. And the word translated 'world' is the Greek word *kosmos*, which is even wider than we might have thought. Yet when I looked closely at how we have done evangelism, even here at Freedom, I uncovered a fear-based system which originates from a wrong perception of God as angry, vindictive and cruel.

Religion has hijacked the gospel, made 'escaping hell' its focus and used the threat of eternal damnation to scare people into the kingdom. "Good news! (But first, the bad news...)". My own conversion experience was like that. I heard sermons about hell and judgment week after week and decided I needed 'fire insurance'.

Hell? Not going there...

For most Christians, an eternal hell is a given, an unquestioned doctrine. Hell fits their doctrinal system. God is love but He is also just. He must punish sin. Hell is the punishment for sin. Simple.

Or is it? I knew it would take a while to address this issue properly and I might be taking the lid off a whole can of worms. I resisted broaching the question of 'hell' for some time, as if it were some kind of 'no-go' area, but God would not let me be. It just kept resurfacing, both in my encounters and as I prepared the 'new versus old' teaching module in the *Engaging God* programme. It is a concept that is generally accepted in most (if not all) religions and wider society, but I knew deep down that something in what I had been taught was not consistent with the Father's love.

Think again

This is where we come back to the scripture from 2 Corinthians which says that God is not counting their trespasses against anyone:

...namely, that God was in Christ reconciling the world to Himself, not counting their trespasses against them... (2 Corinthians 5:19).

The whole cosmos has already been reconciled and no-one's trespasses are counted against them. So from God's perspective what need is there for a 'hell'?

And, despite the limitations of the translations we use there are plenty of other familiar passages which might prompt us to think again too:

But God demonstrates His own love toward us, in that while we were yet sinners, Christ died for us (Romans 5:8). Who is the 'us' that Christ died for, a select few or everyone? The Bible itself answers the question: *For the love of Christ controls us, having concluded this, that one died for all...* (2 Corinthians 5:14).

For if while we were enemies we were reconciled to God through the death of His Son, much more, having been reconciled, we shall be saved by His life (Romans 5:10). God is not angry, even with those who may feel like His enemies.

When you were dead in your transgressions and the uncircumcision of your flesh, He made you alive together with Him, having forgiven us all our transgressions, having cancelled out the certificate of debt consisting of decrees against us, which was hostile to us; and He has taken it out of the way, having nailed it to the cross (Colossians 2:13-14).

For as in Adam all die, so also in Christ all will be made alive (1 Corinthians 15:22). In each part of this statement, 'all' refers to the same people... all people, as Peter confirms: *For Christ also died for sins once for all, the just for the unjust, so that He might bring us to God...* (1 Peter 3:18).

Angry forever?

Pitying and merciful is the Lord; lenient and full of mercy. Not unto the end shall He be provoked to anger, nor into the aeon (age) *will He cherish wrath. Not according to our lawless deeds did He deal with us; nor according to our sins did He recompense to us* (Psalm 103:8-10, Septuagint).

"I shall not punish you into the aeon (age), *nor shall I be provoked to anger with you perpetually"* (Isaiah 57:16, Septuagint).

"I will heal their apostasy (unbelief), *I will love them freely, for My anger has turned away from them"* (Hosea 14:4).

My own experiences of God are characterised by love, grace and mercy, not anger and fear. God does not stay angry forever, so why would He punish people forever? His love is more powerful than all our sin put together. It is far stronger than the lies and deception designed to keep us separated from Him:

"Put me like a seal over your heart, like a seal on your arm. For love is as strong as death, jealousy is as severe as Sheol; its flashes are flashes of fire, the very flame of the Lord. Many waters cannot quench love, nor will rivers overflow it" (Song of Solomon 8:6-7).

Rather than meaning torment and punishment, in this passage fire is a depiction of passion and unrelenting love: God's love is a flame that can never be quenched or extinguished and He is unrelenting in pursuing us for relationship.

There is no fear in love; but perfect love casts out fear, because fear involves punishment, and the one who fears is not perfected in love (1 John 4:18).

How can God punish people if He is love? The two are incompatible. He cannot and He does not. God's justice is always restorative. Discipline and punishment may be indistinguishable terms when viewed with a western mindset but they are totally different when framed by love.

Perpetual Conscious Torment

The idea of 'hell' as a place of perpetual torment is so prevalent in the world's religions and cultures that if you mention 'hell', most people have a pretty clear image of what you are talking about: it probably includes fire, demons with pitchforks and people in torment. This image has been propagated by literature through the ages and more recently by films and TV shows but it was not the view of the early church.

The writings of the Old Testament and Jewish literature throw up various views of the afterlife, including annihilation or sleep until judgment, but eternal torment after death was not a Hebrew concept at all. *The Interpreter's Dictionary of the Bible* comments, "Nowhere in the Old Testament is the abode of the dead regarded as a place of punishment or torment. The concept of an infernal 'hell' developed in Israel only during the Hellenistic [Greek] period" (i.e. beginning in the fourth century B.C.).

There are even some people today who teach that at the resurrection, God will give unbelievers new bodies specifically designed to withstand eternal torture. What kind of a god is that? Is that really the God who was perfectly revealed in Jesus?

To show how extreme the 'hell' mythology gets, I am including some quotes from history by those deceived by this insidious doctrine, collated in a booklet produced by Jerry Onyszczak[13]:

The fruit of eternal conscious torment

Queen Mary of England – "As the souls of heretics are hereafter to be eternally burning in hell, there can be nothing more proper than for me to imitate the divine vengeance by burning them on earth." [This legitimate and logical reasoning exhibits the natural fruits of the doctrine of "eternal" punishment. It is recorded that Queen Mary burned alive 300 Protestants for heresy].

Polybius – The ancient historian says, "Since the multitude is ever fickle, full of lawless desires, irrational passions and violence, there is no other way to keep them in order but by the fear and terror of the invisible world; on which account our ancestors seem to me to have acted judiciously when they contrived to bring into the popular belief these notions of the gods, and of the infernal regions."

Jonathan Edwards – "Reprobate infants are vipers of vengeance, which Jehovah will hold over hell, in the tongs of his wrath, till they turn and spit venom in his face! The view of the misery of the damned will double the ardour of the love and gratitude of the saints of heaven."

Sight of Hell Torments Increases Happiness!

Jonathan Edwards – "The sight of hell torments will exalt the happiness of the saints forever Can the believing father in Heaven be happy with his unbelieving children in Hell... I tell you, yea! Such will be his sense of justice that it will increase rather than diminish his bliss."

Thomas Aquinas – "That the saints may enjoy their beatitude more thoroughly, and give more abundant thanks for it to God, a perfect sight of the punishment of the damned is granted them... In order that the happiness of the saints may be more delightful to them and that they may render more copious thanks to God for it, they are allowed to see perfectly the sufferings of the damned... So that they may be urged the more to praise God... The saints in heaven know distinctly all that happens... to the damned."

Jeremy Taylor – "Husbands shall see their wives, parents shall see their children tormented before their eyes... the bodies of the damned shall be crowded together in hell like grapes in a wine-press, which press on another till they burst..."

Saints Will Be Acquainted With The Eternal Sufferings Of The Lost

John Calvin – [Who had some of his theological enemies burned to death in green, slow-burning wood.]

"Forever harassed with a dreadful tempest, they shall feel themselves torn asunder by an angry God, and trans-fixed and penetrated by mortal stings, terrified by the thunderbolts of God, and broken by the weight of his hand, so that to sink into any gulf would be more tolerable than to stand for a moment in these terrors."

Augustine – "They who shall enter into [the] joy [of the Lord] shall know what is going on outside in the outer darkness... The saints'... knowledge, which shall be great, shall keep them acquainted... with the eternal sufferings of the lost."

Reverend J. Furniss – "The fifth dungeon is the red hot oven. The little child is in the red hot oven. Hear how it screams to come out; see how it turns and twists itself about in the fire. It beats its head against the roof of the oven. It stamps its little feet on the floor."

Gerhard – "... the Blessed will see their friends and relations among the damned as often as they like but without the least of compassion."

Tertullian – "How shall I admire, how laugh, how rejoice, how exult, when I behold so many proud monarchs groaning in the lowest abyss of darkness; so many magistrates liquefying in fiercer flames than they ever kindled against the Christians; so many sages philosophers blushing in red-hot fires with their deluded pupils; so many tragedians more tuneful in the expression of their own sufferings; so many dancers tripping more nimbly from anguish than ever before from applause."

Samuel Hopkins – "This display of the divine character will be most entertaining to all who love God, will give them the highest and most ineffable pleasure. Should the fire of this eternal punishment cease, it would in a great measure obscure the light of heaven, and put an end to a great part of the happiness and glory of the blessed."

Isaac Watts – (1674-1748) America's "Great Awakening" popular hymn writer, even set Christian's feet to dancing with this crisp little verse:

What bliss will fill the ransomed souls,
When they in glory dwell,
To see the sinner as he rolls,
In quenchless flames of hell.

Scriptures have been used to justify some of the greatest atrocities in human history. People were tortured, burned at the stake and multitudes murdered based on somebody's understanding of the Scriptures! Jesus, Paul and believers throughout the ages faced their greatest opposition from those who knew the Scriptures.

Current Modern Day Fruit

Andrea Yates – 2003, on trial for allegedly killing her children.

Media outlets alleged that Michael Woroniecki, an itinerant preacher whom Rusty [Andrea's husband] had met while attending Auburn University, bears some responsibility for the deaths due to his 'fire and brimstone' message and certain teachings found in his newsletter The Perilous Times that they had received on occasion and which was entered into evidence at the trial.

While in prison, Yates stated she had considered killing the children for two years, adding that they thought she was not a good mother and claimed her sons were developing improperly. She told her jail psychiatrist: "It was the seventh deadly sin. My children weren't righteous. They stumbled because I was evil. The way I was raising them, they could never be saved. They were doomed to perish in the fires of hell." She told her jail psychiatrist that Satan influenced her children and made them more disobedient."

[Regardless of Andrea's mental state, where did she get her understanding about perishing "in the fires of hell"? Obviously, someone had taught her.]

Eschatological context

Before going any further, which will inevitably mean looking at various red-letter Bible verses, passages, teachings and parables of Jesus that have been used to affirm that Jesus taught "hell" as a place of eternal conscious torment, I need to provide the eschatological context: everything Jesus was speaking about in

Matthew chapter 24, including the passages referring to Gehenna, were all to be fulfilled in that generation (in AD70) and are not awaiting fulfilment in the distant future.

Jesus made a statement in Matthew 24:34: *"Truly I say to you, this generation will not pass away until all these things take place."* In this chapter, Jesus was giving answers to the questions posed by His disciples following His challenging discourse with the religious leaders of His day recorded in Matthew chapters 21-23. During that discourse, Jesus turned their eschatological beliefs on their head and told them that Jerusalem and the temple would be destroyed and the kingdom would be removed from them. They were understandably incensed by Jesus' assertions that were the culmination of 3 years' worth of teaching and challenges to their preconceived religious and cultural understanding of the kingdom of God and Israel's place within it.

Many times Jesus laid a foundation for the truth that these eschatological events would occur 'in that generation':

"But whenever they persecute you in one city, flee to the next; for truly I say to you, you will not finish going through the cities of Israel until the Son of Man comes" (Matthew 10:23).

For what will it profit a man if he gains the whole world and forfeits his soul? Or what will a man give in exchange for his soul? For the Son of Man is going to come in the glory of His Father with His angels, and will then repay every man according to his deeds. "Truly I say to you, there are some of those who are standing here who will not taste death until they see the Son of Man coming in His kingdom" (Matthew 16:26-28).

"Truly I say to you, all these things will come upon this generation" (Matthew 23:36).

"Truly I say to you, this generation will not pass away until all these things take place" (Matthew 24:34; see also Mark 13:30 and Luke 21:32.)

When Jesus answered those questions posed by His eschatologically confused disciples, He made it absolutely clear that all those things would occur in that generation.

Jesus came out from the temple and was going away when His disciples came up to point out the temple buildings to Him. And He said to them, "Do you not see all these things? Truly I say to you, not one stone here will be left upon another, which will not be torn down." As He was sitting on the Mount of Olives, the disciples came to Him privately, saying, "Tell us, when will these things happen, and what will be the sign of Your coming, and of the end of the age?" (Matthew 24:1-3).

Jesus was referring to literal events which would take place in that generation. The same passages also contain information about literal Gehenna that have been mistranslated as referring to 'hell' and projected into the far future – the 'end of the world' – rather than taken in the same context of being fulfilled in that generation. Once we see that Jesus was referring to that physical, literal generation throughout, it is clear that the passages about Gehenna were also fulfilled and were not referring to the end of the physical world or the end of time itself.

269

Which eschatological belief systems offer a better future and best align with creation being set free from corruption within the restoration of all things?

Happy eschatology probably means different things to different people (and has other names such as realised, fulfilled or covenant eschatology) but my understanding of the term means that all Bible prophecy has already been fulfilled and we are now in the period of the restoration of all things. If we believe in the restoration of all things as a process we are involved in, then everything must get better for us, in us, through us and around us. In happy eschatology, things will get progressively better, not worse, and that gives our beliefs a framework which allows for this better future.

Most eschatological systems have far from happy endings for some or most people and other created beings, as those systems have expectations of fearful judgment, doom, gloom, destruction and failure for mankind to look forward to. However, if the doom and gloom, judgment and destruction are things that have already been fulfilled then we are already in the restorative period where all things will eventually be restored.

"For then there will be a great tribulation, such as has not occurred since the beginning of the world until now, nor ever will." (Matthew 24:21).

Jesus said that the great tribulation would happen in that generation! It was in their near future but is now in our past. Is there any evidence that the audience listening to Jesus believed that He was talking about their generation?

The evidence is clear. All the believers in and around Jerusalem in AD66 knew how to understand the signs of the times, so when the Roman armies were marching on Jerusalem they fled to the mountains of Pella, escaping Jerusalem's destruction and the end of the Jewish world. They knew Jesus was not talking about events thousands of years later.

"...and that He may send Jesus, the Christ appointed for you, whom heaven must receive until the period of restoration of all things about which God spoke by the mouth of His holy prophets from ancient time." (Acts 3:20-21).

Jesus has already come to end the Old Covenant system; this period of the restoration of all things is a present reality and the fulfilment of this prophecy. The future is therefore positive and filled with possibilities of amazing discoveries, blessings, health, wholeness and wellbeing to look forward to.

In a happy eschatology all references to 'the end', 'last days', 'end times', 'last hour' and 'soon to take place' are all referring to the end of the Old Covenant system that Jesus prophesied would occur in that generation, AD 30-70, not to the end of the physical, literal world.

There is nothing to fear for the future, especially if we come into the face to face relationship of intimacy with our Creator Dad. The amazing thing is that as we mature in our sonship we get to participate in creating that future reality.

So many of the doom and gloom destruction prophecies you hear today are framed out of a wrong futurist eschatological perspective and quite frankly they are just plain wrong. How many times over the last 50 years have you heard that Jesus was returning and the tribulation was about to begin? It never happened and it never will happen:

"Truly I say to you, this generation will not pass away until all these things take place." (Matthew 24:34).

There is no need to fear the future based on Biblical prophecy as it is already past for us.

Therefore the end is past, not future; and all Jesus prophesied would happen in that generation did happen:

The gospel was preached to the whole earth in that generation.

The heavens and the earth passed away in that generation.

The new heavens and new earth were established in that generation.

The great tribulation happened in that generation.

Jesus coming on the clouds in power happened in that generation.

The events of the book of Revelation happened in that generation.

The lake of fire, in context, happened in that generation.

'As in the days of Noah' happened in that generation.

They fled from Jerusalem to the mountains in that generation.

The judgment and end of the Old Covenant and the spiritual resurrection of the New Covenant happened in that generation.

The kingdom was established in that generation.

That generation ended in 70 AD with the destruction of the temple and the end of the Old Covenant; and the period of the restoration of all things began in that generation and continues in the New Covenant ages.

In my teaching series on this subject in *Engaging God*, I do present New Testament Bible verses to back up these statements but I will only give one example here, one which is often quoted from a futurist perspective to mean the end of the physical world:

"This gospel of the kingdom shall be preached in the whole world as a testimony to all the nations, and then the end will come" (Matthew 24:14).

But consider these scriptures:

Now there were Jews living in Jerusalem, devout men from every nation under heaven (Acts 2:5).

But I say, surely they have never heard, have they? Indeed they have; "Their voice has gone out into all the earth, And their words to the ends of the world." (Romans 10:18).

...but now is manifested, and by the Scriptures of the prophets, according to the commandment of the eternal God, has been made known to all the nations, leading to obedience of faith; (Romans 16:26)

...because of the hope laid up for you in heaven, of which you previously heard in the word of truth, the gospel which has come to you, just as in all the world also it is constantly bearing fruit and increasing, even as it has been doing in you also since the day you heard of it and understood the grace of God in truth (Colossians 1: 5-6).

...if indeed you continue in the faith firmly established and steadfast, and not moved away from the hope of the gospel that you have heard, which was proclaimed in all creation under heaven, and of which I, Paul, was made a minister (Colossians 1:23)

According to these verses, the gospel of the kingdom was already preached in the whole world – and even in all creation – in that generation.

Realised eschatology inevitably leads to the restoration of all things because all that Jesus prophesied about Gehenna (a real place but often wrongly translated as 'hell') was fulfilled in AD70, not waiting to be fulfilled in a distant future or after people die physically. There is an inevitable conclusion to be drawn from the connection between eschatology and restoration in Jesus' teaching. What Jesus taught an Old Covenant audience using parables has been wrongly used to affirm 'hell' as a place of eternal conscious torment (ECT); Jesus never taught 'hell' as ECT.

"Truly I say to you, this generation will not pass away until all these things take place. Heaven and earth will pass away, but My words will not pass away" (Matthew 24:34-35).

Based on this statement, the great tribulation Jesus prophesied has already occurred and will never again be repeated to fulfil prophecy. The end of the Old Covenant cannot possibly be in our future, as it has already become obsolete and passed away in our past, as the writer of Hebrews affirms:

When He said, "A new covenant," He has made the first obsolete. But whatever is becoming obsolete and growing old is ready to disappear (Hebrews 8:13).

If this event is still future for us, then we are all still obligated to keep the whole law as it must still be in place as Jesus taught them:

"Do not think that I came to abolish the Law or the Prophets; I did not come to abolish but to fulfil. For truly I say to you, until heaven and earth pass away, not the smallest letter or stroke shall pass from the Law until all is accomplished." (Matthew 5:17-18).

I do not think anyone today still wants to be obligated to keep the whole law but that is what a futurist eschatological belief system entails. Are we still under the law? No, we are now under the covering of limitless and unconditional grace.

Believing in realised or fulfilled eschatology does not mean that there will never be any tribulation again throughout history but it does mean that if there is tribulation, it will not be a fulfilment of Bible prophecy or that specific Matthew 24 passage; that 'great tribulation' to end the Old Covenant is in the past and, as Jesus stated, will never be repeated.

And He said to them, "Do you not see all these things? Truly I say to you, not one stone here will be left upon another, which will not be torn down." As He was sitting on the Mount of Olives, the disciples came to Him privately, saying, "Tell us, when will these things happen, and what will be the sign of Your coming, and of the end of the age?" (Matthew 24:2-3).

The judgment of the second coming ended the Old Covenant religious system and finally destroyed the false, old temple wineskin system and literally hundreds of thousands ended up being in outer darkness thrown into the fire of the Valley of Hinnom.

But what about...?

By now, you may be thinking of passages of scripture, even of Jesus' own teaching, which seems to contradict what I am saying. What about the sheep and the goats, or the rich man and Lazarus, or the outer darkness where their worm does not die and their fire is not quenched and there is weeping and gnashing of teeth?

Jesus never warned anyone about 'hell', nor did Paul or any of the other New Testament writers, nor did God tell Adam that he and his descendants would go to 'hell' as a result of the fall. There is no word for 'hell' in the Greek or Hebrew language. It is not a biblical concept at all.

Four separate words have been translated into the single English word 'hell' and in reality, each word has a different meaning:

- *Sheol* (Hebrew) grave or place of the dead

- *Hades* (Greek) unseen world, grave, underworld
- *Tartarus* (Greek) prison for angels
- *Gehenna* (Greek) name of a valley outside Jerusalem used as a fiery rubbish dump.

In English, the word 'hell' comes from Proto-Germanic '*haljo*', whose root '*halija*' means 'a concealed or covered place'. The Norse god Hel is Loki's daughter, and in that mythology, she rules over the evil dead.

Yet our most popular English Bible translations are full of the word, including some which might surprise you:

The Message: 56
King James Version (Authorised Version): 54
New King James: 32
New Living Translation: 19
New Century Version: 15
English Standard Version: 14
New International Version: 14
Amplified Bible: 13
New American Standard: 13

On each occasion that the translators have used the word 'hell' in these versions, they have only done so because they already believed the passage was about 'hell'. Instead of translating what was there, they have read back into the text their preconceived notions of what it meant. Other versions do not include the word at all:

LXX (Septuagint): 0

Young's Literal: o
Concordant Literal: o
Complete Jewish Bible: o
World English Bible: o

The religious institution and its supporters will insist that if you question the doctrine of 'hell', you are rejecting what has always been agreed upon by the Church. It is not so. Orthodoxy is a myth, and it is high time to rethink this subject.

Because if God is love, if God is good, if God is not angry, if God does not require appeasement or sacrifice, if God does not punish us, then what is the purpose of 'hell'?

Does 'hell' as we know it even exist? I will attempt to answer these questions as I seek to help you clear away some of your false preconceptions and assumptions (if you are willing) but I am not going to attempt to convince you to see things the way I do; if you really want to know where people go after they die, you will need to ask God to show you as I did – more of that later.

Pagan myths repackaged

When I began to share my experiences and conversations with God about these issues online it caused quite a stir. Some wrote telling me that Jesus was 'the great theologian of hell' and that He spoke more about hell than about any other single subject. That is factually inaccurate: He absolutely did not. The whole Bible is completely silent about 'hell'. For the first five centuries, few Christians held a doctrine of eternal torment either for the wicked or for unbelievers. But over time, pagan myths about the afterlife were repackaged and passed off as Christian.

We looked briefly at the four Bible words traditionally translated 'hell'. Now I will go into them in more detail. Let's be prepared for the Spirit to reveal the truth to us and not get stuck in tradition.

Sheol (Hebrew)

Strong's Concordance says:

Sheol (H7585) she'ôl From H7592; *Hades* or the world of the dead (as if a subterranean retreat), including its accessories and inmates: – grave, pit, hell.

All good, right up to the last word: 'hell' has been added there, only because the compiler has already decided that some scriptures where this word is used are talking about 'hell'. The true meanings of the word, 'grave' or 'pit' have no context of punishment at all. Most modern Bible versions now translate this word accurately.

Hades (Greek)

Hades (G86) hadēs From G1 and G1492; properly unseen, that is, "Hades" or the place (state) of departed souls: – grave, hell.

'*Hades*' is used only 11 times in the New Testament, including 4 times by Jesus (and some of those are the same story in different gospels). It does not relate to punishment. It is the Greek equivalent of '*sheol*' and has been ascribed the added meaning of 'hell' in exactly the same way.

In these Bible verses, we will use Young's Literal Translation, which is not easy to read but uses 'hades', the actual Greek word in the original texts, and not the invented word 'hell'.

"And thou, Capernaum, which unto the heaven wast exalted, unto hades thou shalt be brought down" (Matthew 11:23 YLT, Luke 10:15 YLT). "Capernaum, you think you're so great but soon you'll be nothing." There is no context of punishment.

"And I also say to thee, that thou art a rock, and upon this rock I will build my assembly [ekklesia]*, and gates of Hades shall not prevail against it"* (Matthew 16:18 YLT). We, the ekklesia, are going to overcome the grave. We do not need to be fearful of death.

There are 2 uses of *'hades'* in Acts, both quoting a single OT reference to *sheol*, that the Messiah's soul was not left to hades, nor did His flesh see corruption (Acts 2:27, 31).

Breaking the power of death: *Where, O Death, thy sting? Where, O Hades, thy victory?* (1 Corinthians 15:55 YLT).

4 times in Revelation:

"...and he who is living, and I did become dead, and, lo, I am living to the ages of the ages. Amen! And I have the keys of the hades and of the death" (Revelation 1:18 YLT). Jesus has the keys of death and the grave – to set people free, not to lock them up!

...and I saw, and lo, a pale horse, and he who is sitting upon him – his name is Death, and Hades doth follow with him (Revelation 6:8 YLT). A personification of 'the grave', or

perhaps the Greek god who, in that mythology, rules over the place of the dead.

...and the sea did give up those dead in it, and the death and the hades did give up the dead in them, and they were judged, each one according to their works (Revelation 20:13 YLT). Again, simply 'the grave' (and according to this verse, judgment comes after the dead come out of it, not before).

...and the death and the hades were cast to the lake of the fire – this [is] the second death (Revelation 20:14 YLT). Death and the grave are not the end. They are to be put somewhere else, and we will look at this 'lake of fire' later in this chapter.

None of these references relates to torment or punishment. The only use of *'hades'* which may appear to do so is in Luke 16:23, in the story of the rich man and Lazarus.

"...and in the hades having lifted up his eyes, being in torments, he doth see Abraham afar off, and Lazarus in his bosom." (Luke 16:23 YLT).

There are several things to say about this passage:

This whole story may not be original to Jesus. Its roots can be traced back to the Hebrew traditional text *Gemara Babylonicum*, which dates from Israel's captivity in Babylon.

The primary characters in the story are not distinguished from one another by righteousness or wickedness but by wealth and social standing.

This whole section in Luke's gospel is a series of lessons about trusting in riches and failing to help the poor, directed primarily at the religious leaders and their supporters. Jesus' purpose in (re-)telling the story was not to give a literal account of what the afterlife looks like.

I will look at this parable again later in this chapter and there are links to articles on the subject in the appendix.

Tartarus (Greek, G5020) *tartaroō*. From *Tartaros* (the deepest abyss of Hades); Greek mythology: the place where the Titans were incarcerated. To incarcerate in eternal torment: – cast down to hell.

The last phrase in this definition was a total invention of the compiler.

'*Tartarus*' is only mentioned once in the New Testament:

For if God did not spare angels when they sinned, but cast them into hell [Tartarus] *and committed them to pits of darkness, reserved for judgment...* (2 Peter 2:4).

If they were 'reserved for judgment' then they had not yet been judged and it would have been unjust to subject them to punishment. This is not 'to incarcerate in eternal torment'.

Gehenna (Greek, G1067) of Hebrew origin ([H1516] and [H2011]); valley of (the son of) Hinnom; *gehenna* (or *Ge-Hinnom*), a valley of Jerusalem.

Gehenna is the Greek word for the Valley of Hinnom, a literal geographical feature outside the gates of Jerusalem. It was an evil and dark place, used for a variety of evil acts (including child sacrifice to Molech); literally a place of perpetual fire, a rubbish dump filled with so much trash (including dead bodies during the time of Isaiah) that the fires never went out and worms would never die from lack of food.

"Therefore, behold, days are coming," declares the Lord, "when this place will no longer be called Topheth or the valley of Ben-hinnom, but rather the valley of Slaughter" (Jeremiah 19:6).

Jeremiah's prophecy was fulfilled with the destruction of Jerusalem in AD70 when dead bodies were literally thrown into Gehenna during the siege by the Roman army. Rather than eternal 'hell', Gehenna was a physical place for dead bodies.

Jesus used the word 'Gehenna' in 11 instances. In all of them, He was talking about kingdom life here and now, not about the afterlife (whether 'going to heaven' or 'going to hell').

Here are all those references:

1. Matthew 5:29
2. Matthew 5:30
3. Matthew 18:9
4. Mark 9:43
5. Mark 9:45
6. Mark 9:47

#1-6 are all the same concept: Jesus is using the imagery of the most disgusting location in Jerusalem to illustrate how destructive sin is (see also #12).

7.   Matthew 10:28

8.   Luke 12:5

#7 and 8 are the same passage in different gospels: "*Do not fear those who kill the body but are unable to kill the soul; but rather fear him who is able to destroy both soul and body in Gehenna.*" Suppose this is referring to God (and there are plenty of other possibilities), it does not say 'punishes' or 'torments', nor mention 'eternal', but only says ' is able to destroy'. Perhaps this might be a good proof-text for annihilationists, but not for those who believe in eternal conscious torment in 'hell'.

9.   Matthew 5:22

"*But I say to you that everyone who is angry with his brother shall be guilty before the court; and whoever says to his brother, 'You good-for-nothing,' shall be guilty before the supreme court; and whoever says, 'You fool,' shall be guilty enough to go into the fiery Gehenna*".

So the difference between saying (1) 'You good-for-nothing' and (2) 'You fool' is enough to make the difference between (1) being sentenced to death by stoning and (2) being tortured for all eternity without hope of reprieve? That seems like an unreasonable escalation in punishment between two offences most of us would struggle to distinguish.

In reality, Jesus is raising the standard of behaviour to include thoughts and emotions, emphasising how powerful our thoughts and words are. He is demonstrating how little it takes to negatively affect us, how just a bit of unresolved anger pollutes our lives and how unforgiveness lands us in a torture chamber of our own making.

10.   Matthew 23:15

"Woe to you, scribes and Pharisees, hypocrites, because you travel around on sea and land to make one proselyte; and when he becomes one, you make him twice as much a son of Gehenna as yourselves".

The Pharisees were all about perceived righteousness. They obsessively followed every directive of the Law and made a show of their piety. They were self-righteous DIY-ers. Jesus was telling them that their own "righteousness" was like dung. They were proud of being 'children of Abraham' but He called them children of the refuse heap and compared them to those who sacrificed to idols.

11.   Matthew 23:33

"You serpents, you brood of vipers, how will you escape the sentence of Gehenna?"

They were going to end up outside the covenant. Some of those listening may actually have had their dead bodies dumped over the city walls into Gehenna during the Roman siege of AD70.

12.   James 3:6

The tongue also is a fire, a world of evil among the parts of the body. It corrupts the whole body, sets the whole course of one's life on fire, and is itself set on fire by Gehenna.

Evil from one body part corrupts the whole body.

Fear and love

Religion uses the fear of an angry god and the fear of hell to keep us in order. But God calls us to simply love Him, ourselves and each other: no religious rules, nothing complicated about it. He is not angry with us, He is always the same: loving, faithful and full of grace and mercy. He has never changed. He has shown us how to love: He loves us so much that He was prepared to come in the flesh and die for us, even when we saw ourselves as His enemies. If we loved like that, the world would be a different place.

I am not saying you should believe what I believe. I am offering you the opportunity to lay aside common misconceptions of what the Bible says so that you can read what it does say and engage with God for yourself to find out what He is really like.

What about the other things Jesus taught that have been used affirm the 'hell' myth?

Weeping, Gnashing of Teeth and Outer Darkness

"Weeping and gnashing of teeth in the outer darkness! That is obviously a reference to suffering eternal physical torture in hell."

Is that so? It is very important to take audience relevance into account: what did Jesus' hearers understand him to be saying to them? His Jewish Old Covenant listeners had background knowledge and context that we do not have today. Jesus also spoke very differently to His disciples than to the religious leaders whose traditions He was challenging.

Look at what happened leading up to Stephen being martyred in Acts 7:54: his accusers (members of the Sanhedrin) became furious and gnashed their teeth at him. Weeping and gnashing of teeth was an expression not of tormented pain and anguish, but rage.

When the chief priests and the Pharisees heard His parables, they understood that He was speaking about them (see Matthew 21:45). The only reason they did not seize Jesus then and there was because they were afraid of the public outcry.

Virtually every time Jesus mentions "gnashing of teeth", He is talking to or about the religious elite and their response to the Gospel which causes them anger and frustration.

This covenantal language is about the consequences of breaking covenant and Jesus is focusing on those who would identify themselves as 'sons of the kingdom' while rejecting His ministry. They were the Pharisees, Sadducees, Priests, Levites, Lawyers, Rabbis etc. Jesus' figurative warnings are not directed towards the 'sinners' He hung out with but the self-righteous religious leaders who were trying to kill Him.

He said, "*I did not come to call the (self-) righteous, but sinners*" (Matthew 9:13) and His response to the adulteress was, "*I do not condemn you either. Go. From now on sin no more.*" (John 8:11).

Why would we think 'weeping and gnashing or grinding of teeth' is a reference to physical torture in 'hell'? Jesus tells the

Pharisees, the religious elite, that they cannot escape Gehenna and offers parable after parable warning that weeping and gnashing of teeth will ensue when they discover they have missed out on the kingdom that they believed was theirs by right.

So to be 'cast out' meant to be outside of the covenant relationship and therefore figuratively to be in outer darkness where they would weep and grind teeth in self-righteous anger and anguish, having failed to heed Jesus. They were angry and frustrated when Jesus preached that their religious system of laws and works would become obsolete in that generation. They continued to use the temple and the veil of separation and persecuted the early church and tried to get them back under the law through Judaisers. There is nothing in these texts about 'hell' or eternal punishment.

It was not the general mass of humanity that Jesus was speaking of when He talked about gnashing of teeth and the outer darkness in Matt 8:12, 13:42, 13:50, 22:13, 24:51, 25:30 and Luke 13:28. It was this group of self-righteous individuals who would find themselves outside the covenant they were so sure was their birthright. In that 'outer darkness', having failed to heed Jesus' warnings, they would respond with defiant anger.

Jesus spoke about many things in parables, which are short stories which illustrate one or more points, lessons or principles. These parables need sincerely seeking to find the truth behind them as their meanings are not always obvious, especially for us today. A parable uses metaphors or figures of speech or similes, i.e. something is said (or implied) to be "like" something else (e.g. "The just man is like a tree planted by streams of water").

We should be careful not to just assume a literal meaning, nor to accept the traditional interpretation either. Medieval interpreters of the Bible often treated Jesus' parables as allegories, with symbolic meanings found for every element in His parables. Most modern scholars regard their interpretations as incorrect and instead suggest that Jesus' parables are mostly intended to make a single important point.

Given the symbolic nature of parables, we really should not use them to create or prove a doctrinal position beyond their intended purpose because it is so easy to make confirmationally biased interpretations. Unfortunately, this is exactly what has happened. Parables have been wrongly used to affirm important theological issues like:

The nature of divine judgment.

The state of the afterlife.

'Hell' (*sheol, hades*) as an inescapable place of God's fiery judgment and punishment. And how we preach the gospel has been greatly influenced by the 'hell' concept.

When looking at parables we need to be open to look with fresh eyes so we can understand what Jesus is actually meaning, by asking certain questions:

- Who is being addressed? - Jews, Gentiles, the religious leaders, everyone in Jesus' day, everyone throughout history?
- Was the context specific to that time or is it applicable now?
- Was it using Old Testament or local symbolism?
- Was it referring to pre-cross resurrection issues and Old Covenant ideas and concepts?
- What is the true meaning of the actual words used in these stories? Are the words translated accurately, and do they keep their original meanings? Or have the Greek words been mistranslated or misinterpreted because of modern pre-existing views and confirmation bias?

Jesus used parables to subvert the traditional thinking and understanding of His hearers by using them to contrast kingdom values. He often used subversive language towards the common ideas of the Rabbis, Pharisees, Zealots, Essenes etc. *"You have heard it said... Now I say unto you..."*

When we read the parables today, we need the Holy Spirit to lead us to their truth, relationally and experientially. The context of many parables was that they were directed towards religious leaders of Jesus day and those who followed them.

- They challenged their DIY religion.
- They challenged their traditions.
- They challenged their religiosity.
- They challenged their attitudes.
- They challenged their heart motives and values.

The overall point of the parable is a warning that when Jesus is enthroned, rejecting Him (by treating His followers badly) will result in the fire of Gehenna when Jerusalem is destroyed at the end of that age. The fire was figuratively the fiery pit or lake of fire that was literal Gehenna, not an eternal afterlife 'hell' concept.

Parable of the sheep and goats

"These will go away into eternal punishment, but the righteous into eternal life." (Matthew 25:46).

To understand what this parable means we need to look at the real meaning of the phrases 'eternal fire' and 'eternal punishment' in their true context.

Matthew 25:41 ... "Eternal punishment" and into the eternal fire originally for the devil and his angels – surely this must mean "hell"? What else could it mean?

The English words 'eternal', 'fire', 'punishment' and 'devil and angels' do not have the same meaning in Greek. The original Greek meanings of the words eternal and punishment, will reveal that what seems obviously to mean 'hell' is actually far from it. The traditional English rendering of the words is not always found within the original Greek: some are mistranslations, particularly the English words 'eternal', 'everlasting', 'forever', 'punishment', 'fire', 'torment', 'judgment', 'wrath'.

It is vitally important to understand the meaning of these words, not just in this parable but in the whole of the New Testament writings. They can be interpreted differently, as shown in a literal Bible version such as Young's Literal translation (YLT) and if the real root meanings are used (as in the Mirror Bible) rather than common or modern idioms often chosen by other translators.

It is a religious tradition that conditions us to believe in a 'hell' that God uses to punish and torment His children forever and ever. We have been taught that there is eternal, everlasting, forever and ever judgment that results in God's children being separated from Him in the fire of 'hell', being punished as a result of the verdict of an angry, unforgiving judge. This deception is caused by the mistranslation and misinterpretation of the words 'eternal' and 'punishment'. Using the direct meaning of the words, we will see that they do not mean 'eternal' and they do not have to mean 'retributive punishment' either.

A New Covenant

I was taught many so-called foundational teachings and even delivered an entire 'Foundations' teaching series, based on a passage in Hebrews 6, that I now realise was a completely wrong understanding of the text. I took the passage in isolation and turned it into a set of foundational doctrines that we need to build our lives on today. That was not the purpose of the book of Hebrews, which was written to reveal the end of the Old Covenant as it faded away during that generation and became obsolete. What I taught was a set of doctrines that were Old Covenant, no longer relevant for today, and were really to be avoided, not embraced.

*For if that first covenant had been faultless, there would have been no occasion sought for a second. For finding fault with them, He says, "Behold, days are coming, says the Lord, when I will effect a new covenant with the house of Israel and with the house of Judah; Not like the covenant which I made with their fathers on the day when I took them by the hand to lead them out of the land of Egypt; for they did not continue in My covenant, and I did not care for them, says the Lord. "For this is the covenant that I will make with the house of Israel after those days, says the Lord: I will put My laws into their minds, and I will write them on their hearts. and I will be their God, and they shall be My people. "And they shall not teach everyone his fellow citizen, and everyone his brother, saying, 'Know the Lord,' for all will know Me, from the least to the greatest of them. "For I will be merciful to their iniquities, and I will remember their sins no more." When He said, "A new covenant," He has made the first obsolete. But whatever is becoming obsolete and growing old is ready to disappe*ar (Hebrews 8:7-13).

This is an amazing promise that in the New Covenant all will know God as, in His great and wonderful mercy, He remembers their sins no more. Unfortunately, mankind has a memory that still remembers its lost identity and lives according to the knowledge of the tree of good and evil rather than the path of the tree of life.

The context of Hebrews 6:1-2 is that the doctrines of the Old Covenant are obsolete in the new but reading it at face value in English, as I did, could give you the opposite idea. Below is the passage Hebrews 6:1-2 in the NASB and by comparison the Mirror Bible. As you read them you will see that the ideas conveyed have completely opposite meanings; so which is correct, laying a foundation of Old Covenant doctrines again or avoiding those old doctrines and entering into a new relationship?

Therefore leaving the elementary teaching about the Christ, let us press on to maturity, not laying again a foundation of repentance from dead works and of faith toward God, of instruction about baptisms and laying on of hands, and the resurrection of the dead and eternal judgment (Hebrews 6:1-2 NASB).

Consequently, as difficult as it may seem, you ought to divorce yourselves from sentimental attachment to the prefiguring doctrine of the Messiah, which was designed to carry us like a vessel over the ocean of prophetic dispensation into the completeness of the fulfilled promise. A mind shift from attempts to impress God by your behaviour, to faith-righteousness in Christ, is fundamental. There is no life left in the old system. It is dead and gone; you have to move on. All the Jewish teachings about ceremonial washings (baptisms), the laying on of hands (in order to identify with the slain animal as sacrifice), and all teachings pertaining to a sin consciousness, including the final resurrection of the dead in order to face judgment, are no longer relevant. (All of these types and shadows were concluded and fulfilled in Christ, their living substance. His resurrection bears testimony to the judgment that he faced on humanity's behalf and the freedom from an obstructive consciousness of sin that he now proclaims.) (Hebrews 6:1-2 Mirror).

How different that is to what I was taught and taught others myself! When it comes to concepts like eternal judgment and resurrection from the dead, those Old Covenant concepts are fully realised in Jesus and His resurrection. Trying to live under an Old Covenant system in the New Covenant age produces self-inflicted guilt, shame and condemnation for those trying to live by religious dead works – and that condemnation is projected onto the world. The church has condemned those in the world for not yet believing, calling them unbelievers and assigning them an eternal punishment in 'hell' if they do not repent. That is turning the amazing good news of a merciful, loving Father who has reconciled the world to Himself into incredible fear-inducing bad news of an angry God who needs appeasing with our dead works.

So often today when people think of judgment they associate it with other words (just as I did), such as justice, penal, penalty, punishment, condemnation, a custodial sentence. Those are man's idea of judgment but we should not assume them to be associated with God's type of judgment.

If you have been before a judge or magistrate and stood in the dock, which fortunately I have not (although I have been a witness and part of a jury) when the verdict is given based on the evidence heard, you would hope that the verdict is 'not guilty'. A guilty verdict means punishment: that, we see as justice in our modern-day judicial system, which is largely punitive and not restorative as it is based on Old Covenant principles.

There is no mercy in our justice system but that is not the case with heaven's justice system: the whole judgment-justice cycle is based on mercy to such an extent that, from God the Father's position as the judge, mercy and justice are synonymous terms. In fact, the Father gave judgment into the hands of Jesus and to us as co-heirs. All judgment and justice are now based on the merciful loving-kindness of the verdict of the cross which declares all mankind not guilty, innocent, justified and righteous.

The Greek words translated judgment are variations of *krimatos*, *krima* and *krino* which just mean a decision, a verdict or a discernment, never a punishment. The mythical 'hell' concept assumes that God's verdict as judge is everlasting damnation (torment) for the unredeemed lost and eternal safety for the redeemed saved.

The individual words and their meaning below have no concept of punishment or torment.

krino – judge, decide, think good, to separate (distinguish), i.e. judge; come to a choice or decision by making a judgment.

krima (a neuter noun derived from 2919 /*krínō*, "to distinguish, judge") – judgment, emphasizing its result (note the *-ma* suffix). This is everlasting damnation (torment) for the unredeemed (the usual implication of 2319 /*theostygḗs*) – or the eternal benefits that come from the Lord's judgment in favour of the redeemed (cf. Rev 20:4). See 2919 (*krínō*). 2917 /*kríma* ("the results of a judgment") dramatically links cause-to-effect.

Indeed, every decision (action) we make carries inevitable eternal results (cf. Ecclesiastes 12:14).

Usual usage: a judgment, a verdict; sometimes implying an adverse verdict, a condemnation, (b) a case at law, a lawsuit.

The NASB interprets that word *krino*, its root word *krima* and *krimatos* (which in reality just means a judicial verdict, that is to decide and select) as condemnation (8), judgment (15), judgments (1), lawsuits (1), sentence (1), sentence of condemnation (1), way (1).

There is no punishment indicated here, just an evidence-based verdict, contrary to the religious opinion of the translators who add condemnation.

Even in our retributive and punitive western judicial system, you must be found guilty to receive a negative judgment and be sentenced. Is there evidence against mankind that requires God to give us a custodial sentence in 'hell' forever? I believe the opposite is, in fact, true: there is overwhelming evidence that the whole of mankind (and in fact the whole of creation) has been reconciled and found not guilty. In 2 Corinthians chapter 5 Paul clearly states that God was in Christ reconciling the cosmos and not counting their trespasses against them.

The Greek word translated 'trespasses' is *paraptóma* its meaning is (from 3895 /*parapíptō*, see there) – properly, fall away after being close-beside, i.e. a lapse (deviation) from the truth; an error, "slip up"; (Strong's).

When Adam chose to follow Eve along the wrong tree path he lost his identity and image as a son of God and became an orphan: that is what 'the sin' is. Mankind has been living in lost identity, desperately seeking to discover who he is by religious and humanistic dead works. All the bad behaviours we consider as sins are the symptoms of our lostness.

So God in Jesus, through the cross, did not come to condemn mankind to eternal separation in conscious torment but to reconcile mankind and by implication all creation to Himself by not counting that walk of independence against them. Below is the NASB and Mirror Bible, again for comparison purposes; as you read these passages you will see no guilty verdict has been imposed upon the cosmos.

Now all these things are from God, who reconciled us to Himself through Christ and gave us the ministry of reconciliation, namely, that God was in Christ reconciling the world to Himself, not counting their trespasses against them, and He has committed to us the word of reconciliation (2 Corinthians 5:18-19 NASB).

The idea of mankind's co-inclusion in the death and resurrection of Jesus Christ is entirely God's doing! To now realize that God has indeed brought final closure to the old and for us to see everything and everyone in this new light is to simply see what God has always known to be true about us in Christ; we are not debating human experience, opinion, or their contribution; this is exactly what God believes. In Jesus Christ, God exchanged equivalent value to redeem us to himself. He went to the highest extreme in this act of reconciliation to persuade us of our original worth! This God has given us as the mandate of our ministry.

(The word, *katalasso*, translates as reconciliation; it is a mutual exchange of equal value. This transaction was not to buy us back from "the devil"; a thief never becomes an owner; it was God redeeming our minds from the lies that we believed about ourselves - reconciliation is the bold unveiling of the value of the hidden treasure in everyone! See 2 Cor 4:7 and Matt 13:44). *Our ministry declares that Jesus did not act independently of his Father. God was present in Christ when he reconciled the total kosmos to himself. Deity and humanity embraced in him; the fallen state of mankind was deleted; their trespasses would no longer count against them! He now announces his friendship with every individual from within us!* (The incarnation did not separate the Father from the Son and the Spirit. In him dwells the fulness of God in a human body. Col 2:9. As a human person, Jesus felt the agony of fallen humanity on the cross when he echoed Psalm 22, "My God, my God, why have you forsaken me! Why are you so far from helping me, from the words of my groaning?" But then in verse 24, David declares triumphantly: "He has not despised or abhorred the affliction of the afflicted; and he has not hid his face from him, but has heard, when he cried to him.") (2 Corinthians 5:18-19 Mirror).

The reconciliation of the cross is not just for mankind but, as Colossians 1:16-20 reveals, for the 'all things' of creation.

For by Him all things were created, both in the heavens and on earth, visible and invisible, whether thrones or dominions or rulers or authorities—all things have been created through Him and for Him... For it was the Father's good pleasure for all the fullness to dwell in Him, and through Him to reconcile all things

*to Himself, having made peace through the blood of His cross;
through Him, I say, whether things on earth or things in heaven.*
(Colossians 1:16, 19-20 NASB).

*Everything that is begins in him whether in the heavenly realm
or upon the earth, visible or invisible, every order of justice and
every level of authority, be it kingdoms or governments,
principalities or jurisdictions; all things were created by him and
for him... He initiated the reconciliation of all things to himself.
Through the blood of the cross God restored the original
harmony. His reign of peace now extends to every visible thing
upon the earth as well as those invisible things which are in the
heavenly realm.* "Not only that, but all the broken and
dislocated pieces of the universe, people and things, animals and
atoms, get properly fixed and fit together in vibrant harmonies,
all because of his death." – The Message. (Colossians 1:16, 20
Mirror).

This reality of a 'not guilty' verdict is further confirmed in
Colossians chapter 1.

*When you were dead in your transgressions and the
uncircumcision of your flesh, He made you alive together with
Him, having forgiven us all our transgressions, having cancelled
out the certificate of debt consisting of decrees against us, which
was hostile to us; and He has taken it out of the way, having
nailed it to the cross* (Colossians 1:13-14 NASB).

*He rescued us from the dominion of darkness (the sense-ruled
world, dominated by the law of performance) and relocated us
into the kingdom where the love of his son rules.* (Darkness is not

a force, it is the absence of light. [See Eph 4:18] A darkened understanding veiled the truth of our redeemed design from us. 2 Cor 4:4. What "empowered" darkness was the lie that we believed about ourselves! The word, *exousia*, sometimes translated authority, is from *ek*, origin or source, and *eimi*, I am. Thus, I was confused about who I am until the day that I heard and understood the grace of God in truth, as in a mirror. See 2 Corinthians 3:18, John 1:12.) *In God's mind mankind is associated in Christ; in his blood sacrifice we were ransomed; our redemption was secured; our sins were completely done away with.* (The word sin, is the word *hamartia*, from *ha*, negative or without and *meros*, portion or form, thus to be without your allotted portion or without form, pointing to a disorientated, distorted, bankrupt identity; the word *meros*, is the stem of *morphe*, as in 2 Corinthians 3:18 the word *metamorphe*, with form, which is the opposite of *hamartia* - without form. Sin is to live out of context with the blueprint of one's design; to behave out of tune with God's original harmony. See Deuteronomy 32:18, "You have forgotten the Rock that begot you and have gotten out of step with the God who danced with you!" Hebrew, *khul* or *kheel*, to dance. Sin distorts the life of our design. Jesus reveals and redeemed our true form.) (Colossians 1:13-14 Mirror).

How can there be punishment, let alone eternal torment, if there is nothing held against us? If everyone has had their transgressions taken out of the way and all debts are cancelled, how can there be a negative judgment and eternal punishment?

When God, as a righteous judge, makes a verdict, it does not come with condemnation, it always comes with an opportunity to respond and be restored. Even when God judges something in someone as wrong, it is not to punish them but it is so they can choose something that is right. God's judgment of our lives is always to bring life and restoration, never death. God, our loving Father, is a righteous judge and therefore His judgments are righteous and His justice is His mercy.

The Greek word for righteous, *dikaiokrisias*, has *krisias* (judgment) within it and means just, righteous, impartial. Judgment is based on God's love, mercy and grace but the Old Covenant idea of a wrathful God of vengeance is ingrained in the minds of mankind. So when we read a Bible verse that contains the words judgment and wrath we are preconditioned to think of a future in 'hell' after a final judgment. As an example, Romans chapter 2 talks of wrath and righteous judgment: let's compare the NASB and Mirror Bible translations.

Or do you think lightly of the riches of His kindness and tolerance and patience, not knowing that the kindness of God leads you to repentance? But because of your stubbornness and unrepentant heart you are storing up wrath for yourself in the day of wrath and revelation of the righteous judgment of God, who will render to each person according to his deeds (Romans 2:4-6 NASB).

Do not underestimate God's kindness. The wealth of his benevolence and his resolute refusal to let go of us is because he continues to hear the echo of his likeness in us! Thus his patient passion is to shepherd everyone into a radical mind shift. (It is the revelation of the goodness of God that leads us to repentance; it is not our "repentance" that leads God to goodness! The word "repentance" is a fabricated word from the Latin word, penance, and to give religion more mileage the English word became re-penance! That is not what the Greek word means at all! The word, *metanoia*, comes from *meta*, meaning together with, and *nous*, mind; thus, together with God's mind. This word suggests a radical mind-shift; it is to realise God's thoughts towards us. *In Jesus Christ, God has measured mankind innocent, he is the blueprint of our design! A calloused heart that resists change accumulates cause to self-destruction, while God's righteous judgment is revealed in broad daylight.* (The gospel openly declares that God declared mankind innocent.) By resisting him you are on your own; your own deeds will judge you. (Rejecting his goodness [v 4] keeps you snared in a lifestyle ruled by sin-consciousness and condemnation.) (Romans 2:4-6).

Wrath: Greek *orge* anger, wrath, passion; from *oregomai* violent passion.

God has passionate feelings against the sin (our inherited lost identity) that so easily entangles us but that wrath is not directed towards us as His children. God is a consuming fire and He is passionate against anything that robs us of our sonship identity. God's wrath, which is His passion, will consume the sin, not the sinner who is already declared not guilty. Why do we assume that God would make a judgment and then take away our ability to respond to it? Because God has been wrongly portrayed as being angry, needing appeasing and ready to punish us forever if we reject Him.

Justice is based on the finished work of the cross. It does not excuse sin or mean there are no consequences for our behaviour but God's mercy always triumphs over man's version of justice. Our religious programming causes us to see the word 'wrath' or 'judgment' and immediately jump to the conclusion that this must be referring to final judgment at the end of the world and a sentence of eternal punishment. The fact that these New Testament verses never refer to 'hell' concerning judgment is completely overlooked.

The truth is that there are consequences for our negative behaviour in that when it comes to receiving mercy, we will reap what we sow – but that is in this life. Jewish thought viewed sin as self-inflicted judgment. In other words, when you sin, you inflict judgment upon yourself. Sin has its own reward in this life, not in the afterlife: living with no identity, in anonymity, enjoying no relationship with God is really 'hell' on earth. Sin isn't meaningless; it's literally inviting 'hell' into your life now, living 'less than' kind of lives.

God the judge is our Father and the evidence used in any case against us is what Jesus did for us and as us on the cross: the verdict is 'not guilty'. We are innocent and our Father's desire is reconciliation, not separation and restoration, not retribution. God does not count our sins against us therefore there is no punishment but there are consequences and we will all have the consuming fire of His loving presence to face.

What if we choose to reject God's mercy in this life and physically die? An age-enduring righteous judgment can therefore only be an opportunity for the continuing ability to choose to accept Jesus, and that choice never ends, even after physical death. If anyone chooses death and not life, God respects their choice but never gives up on them as love never fails. I will go deeper into this truth later but for now, let's look at other words that have been misinterpreted and therefore wrongly translated in English.

'Eternal punishment'

So much of the wrong understanding of 'hell' comes from linking it with the words 'eternal' and 'punishment', so what are those words and what do they mean in the original Greek?

Eternal

'Eternal' in English means lasting or existing forever; without end, with synonyms such as everlasting, never-ending, endless, without end, perpetual, undying, immortal, deathless, indestructible, imperishable, immutable, abiding, permanent, enduring, infinite, boundless, timeless;

The Greek words that have usually been translated into English as 'eternal', 'everlasting' or 'forever' are *aiōniou* and *aiōnios*.

For example in Matthew chapter 25.

"These will go away into eternal punishment, but the righteous into eternal life." (Matthew 25: 46).

From Strong's concordance:

Definition: agelong, eternal.

Usage: age-long, and therefore: practically eternal, unending; partaking of the character of that which lasts for an age, as contrasted with that which is brief and fleeting.

Eternal is not the correct usage and implies life without end.

HELPS Word-studies in Biblehub's online Greek interlinear states:

Cognate: *aiōnios* (an adjective, derived from 165 /*aiōn* ("an age, having a particular character and quality") – properly, "age-like" ("like-an-age"), i.e. an "age-characteristic" (the quality describing a particular age); (figuratively) the unique quality (reality) of God's life at work in the believer, i.e. as the Lord manifests His self-existent life (as it is in His sinless abode of heaven).

That is an excellent definition of *aiōnios* but using the words eternal, everlasting or forever is a not good interpretation in English. *Aiōnios* means aeon or age: there is no concept of without end, infinite or timeless and no primary focus on the future, but rather on the age (*aiōn*) it relates to.

Actually, believers live in 'eternal (*aiōnios*) life' right now, experiencing the quality of God's life now as a present possession. In Greek, an age could refer to a generation, lifetime, or a longer, finite length of time. It's where we get our word "aeon"; it is not infinite or eternal. It also correlates with the Hebrew word *olam*, hidden or unknown time, which denotes anything from a 24 hour period to an epoch or season. Greek translations use the present tense of 'having *aiōnios* (eternal) life now' in John 3:36, 5:24, 6:47 and Romans 6:23.

Aiŏnios refers to the length of an age, 'from age to age' or age-enduring, a life that can be experienced continually and continuously now, not just in heaven in the future after death.

Questions that often get asked are "If it does not mean 'eternal' does that not diminish the life we have in God?" and "If it does not mean everlasting does that mean it can end"?

I truly believe, both by revelation and personal experience, that the answer to both questions is 'no'. Seeing eternal life as something we have now only enhances it by not putting it off to the future and makes the quality and abundance of the life we have now the focus rather than just its length.

To be clear, *aiŏnion* and *aiŏnios* never mean eternal, forever or everlasting when referring to anything at all – let alone 'hell' punishment or torment. This is a wrong interpretation, influenced by a wrong view of God and the nature of His judgment by associating it with punishment.

Aiŏnion, aiŏnios is not translated 'eternal' or 'forever' even once and as 'everlasting' only once in a literal Bible version such as Young's Literal Translation:

eternal	YLT 0	NASB 75
everlasting	YLT 1	NASB 110
forever	YLT 0	NASB 323

The true meaning is, therefore, 'age-enduring' and not 'eternal', 'everlasting' or 'forever'; for example, in probably the most well-known Bible verse of all:

For God so loved the world, that He gave His only begotten Son, that whoever believes in Him shall not perish, but have eternal life (John 3:16 NASB).

...but may have life age-during (John 3:16 YLT).

The word 'perish' in John 3:16 actually means 'lost' (as in sheep, coin and son) and should not be linked to eternal punishment either, as it refers to living in a continual state of lost identity in this life.

The entire cosmos is the object of God's affection! And he is not about to abandon his creation - the gift of his son is for humanity to realize their origin in him who mirrors their authentic birth - begotten not of flesh but of the Father! In this persuasion the life of the ages echoes within the individual and announces that the days of regret and sense of lost-ness are over! (John 3:16 Mirror).

This *aiónios* life is not the quantity of life but the quality of knowing who God truly is, through knowing who Jesus is, and therefore knowing our sonship identity in this wonderful love relationship.

This is age-enduring (eternal) life, that they may know You, the only true God, and Jesus Christ whom You have sent (John 17:3).

Any time we see the term 'eternal life' in the New Testament, it should be translated as 'life of the age'. It means that this phrase 'eternal punishment' should more accurately be viewed as 'discipline or correction for the length of the age'.

Punishment

Let's move on to the word 'punishment' in English, meaning: the infliction or imposition of a penalty as retribution for an offence. Suffering, pain, or loss that serves as retribution, a penalty inflicted on an offender through judicial procedure. Severe, rough, or disastrous treatment.

There are three Greek words translated as 'punishment' in the New Testament; they are *epitima, timoreo* and *kolazo* and are only used seven times.

The word *epitima*, translated 'punishment', is only used once in 2 Corinthians 2:6 and means 'to turn a situation in the right direction' – the fitting (appropriate) response necessary to turn someone in the right direction. Paul used the word to refer to the sorrow of correction caused by his letters, nothing to do with the punishment of eternal conscious torment in the 'hell' mythology.

The Greek word *timoreo* is also only used once, in Hebrews 10:29, comparing man's law-based retribution to God's restorative grace.

The associated word *timória* means: to be authorized to administer recompense, punishment – punishment, meted out from the view of the offended party. This form of punishment, penalty or vengeance is never used in connection with God and only refers to man's notion of punishment.

With how much closer scrutiny do you suppose someone will be viewed who has trampled the Son of God underfoot and scorned the blood of the Covenant by publicly insulting the Spirit of grace. (Preferring the law above the revelation of grace brings you back under the judgment of the law without the possibility of further sacrifice. There is no alternative mercy outside of God's grace gift in Christ.) (Hebrews 10:29 Mirror).

The other five occasions are where the Greek word *kolazo* is translated as 'punishment'. That word is derived from the Greek root word *kolos* which originally meant to correct by pruning or restricting. The retributive or punitive modern meanings are not found in the original root meanings. In my opinion, the word 'chastisement' would be a better translation of *kolazo*, meaning restorative correction and not vengeance.

When reading Strong's concordance it translates *kolazo* as punishment but rather than look at the original Greek root concept it adds its own biased meaning of 'condemnation, damnation' to the correct meaning of chastisement. It is not condemnation or damnation: this is only a modern, religious Christianese Greek translation and not its real original meaning

The NASB lexicon has a definition for *kolasin, kolazo, kolos* as to lop or prune, as trees and wings; to curb, check, restrain; to chastise, correct, punishment.

Strong's concordance says 'chastisement, punishment' but then adds 'torment, perhaps with the idea of deprivation'. Strong's also adds its own interpretation of 'the penalty of a punishment which brings torment'. Only in the religious world would you think that you prune plants to punish them rather than make them more fruitful!

The real meaning is 'being restrained for disciplinary correction'. Which idea better reflects God's loving character and nature? Do you think God wants to punish or correct His children?

It is for discipline that you endure; God deals with you as with sons; for what son is there whom his father does not discipline? But if you are without discipline, of which all have become partakers, then you are illegitimate children and not sons... All discipline for the moment seems not to be joyful, but sorrowful; yet to those who have been trained by it, afterwards it yields the peaceful fruit of righteousness (Hebrews 12:7-8, 11).

If there is any sense of torment in the afterlife, in the consuming fire of God's loving presence as a result of our own choice, what causes it: torment as a result of God's punishment or the anguish of soul and regret that comes from recognising the consequences of our past behaviour and choices? I would be more likely to be tormented by my own stupidity than by God.

Sin is the loss of our identity and original image: it does have its own consequences but they are mostly manifested now, in this life. In the Matt 18 parable, it states that unforgiveness brings torment or even torture now in this life, not in the future, and definitely not by God.

Let's look at the two parables that have been used to affirm 'hell' as eternal conscious torment, the parables of the sheep and the goats and Lazarus and the rich man.

Sheep and goats

To be fair, you can understand why people tell us 'the Bible clearly says...' – our English Bibles certainly seem to. However, in this parable, as we have seen, the words themselves do not mean what we have been taught. The life being promised is the-God-kind-of-life: and the *aiōnios* punishment, therefore, is the-God-kind-of-punishment: that is, restorative and corrective, not retributive.

But what about the actual meaning of the parable itself?

"But when the Son of Man comes in His glory, and all the angels with Him, then He will sit on His glorious throne. All the nations will be gathered before Him; and He will separate them from one another, as the shepherd separates the sheep from the goats; and He will put the sheep on His right, and the goats on the left. "Then the King will say to those on His right, 'Come, you who are blessed of My Father, inherit the kingdom prepared for you from the foundation of the world. For I was hungry, and you gave Me something to eat; I was thirsty, and you gave Me something to drink; I was a stranger, and you invited Me in; naked, and you clothed Me; I was sick, and you visited Me; I was in prison, and you came to Me'... "Then He will also say to those on His left, 'Depart from Me, accursed ones, into the eternal fire which has been prepared for the devil and his angels. Then He will answer them, 'Truly I say to you, to the extent that you did not do it to one of the least of these, you did not do it to Me.' These will go away into eternal punishment, but the righteous into eternal life." (Matthew 25:31-46).*

Jesus' meaning in this parable (as in all the parables) was not literal but figurative. The sheep and goats in the parable are said to be nations, not individuals. The criterion for escaping 'eternal punishment' is good works, not faith in Jesus. So you can only reasonably use this passage to argue your case for an 'eternal hell' if you are prepared to assert that whole nations will be sent to heaven or hell, and based on their works, not on faith. So far I have not come across anyone in any theological stream who is prepared to do so.

This is not describing a corporate judgment where entire nations themselves are sent to heaven or hell in the future. It is not about the end of the world where people are to be judged based on how they treated the Jews or Christians (depending on what doctrinal version you have been taught).

The separation of the figurative sheep and goats took place in AD70 when all the believers left Jerusalem as Jesus warned them to when they recognised the signs of the times Jesus prophesied. The goats represent the religious, unbelieving Jews, who persecuted the early church until the end came, as Jesus prophesied it would, in that generation. Hundreds of thousands of these figurative goats then ended up being cast into the fires of a literal Gehenna.

I believe if we look at what Jesus said about Gehenna in context, we will see that he was not talking about eternal conscious torment at all but the end of the Old Covenant system and the fate of those who continued to follow Judaism. This was the end of their world and the end of 'the heavens and the earth', the nickname for the temple.

All the scriptures you will find quoted to affirm the belief in 'hell' as penal retribution in eternal conscious torment are already eschatologically realised and fulfilled. Therefore they have never applied to anyone's afterlife experience or expectation, even in the past, and certainly not to that of any of God's children today. That really is good news, rather than the fear-inducing bad news often preached today.

Another objection: "The eternal fire prepared for the devil and his angels? That's clear enough."

The more I consider this phrase, the more I am inclined to Chuck Crisco's view that it refers to 'the accuser and his messengers', which is a perfectly valid translation of the Greek words used. The Law, the religious system and those who fought to preserve it were heading for the fires of the Temple Mount and Gehenna at the end of the Old Covenant age (*aiōn*) in the destruction of Jerusalem by the armies of Rome (AD70).

But if that is a step too far for some, let's consider the purpose of fire. The Greek word is *pur*, from which we get words like 'pure' and 'purify'. Jesus came baptising with the Holy Spirit and with fire and Paul said that everyone's work will be tested with fire. I believe we will all go through the fires of purification to restore us to our original design and identity as sons by removing anything that distorts that image. We can engage with that fire now, or wait until we die (I advise option 1). There is a fire which awaits everyone who has not gone through it already but it is for purifying and correcting, not for destroying. It is the consuming fire of God's passionate love. And my testimony is that even those who did not accept Jesus while alive will still get to choose when they experience that fire after death.

So what was Jesus' point in this story of sheep and goats? 'Brothers' was a term used by Jews to refer exclusively to other Jews. Again (as throughout these chapters of Matthew's gospel) I would suggest that in His love He was setting out a warning to the religious-yet-unbelieving Jews, especially the leaders, who instead of serving 'the least of these my brothers' (the believing Jews) would imprison and kill them instead.

Lazarus and the rich man

There is really only one mention of an afterlife of torment in the whole of scripture, and it is found in the parable of Lazarus and the Rich Man in Luke chapter 16. We touched on this before, and for an in-depth look into this parable we recommend Brad Jersak's analysis in the Brazen Church publication *Putting Hell Back in the Handbasket*[14]. But what is the context of the parable? It comes just after this passage about the use of wealth:

"Now there was a rich man, and he habitually dressed in purple and fine linen, joyously living in splendour every day. And a poor man named Lazarus was laid at his gate, covered with sores, Now the poor man died and was carried away by the angels to Abraham's bosom; and the rich man also died and was buried. In Hades he lifted up his eyes, being in torment, and saw Abraham far away and Lazarus in his bosom. And he cried out and said, 'Father Abraham, have mercy on me, and send Lazarus so that he may dip the tip of his finger in water and cool

off my tongue, for I am in agony in this flame.' But Abraham said, 'Child, remember that during your life you received your good things, and likewise Lazarus bad things; but now he is being comforted here, and you are in agony. And besides all this, between us and you there is a great chasm fixed, so that those who wish to come over from here to you will not be able, and that none may cross over from there to us.' And he said, 'Then I beg you, father, that you send him to my father's house – for I have five brothers – in order that he may warn them, so that they will not also come to this place of torment.' But Abraham said, 'They have Moses and the Prophets; let them hear them.' But he said, 'No, father Abraham, but if someone goes to them from the dead, they will repent!' But he said to him, 'If they do not listen to Moses and the Prophets, they will not be persuaded even if someone rises from the dead.'" (Luke 16:19-31).

This parable seems to indicate that there is a possible afterlife of eternal conscious torment and separation from God. However, we need to consider two things: firstly what Jesus' main point is in this parable; and secondly, that it refers to a situation which took place before His death and resurrection.

The use of wealth

From the beginning of Luke 16, Jesus is speaking about the management of wealth.

Therefore if you have not been faithful in the use of unrighteous wealth, who will entrust the true riches to you? And if you have not been faithful in the use of that which is another's, who will give you that which is your own? No servant can serve two masters; for either he will hate the one and love the other, or else he will be devoted to one and despise the other. You cannot serve God and wealth.

Now the Pharisees, who were lovers of money, were listening to all these things and were scoffing at Him... And He said to them, "You are those who justify yourselves in the sight of men, but God knows your hearts; for that which is highly esteemed among men is detestable in the sight of God..." (Luke 16: 11, 15).

Like many of his teachings, this whole discourse was aimed at the religious elite, who were rich and powerful but abused their position. It fits with His other stories about a good Samaritan, the invitation to the banquet and the wise and foolish builders, and His warnings about a camel being unable to pass through the eye of a needle (a play on the name of a gate in Jerusalem), and having the whole world but losing your soul.

Their abuse of money (in the same context) could be seen in how they were 'putting away' their wives (rather than divorcing them – many of our Bible versions miss the whole point by mistranslating this) to avoid having to return the dowry. This left their abandoned wives destitute; and if they remarried, it caused them to commit adultery. Jesus challenged this practice in Luke 16:18, the previous verse to the parable we are looking at.

Jesus was telling the Pharisees that just because they were natural descendants of Abraham, that did not mean they were going to obtain the spiritual inheritance of the kingdom. In contrasting the fortunes of Lazarus and the rich man, He was looking forward to the great role reversal soon to take place when the sceptre would be taken out of the hands of Judah and officially belong to Jesus alone, who would then give the kingdom to His New Covenant people, the Ekklesia. This happened in AD 70 when the natural kingdom was taken away and the kingdom of God became spiritual, with Christ ruling from heaven, not physical Jerusalem.

Come now you rich, weep and howl for your miseries that are coming upon you... you have heaped up treasures in the last days! (James 5:1-3) is the same warning.

The 'chasm' in the story may have been culturally symbolic of the great cultural divide between Jew and Gentile in contemporary Judaism (and it has been suggested that it is most likely a reference to the Jordan Rift Valley which separated the land Abraham was promised from Gentile lands). Uncircumcised Gentile proselytes of Judaism were referred to as "gate proselytes" or "strangers inside the gate" and they enjoyed certain rights and privileges under the Mosaic Law. In the parable, the rich man left Lazarus outside when he should have provided for him inside. Looking out for the poor is part of the good news (as seen in Isaiah 61:1-2 and in the injunction to love our neighbour as ourselves).

Jesus came saying "You have heard it said" (rabbinical tradition) "but now I say unto you", turning their traditions on their head. His parables do the same thing, often referring to Jewish beliefs in order to challenge them. His purpose in this parable was not to offer a definitive revelation on the nature of hades but to make a profound ethical point in a story which incorporates some contemporary Jewish imagery of what happened to people after death.

So this is primarily a parable about the way the rich treat the poor and perhaps about racial division. It is not about heaven and hell: neither are even mentioned.

Abraham's bosom

Secondly, the scenario it describes took place before Jesus' death and resurrection and does not indicate the situation after that event. It also refers to a culturally accepted view of the afterlife which is not found in the Old Testament at all. 'Abraham's bosom' is not a biblical phrase but something they picked up while in captivity in Babylon and is only found in the Babylonian Talmud.

The idea is that there might be two places in *sheol*: one for the righteous to await resurrection (which Jesus perhaps referred to on the cross as 'Paradise', where the thief would be with Him that day), the other supposedly for the unrighteous to await judgment. However, after his death Jesus actually went to *sheol* and preached and executed that judgment; and the verdict was 'not guilty'.

The rich man's desire is to send a warning to his brothers before it is too late. Since his brothers were still alive, this must be before any 'judgment day' at the 'end of the world' and therefore whatever he is experiencing, it is not the 'eternal fires of hell'.

And as Brad Jersak points out,

"... aspects of the story make a crass literalism awkward: how does the rich man communicate with Abraham across the chasm? Does everyone there have a direct line to the patriarch? Does someone being incinerated in a furnace care about thirst? Are these literal flames? And since hades precedes the resurrection of the body, do we have literal tongues with which to feel thirst? Is this also the literal Abraham? Do the millions in his care take turns snuggling with him? Or is his bosom big enough to contain us all at once? How big he must be! And so on into implausibility. Taking the parable seriously means we mustn't take it so literally."

Do we really think that from heaven we will see our loved ones in 'hell' and talk to them but offer them no hope, yet we are going to be happy and call heaven a place of peace? Are we going to eternally see the suffering of our mum or grandmother or a child that died at 16 years of age in an accident, and be filled with joy?

In summary, the context of Luke 16 is all about wealth and true riches. In the verses immediately preceding this parable Luke tells us that the Pharisees were lovers of money. Jesus is not offering a treatise on the afterlife, but a warning about putting your trust in riches and failing to help the poor.

Away from the presence

This passage in 2 Thessalonians is often quoted in support of 'hell':

...when the Lord Jesus will be revealed from heaven with His mighty angels in flaming fire, dealing out **retribution** *to those who do not know God and to those who do not obey the gospel of our Lord Jesus. These will pay the* **penalty** *of* **eternal destruction, away from** *the presence of the Lord and from the glory of His power* (2Thessalonians 1:7-9).

If you believe in hell as eternal conscious torment, the word 'destruction' does not work for you. If you believe in the annihilation of the wicked, the combination of 'eternal' and 'destruction' makes no sense. However you look at it, we need to delve deeper.

The English words in bold are all poor translations: *diké* (translated penalty) means justice, judicial hearing, legal decision; the related word *ekdikesis* (retribution) means that which arises out of justice; *aionion* (eternal) we know means pertaining to the age; *olethros* (destruction) means the state of being lost; *apo* (away from, from) does indeed mean 'from', but in the sense of 'coming out of' or 'coming from' and not 'separated from'. Matthew Distefano points out that the phrase 'eternal destruction from the presence of the Lord' (*olethron aionion apo prosopou tou Kyriou*) in 2 Thessalonians 1:9 echoes exactly that in Acts 3:19: 'times of refreshing from the presence of the Lord' (*kairoi anapsyxeos apo prosopou tou Kyriou*). No one translates that as 'times of refreshing away from the presence of the Lord'. So Paul was encouraging the Thessalonians that there was a judicial decision about to come from the Presence of the Lord which would have a consequence for those who were persecuting them: it would involve a state of lostness pertaining to the age. Or you can read it as God's consuming-fire-presence delivering a justice that totally ruins their lostness.

This is not about some future end of the world event or afterlife experience but what Jesus prophesied would occur in that generation (and did occur in AD70) – and even then, God's justice is always restorative for everyone.

The Lake of Fire

Four verses mention 'the lake of fire' in the Bible, all in Revelation chapters 19 and 20. Revelation is an apocalyptic book, symbolic and cryptic in nature, the only one of its kind in the New Testament but very common in Jewish and Greek literature. Only those 'in the know' and immersed in the culture in which it is written can fully understand the symbolism. Symbols can represent multiple concepts. One thing is certain: apocalyptic literature is never intended to be read literally. We can get clues about some of the symbols because they also appear in the book of Daniel, including the beast being cast into the blazing fire (Dan 7:11). Just as Daniel's beasts were figurative, representing various nations, so too is the lake of burning sulphur figurative. The book of Revelation is not a prophecy for the far distant future but was an immediate warning to first-century Israel that just as Sodom and Gomorrah fell in fiery destruction, so too the Jewish religious system was in danger of ending in the same manner.

The 'book of life' mentioned is a commonly understood concept in the Jewish tradition and refers back to the law where according to the Talmud this book is opened every Jewish new year on Rosh Hashanah.

In Revelation 20:14, we see death and hades thrown into the lake of fire. Here, the lake of fire may well represent God's (completed) triumph over evil, sin, the grave and death through the power of the cross. Many of the early church Fathers saw the lake of fire as a spiritual place where everyone in humanity was purged of their unbelief and sins so that they could eventually believe in God. I believe it is fed by the river of fire which flows from God's throne.

And the devil who deceived them was thrown into the lake of fire and brimstone, where the beast and the false prophet are also; and they will be tormented day and night forever and ever (Revelation 20:10).

'Forever and ever' is a poor translation of 'to the ages of ages'. Brimstone (Greek: *theios*, closely related to the word for 'God') was regarded as having the power to heal and purify. *Basanizo* (translated torment) is 'testing with a touchstone' (in other scriptures it is translated as tossed or battered by waves, straining at the oars of a boat, and being in labour while giving birth).

Go to God

No matter how many objections we address, how many scriptures we dig into, we know that some will not be persuaded. This book and specifically this chapter are not intended for them but for those who discover that God is already on their case – and even they will probably come up with other verses or passages not included in this brief survey. There are far more comprehensive treatments of the subject elsewhere; we have referenced some of them in the text. But ultimately all of us are going to need to go to God, in whatever way we know how, and hear what He has to say to us about the questions we have.

Fire and passion

I believe we will all go through the fires of purification to restore us to our original design and identity as sons by removing anything that distorts that image. The questions are why, when, where and how will we all engage the consuming fire of God's love, and will we do so willingly? In our minds the fire is often associated with judgment but, because of the cross, that judgment is nothing to be feared and only needs to be embraced.

There is a fire in the afterlife but it is for purifying and correcting. Even those who rejected Jesus whilst alive will still get the continuing opportunity to choose Jesus and life after physical death because love never fails and never gives up.

God is love. He never has been and never will be anything other than perfect love. We all need to experience the passion of God's love that is stronger than death and to know by experience that love which will not relent, will never cease, and will never let go of any of His children.

I have experienced such love in places of fire during my many encounters in the heavenly realms. Those experiences were initially terrifying to my soul as I engaged in a river of fire, the judgment seat of fire, the fire stones, the fire of the altars, and the passionate fire of God's presence. I believe we will all have our own burning bush encounters that will awaken us to our identity and destiny as Moses' encounter did for him.

The wrong concept of 'hell' has made fire something to be feared and to be avoided but when we know God's fire is His love, we can embrace the consuming, purifying, correcting fire of His presence where we are all tested and purified, even today.

The fire of God's love consumes our selfish motives and burns up our deepest regrets. At the Judgment Seat, I saw that there is a fire in His eyes that penetrates deep into the very core of our being with the most piercing, passionate love. Let's all embrace the fire of God's presence to consume everything that robs us from our identity and relationship so we can be restored.

The restoration of all things is the heart of God who is Love, Light, Spirit and Fire and all these terms are synonymous and reflect the loving nature of a good God who passionately desires our restoration.

Now if any man builds on the foundation with gold, silver, precious stones, wood, hay, straw, each man's work will become evident; for the day will show it because it is to be revealed with fire, and the fire itself will test the quality of each man's work. If any man's work which he has built on it remains, he will receive a reward. 15 If any man's work is burned up, he will suffer loss; but he himself will be saved, yet so as through fire (1 Corinthians 3:12-14 NASB).

Everyone's work shall be tested in the scrutiny of real life; it shall be made apparent as in broad daylight just as gold is tested in fire: what you teach will either burn like stubble or shine like gold. (The revelation of mankind's co-crucifixion and co-resurrection with Christ is the gold of the gospel!) (1 Corinthians 3:13 Mirror).

Realize that your life is God's building; his sanctuary, designed for his permanent abode. His Spirit inhabits you! (He designed every cell in your body to accommodate and express him.) *Just like fire would burn away the dross, any defilement of God's temple would be destroyed in order to preserve human life as his permanent sanctuary.* (1 Corinthians 3:16-17 Mirror Bible).

We can all experience the fire and passion of God's love today for ourselves. Let's not hide from it or try to avoid it.

"Son, it is time for everyone to embrace the fire to experience deeper love and the purification that My consuming fiery love brings.

"Son, call on Me to stoke the fires and increase the intensity of the heat to reveal hearts, minds and motives. "

– So I call for the purification of fire.

– I call for the fire of love to penetrate the hardest, darkest areas of our hearts.

– I call for the refiner's fire to burn away the dross of self.

– I call for the light to shine, to expose the things hidden because of shame.

– I call for love's overcoming power to reveal and break every chain tethering God's people to the DIY path.

– I call for the passion of God's heart to be revealed in His wrath directed towards all brokenness and lost identity.

Let the consuming fire of God's love burn in our hearts and minds to restore us to true sonship.

Can we see the truth or are our minds veiled in the darkness of religious deception as mine was? Those veils need to be removed for the truth to be revealed.

And even if our gospel is veiled, it is veiled to those who are perishing, in whose case the god of this world has blinded the minds of the unbelieving so that they might not see the light of the gospel of the glory of Christ, who is the image of God (2 Corinthians 4:3-4).

... for their minds have been blinded by the god of this age, leaving them in unbelief. Their blindness keeps them from seeing the dayspring light of the wonderful news of the glory of Jesus Christ, who is the divine image of God (2 Corinthians 4:4 TPT).

The 'god of this age' refers to the religious systems, governing structures and self-help solutions of this world. A religious veil has blinded many to God who is love, light, spirit and fire. The true image of God has been veiled, with the result that some people, perhaps ourselves included, have not been able to see the reality of who He truly is. Does our 'God' look exactly like Jesus? Does our 'God' look exactly like love?

The DIY tree path

This veil began to be drawn over the truth when Adam and Eve chose to follow the wrong path, the path of the tree of knowledge of good and evil, what I have called the DIY tree path. In losing sight of God they also lost sight of themselves and the true image of their sonship. They became slaves to their own do-it-yourself efforts to restore what they already had: love, acceptance, approval, affirmation, significance and purpose in the relationship.

Mankind has been doing the same ever since. We have tried many solutions, including power, position, money, materialism, religion and other relationships. All that DIY has done is cause us more pain, leading to more unsuccessful self-medication. All our religious systems are DIY attempts to please or appease God, hoping to get back what was lost. Sadly, if we do not know the relational truth about God and ourselves, we are actually helping to keep the veils in place:

"You are the light of the world. A city set on a hill cannot be hidden" (Matthew 5:14).

We are supposed to be the light that enables people to see God but that light will be dimmed or distorted if we are hidden behind a mask or a veil of religious deception ourselves.

False reality

Our own minds are inevitably veiled by the things we already believe. Our mindsets, world-views and strongholds can all be veils or filters over our minds that obstruct and filter how we process reality. These constructs within our minds and consciousness frame our world, what we believe and how we interact. We see the world – and God – through the lens of our understanding. It is a distorted view, a false reality, but while it persists it is real to us.

To make matters worse, we often have confirmation bias operating. Defined as 'the tendency to interpret new evidence as a confirmation of one's existing beliefs or theories', confirmation bias is particularly prevalent in the area of religious beliefs. Our theology and doctrines tend to cause us to interpret everything through their filters. It takes a significant experience, often almost a trauma, to shake us loose from the limitations of what we already believe.

Trust in the Lord with all your heart, and do not lean on your own understanding (Proverbs 3:5).

God is wooing us into a deeper level of intimacy with Him in a relationship. When we encounter God we want to make sure that we are not relying on our existing understanding but only on a continual living relationship (so we must beware of replacing our existing understanding with a new, equally flawed one). There is a new level of experiential relationship with God (Father, Son and Spirit) that is being unveiled to us, a new level of communication with God (the ability to hear and see what God is revealing); a new mind, the mind of Christ, continually flowing from our relationship with Him rather than just new theology or doctrines (a new DIY construct).

Metanoia, a radical shift

When we can behold God (Father, Son and Spirit) as He really is, then we can become conformed to the image of sonship that we see within Him.

And do not be conformed to this world, but be transformed by the renewing of your mind, so that you may prove what the will of God is, that which is good and acceptable and perfect (Romans 12:2).

In the past, I believed I could renew my mind by memorising Bible verses and confessing them, trying to believe them. I have come to understand that we are renewed from within, not from the outside, as we relate to God who is Father, Son and Spirit in us (and we are in Him). This is my testimony of how this came about for me. Early in 2016, I heard God say:

"The mists around the closed and clouded minds must be dissipated. The hindrances and entanglements must be removed so that the limitations of minds that are stuck in what has been can become free to embrace what can be so that it can become what will be. The veils must be removed and restrictions lifted to embrace the limitless potential of My reality. The Way, Truth and Life are to be experienced not conceptualised and contained.

"The limits of what is possible must be removed for My purpose to be achieved. You must begin to entertain limitless grace and mercy to be able to grasp what is true reality, beyond all expectations. New dimensions of everything can be yours if you are willing to let go of the old and embrace the challenge of the new."

To know God who is Father, Son and Spirit, and to know our identity in sonship in Him, we need our minds deconstructed from the wrong frameworks, from all our limited, restricting belief systems.

Or do you think lightly of the riches of His kindness and tolerance and patience, not knowing that the kindness of God leads you to metanoia? (Romans 2:4).

We need a *metanoia*, a radical shift of thinking, to enable a relationship with the Truth to reveal true reality. Most Bible versions translate the word as 'repentance', but *metanoia* has nothing to do with saying sorry or doing penance for our past: Jesus dealt with that on the cross and made us righteous once and for all.

He called me to make some laws and legislative decrees based on what He had told me. As I did, I expected Him to use them to free others from their worldly and religious mindsets. I had no idea that He was instead going to use my own words to iconoclastically deconstruct my conscious, subconscious and unconscious mind!

It began with Brexit, the vote about whether the UK should remain within the European Union or leave it. I was pondering how to vote when He asked me "Why do you normally vote the way you do?"

In the conversation that followed, I realised that I had made huge assumptions about which party He would want me to support, not only over this issue but more generally. I had always voted on principle, but God showed me that the principles I was voting on were my own, not His.

So I asked Him which way the Brexit vote would go. He told me and asked me which way I was going to vote. "Leave," I replied, "because You have told me that is the way the vote is going to go." Another assumption! It turned out that God wanted me to vote the opposite way so that He could teach me how to respond when my choice was defeated.

This series of conversations with God (I wrote about them in more detail in my previous book, *My Journey Beyond Beyond*) revealed that I had many more assumptions and presumptions about God, the Bible, theology and doctrine than I thought, and that they were acting as veils and filters in my mind.

So the process of my deconstruction and renewal began in earnest.

Cognitive dissonance

It is impossible to see Him as He is when our minds are confused with our distorted ideas about Him. Every time a stronghold in the mind is broken down, it makes way for a resurrection of fresh revelation. This is not an easy process; there is a lot of eating humble pie to do. And some of those strongholds are beliefs deeply cherished by ourselves and by others; one reason I initially held back was that I knew this was going to cause trouble.

Cognitive dissonance is the mental stress or discomfort we experience when we realise that we hold two or more contradictory beliefs, ideas, or values simultaneously. This often happens when new information manages to get through the filter of confirmation bias and threatens to disrupt the balancing act in our minds.

The encounters I had with God challenged what I believed about Him. This put a stress on my brain that felt like a restrictive band around my head. The pressure was only released when I gave in and stopped trying to hold on to my old way of thinking.

Renew and transform

As we saw, Jesus Himself constantly challenged the accepted thinking of His day: "You have heard it said... but I say to you..." He turned their religion on its head; love replaced religious duty and obligation.

C. S. Lewis called God 'the Great Iconoclast' and wrote, "There are three images in my mind which I must continually forsake and replace by better ones: the false image of God, the false image of my neighbours, and the false image of myself." (*The Great Divorce*)[16]. John Crowder[2] says, "It is only at this place where our ideas and our faith are completely devastated that we have an opportunity to meet the God who transcends all our ideas about God."

Are we ready to let God renew and transform our thinking? As I wrote in '*My Journey Beyond Beyond*',

> I began to discover that God will not be confined to our limited, static perceptions of Him. We cannot keep an infinite God in a box constructed within the finite capacities of our understanding. All that will do is limit

ourselves. God does not dwell in manmade temples, theological constructs or ideologies; He dwells in our spirits and in our hearts. We need to encounter Him so that we can have a transformation, a revolutionary change of mind. We need the veils of our understanding stripped away. This can only happen through our relationship with the living Word of Truth, the ultimate source of revelation who searches the deep things of God and makes them known to us.

Do not allow your current understanding to keep you in bondage to the limitations of your past experience. Insanity is to keep doing the same things expecting different results; it is to live trapped in our own limitations. Everything we receive must come through personal encounters with God. Those encounters will never contradict the record of God's nature and character revealed in the Bible but may not be directly found in it. They will definitely challenge religious belief systems which limit what the Bible actually says, by reducing it to a set of rules or doctrines.

Our old mindsets, thinking patterns and religious world views will keep us in old trusted ways of behaviour and will limit our ability to engage in the heavenly spiritual realities that are being unveiled in our day. Are we prepared to embrace and spread the revolution? Some of the doctrines and beliefs we once deemed foundational may turn out to be just the skewed projections of our own fearful, fallen assumptions about God. He is about to explode the DIY myths we have invented; myths which obscure who He really is from our view.

Love bombs

I saw angels with light wands marking us out, and others, for laser-guided love bombs. God wants to explode those love bombs over you, penetrating your mind, your heart, your whole being with His love for you, revealing your true identity as a beloved son.

Live loved, love living and live loving.

Invite Him to release those love bombs over you. Let your heart and mind be cocooned in love. Let Jesus reveal His love for you. Let the Father reveal His love for you. Let the Spirit explode His love in you. Let the love of God touch your mind. Let Him encounter you with love that will explode and destroy any wrong image of Him. Let Him remove the veils that obscure and distort Him.

Let Him explode your limited reality.

To reconcile all things

...and through Him to reconcile all things to Himself, having made peace through the blood of His cross; through Him, I say, whether things on earth or things in heaven. And although you were formerly alienated and hostile in mind, engaged in evil deeds, yet He has now reconciled you in His fleshly body through death, in order to present you before Him holy and blameless and beyond reproach (Colossians 1:20-22).

According to what most of us have believed, Jesus has reconciled only a certain, select group of people, in order to present us blameless and beyond reproach. We have limited the scope of this reconciliation, thinking it could not possibly include everyone and everything. Inevitably, different groups have had different opinions about who is in and who is out.

Everyone and everything is included. Jesus reconciled all things to Himself. If Jesus did it already, no one needs to do anything more. There is nothing we can do to make ourselves holy and blameless and beyond reproach, because He already did it. He died our death, dealt with our separation and brought us back into a restored relationship.

...namely, that God was in Christ reconciling the world (Greek: kosmos) to Himself, not counting their sins against them, and He has committed to us the word of reconciliation (2 Corinthians 5:19).

God is not counting anyone's sins against them. That is forgiveness. Psalm 103 tells us that as far as the east is from the west, so far has He removed our transgressions from us. No matter how far you travel trying to find them, you never will.

Vine's dictionary will tell you that kosmos means 'the sum-total of human life in the ordered universe, considered apart from, and alienated from, and hostile to God, and of the earthly things which seduce from God.' Even if you do believe the part about 'alienated' and 'hostile', the kosmos is still what 'God so loved' in John 3:16 and what 'God was in Christ reconciling' in 2 Corinthians 5:19. It has all been reconciled.

We have this word, that Jesus has reconciled everyone, but what have we done with it? Have we shared with people the good news of what God has done for them, or bad news, that they are not reconciled with, and still separated from, a God who doesn't even like them?

The final judgment

For the wages of sin is death, but the free gift of God is age-enduring life in Christ Jesus our Lord (Romans 6:23).

Jesus died our death and now there is no longer any sin, and therefore no wages due. If no one's sin is counted against them, based on the power of the cross, then all subsequent judgments must produce life and not death. As Francois Du Toit says in the Mirror Bible translation of 2 Corinthians 5:19, "the fallen state of mankind was deleted." There is no double jeopardy in God's kingdom: you cannot be tried for the same thing twice. No one can be judged again for what Jesus already died for. The cross is the final judgment. There is no future 'judgment day': it already happened at the cross and we have all been declared blamelessly innocent.

Sadly, we judge people all the time, based on their behaviour and what we consider to be right or wrong rather than looking at them in love through the eyes of Jesus. Whilst we do not necessarily condone everyone's behaviour, we need to be careful not to think that it can exclude them from God's love and reconciliation.

Pleased to reveal His Son in me

Paul recounts his encounter (as Saul) on the road to Damascus:

337

But when God, who had set me apart even from my mother's womb and called me through His grace, was pleased to reveal His Son in me so that I might preach Him among the Gentiles... (Galatians 1:15-16).

He does not say that God revealed His Son in the bright light that blinded him, but that "God was pleased to reveal His Son in me". God had been at work in him all along; Jesus had been in Him all along; now God revealed that to him. God is not separated from people, even from someone like Saul who was implacably opposed to Him. He is at work in all people to reveal Himself as love and light – and through them to others.

For too long the good news has been presented something like this: "There is a big gulf between you on one side and God on the other. The cross bridges the gap and you can walk across that bridge and engage God." The real good news is that there is no gulf. God is already at work in everybody, and our job is to help them see that (not to tell them that they are dirty, rotten sinners who deserve to suffer eternal conscious torment as their punishment in hell). There is no separation.

Let us not imagine that the incarnation separated Father, Son and Spirit; nor even the crucifixion. Scripture tells us that all the fullness of God's being dwells bodily in Christ (Colossians 2:9) and that God was in Christ, reconciling the world to Himself (2 Corinthians 5:19). On the cross, Jesus felt the agony of fallen humanity when he quoted the opening line of Psalm 22, *"My God, my God, why have you forsaken me?"* But every Jewish person who heard Him knew where the Psalm was going, with David crying triumphantly *"He has not despised nor abhorred the affliction of the afflicted; Nor has He hidden His face from him; But when he cried to Him for help, He heard."* (Psalm 22:24).

Victory of the cross

The restoration of all things is based on the victory of the cross over all things that would hinder our reconciliation and restoration to a relationship.

All judgment and justice are based on the victory of the cross over sin, death and the grave; every hindrance or legal obstacle is overcome. Jesus holds the keys of death and hades (Revelation 1:17) and He is using them to unlock the door, not lock it. That is contradictory to some of our belief systems. God has opened access to everyone. The gates of the New Jerusalem are never shut. Everyone is included, no one excluded.

...so that, as sin reigned in death, even so grace would reign through righteousness to age-enduring life through Jesus Christ our Lord (Romans 5:21).

The power of the resurrection has defeated death (and it is what enables everything to be restored). The resurrection has overcome death and grace now reigns.

All will be made alive

For since by a man came death, by a man also came the resurrection of the dead. For as in Adam all die, so also in Christ all will be made alive (1 Corinthians 15:21-22).

Take note of the 'all' in both parts of that last sentence. It seems that no one has much trouble with the first 'all' meaning 'all'.

The second 'all' is where the trouble begins, because if it is the same 'all' then much of our theology bites the dust. So we have made 'in Christ' conditional, in a way that we do not with 'in Adam': so that only those who are 'in Christ' will be made alive. And we have gone on to define what being 'in Christ' looks like, according to our various denominations and streams.

Both mentions of 'all' are the same 'all'. Christ was the last Adam and the Adamic race ended with Him. From this side of the cross, no one is descended from Adam any more but from Christ. From that point on, all are 'in Christ' (though some do not know it and the 'gospel' we have preached has consistently told them that they aren't). And Paul says that 'in Christ' all of us are going to be made alive.

The sting of death is sin, and the power of sin is the law; but thanks be to God, who gives us the victory through our Lord Jesus Christ (1 Corinthians 15:56).

For the law of the Spirit of life in Christ Jesus has set you free from the law of sin and of death (Romans 8:2).

Those are very familiar scriptures and we read them as if they apply exclusively to 'us' (those we consider as being 'in Christ'). But who is under the law, since the cross? No one, not even the Jewish people who were the ONLY ones under the law in the first place!

Everyone has victory over death and sin through the power of the cross.

...who has saved us and called us with a holy calling, not according to our works, but according to His own purpose and grace which was granted us in Christ Jesus from all eternity [literally, from before the times of the ages] *but now has been revealed by the appearing of our Saviour Christ Jesus, who abolished death and brought life and immortality to light through the gospel* (2 Timothy 1:9-10).

Death is abolished. It no longer has power over anyone. This was already decided 'from before the times of the ages' but has been 'brought to light' by the gospel.

God is not holding anything related to sin against the world and is restoring all things, first to original condition and then to His original intention. God is looking for all things to grow and mature from their original condition to fulfil their potential, His original intention. Original condition is just the start: there is more to come!

We have seen that restoration deals with the sin that occurred at the fall when mankind lost their identity and with the death which came as a result. In fact, Jesus' death and resurrection dealt with everything that happened because we chose the DIY path.

Now if we have died with Christ, we believe that we shall also live with Him, knowing that Christ, having been raised from the dead, is never to die again; death no longer is master over Him. For the death that He died, He died to sin once for all; but the life that He lives, He lives to God. Even so consider yourselves to be dead to sin, but alive to God in Christ Jesus... For sin shall not be master over you, for you are not under law but under grace (Romans 6 8-11, 14).

Death and resurrection

"Blessed and holy is the one who has a part in the first resurrection; over these the second death has no power" (Revelation 20:6).

There are several questions to consider here:

* What is the second death?
* What is the first death?
* Who has a part in the first resurrection?

Some see the second death as eternal separation from God. They believe that when the 'unsaved' physically die they will either go to eternal conscious torment in hell (ECT) or they will cease to exist (annihilation). Neither of these views allows for 'the restoration of all things', nor do they accurately reflect the merciful, just, loving nature of God.

The Bible itself tells us what the second death actually is:

Then death and Hades were thrown into the lake of fire. This is the second death, the lake of fire (Revelation 20:14).

The lake of fire is not 'hell'. In fact, if you insist on translating the Greek word *hades* as 'hell' then it is where 'hell' ends up! It is the death of death itself, the destruction of all that prevents us from experiencing the fullness of life. In the first death, Christ died the death of all men, receiving the 'wages of sin' on our behalf. The second death cannot mean some kind of endless death, because Jesus destroyed death and "death is swallowed up in victory" (1 Corinthians 15:54).

We are not subject to the second death if we have experienced the first death (being co-crucified with Jesus) and the first resurrection (being made alive together with Him). Death is defeated. It will not triumph over billions of people forever by consigning them to a 'lost eternity'. Jesus' resurrection life brings an end to death, either through water (baptism) in this life or through fire (the consuming fire of God's love) after this life is over. In place of death, He has given us life:

The wages of sin is death. But the gift of God is age-enduring life, through Christ Jesus our Lord (Romans 6:23).

We can voluntarily embrace being buried and resurrected with Jesus (which we acknowledge and with which we identify in baptism) or through fire. God Himself is that consuming fire. If we have died to self in this life, the second death has no jurisdiction over us.

Consuming fire

But many people are blind to the truth and are unnecessarily living in their own DIY mindsets of lostness. They continue to live separated from God, although He has done everything necessary for their reconciliation, therefore they continue to experience the resultant sin and death. So what happens to them when they die physically and end up in the consuming fire of God's love?

What is the purpose of the fire? Fire refines and makes pure. The dross in their lives will be burned away until each person chooses life through Jesus and receives their new name which was written in the book of life from the foundation of the world. What has been stolen from them is restored to them. How long it takes is dependent on each individual's resistance to the working of that consuming fire.

The end of choice?

...then the dust will return to the earth as it was, and the spirit will return to God who gave it (Ecclesiastes 12:7).

The physical body of everyone who dies returns to the earth and everyone's spirit returns to God. But what happens to the soul, our conscious understanding of who we are?

If people do not choose life through Jesus in this life, there is not an automatic 'free pass' to a relationship with God in the next. But I cannot find even one Bible verse which indicates that physical death is the end of choice. I have asked others, especially those who contend that unbelievers go straight to the eternal conscious torment of hell when they die, and none of them can come up with anything except a verse taken entirely out of context:

And inasmuch as it is appointed for men to die once and after this comes judgment... (Hebrews 9:27).

It is a verse which many use to object to the restoration of all things. In context, the 'once' is the death of Jesus, with which we identify. The word 'judgment' is not a synonym for 'punishment', it means 'reaching a verdict'; and the verdict is 'blamelessly innocent'. The only death that everyone needs to experience is inclusion in Jesus' death.

J. W. Hanson, in his book, *Bible Threatenings Explained*[16], tells us what this passage actually means.

> "*And as it is appointed unto men once to die; but after this the judgment; so Christ was once offered to bear the sins of many; and unto them that look for him, shall he appear the second time, without sin unto salvation.*"– Hebrews 9:27-28.

This text is usually misstated in this shape, "it is appointed unto all men once to die, and after death the judgment." But the reader of the context will perceive that Paul was not speaking of the physical death of mankind, but of the sacrificial death of the high priest, and was contrasting with the death of Christ, the ceremonial death of the Aaronic priesthood. The language of the original shows this more clearly than does the language of our version. In the Greek, the definite article *tois*, (the or those) precedes the word translated men, (*anthropois*), and thus it reads, "it is appointed unto the (or those) men once to die." What men? The context shows:

> 24 *For Christ did not enter a holy place made with hands, a mere copy of the true one, but into heaven itself, now to appear in the presence of God for us; 25 nor was it that He would offer Himself often, as the high priest*

enters the holy place year by year with blood that is not his own. 26 Otherwise, He would have needed to suffer often since the foundation of the world; but now once at the consummation of the ages He has been manifested to put away sin by the sacrifice of Himself. 27 And inasmuch as it is appointed for men to die once and after this comes judgment, 28 so Christ also, having been offered once to bear the sins of many, will appear a second time for salvation without reference to sin, to those who eagerly await Him.–Heb. 9:24-28.

This is a literal translation. The plain statement is: As the high priests, the antitypes, died a figurative death, annually, (see Ex. 28:29--30), so Christ was offered once for all in the sinner's behalf. The ordinary reference to the dying of all men leaves the "as" and "so" without meaning or application. But when we see that the apostle was showing the superiority of the mission of Christ over the annual sacrifices of the Jewish high priest, the meaning becomes plain. He employed "the men" as types of the superior sacrifice of Christ.

The reader cannot fail to see that it is not mankind, but certain men, "the men" who all the way through this chapter and the next are compared to Christ, who are said once to die. These men are the priests, or the successors of the high priests under the law. They died, figuratively, once a year, on the great day of atonement in the offering of sacrifices. Ex. 30:1-10, Ex. 25:22

The priests represent Christ, and their death illustrates and prefigures the death of Christ; but man's death, and an after death judgment bears no relation to the death of Christ. The common use of this text is but little less than an outrage on the sense of the apostle. No one can carefully read this and the following chapter, and fail to see that the language is exclusively applicable to the Jewish high priests and the death of Christ, and has no reference to an after-death judgment.

Rescue from the grave

On the other hand, there are plenty of Bible verses which speak of God rescuing people from the grave.

The Lord kills and makes alive; He brings down to Sheol and raises up (1 Samuel 2:6).

For the Lord will not reject forever, For if He causes grief, Then He will have compassion according to His abundant loving kindness. For He does not afflict willingly or grieve the sons of men (Lamentations 3:31-33).

For we will surely die and are like water spilled on the ground which cannot be gathered up again. Yet God does not take away life, but plans ways so that the banished one will not be cast out from him (2 Samuel 14:14).

Jesus went into hades, preached there and led captivity captive: see Eph 4:8,9; Psalm 68:18; 1 Peter 3:18-20. Death is not the end of God's power or desire to save.

A covenant with death

Jesus has restored what death robbed us of: access into God's loving presence to experience restored face-to-face relationship. Religion, meanwhile, has a covenant with death. To enter heaven and experience eternity, it teaches, you have to die. So even believers are expecting to have to die before they go to heaven.

Heaven is open now because we already died with Christ! The covenant with death needs to be broken so that we can live the abundant life that God intends. If you have a covenant with death, go ahead and break it! Do not agree that you have to die.

"Truly, truly, I say to you, he who believes has eternal [lit: age-enduring] *life. I am the bread of life. Your fathers ate the manna in the wilderness, and they died. This is the bread which comes down out of heaven, so that one may eat of it and not die. I am the living bread that came down out of heaven; if anyone eats of this bread, he will live forever* [lit: to the age]*; and the bread also which I will give for the life of the world is My flesh."* (John 6:47-51).

More questions

What does happen to people after they die, as believers or not yet believers?

• Are they just soul sleeping?
• Are they watching over us?
• Are they suffering?
• Can we help them?
• Will we ever see them again?

348

- What happens after we die?
- What is death?
- What is life?

These are questions that are worth answering before looking at my testimony concerning engaging that fiery place.

Who are we, what are we, and are there different endings and places for the different parts of us? We are a spirit, we have a soul and we live in a body. Our spirit was created outside of time and space and pre-existed before this life. Adam became a living being/soul when God breathed His breath, His Spirit, into him:

Then the Lord God formed man of dust from the ground, and breathed into his nostrils the breath of life; and man became a living being. (Genesis 2:7).

Adam lived with his spirit clothing his body and soul in total God-consciousness: he was literally clothed with light, the glory of his spiritual identity. I believe transfiguration will mean a return to this primordial state, with abilities that we currently term 'supernatural' becoming normal.

When I consider Your heavens, the work of Your fingers, the moon and the stars, which You have ordained; What is man that You take thought of him, and the son of man that You care for him? Yet You have made him a little lower than God, and You crown him with glory and majesty! You make him to rule over the works of Your hands; You have put all things under his feet (Psalm 8:3-6).

When Adam sinned, he lost his identity in sonship and his spirit became separated relationally both from God and from his soul: this was spiritual death. Adam eventually died physically, aged 930, in time and space because he walked independently in DIY mode.

"...but from the tree of the knowledge of good and evil you shall not eat, for in the day that you eat from it you will surely die" (Genesis 2:17).

The restoration of all things must include the total restoration of our being, spirit, soul and body, in union with the oneness of Father, Son and Spirit with *perichoresis* relationship.

Now may the God of peace Himself sanctify you entirely; and may your spirit and soul and body be preserved complete (1 Thessalonians 5:23).

This sanctification process that we all have to go through is to bring life and immortality back into the light of revealed truth that we all will live by.

What happens after we die?

When we talk of death, what death are we referring to? Is it spiritual death, physical death, the death of self as we embrace being crucified with Christ, or is it the second death? Confusing, isn't it? The last enemy is death, and death has already been defeated, conquered and abolished by Jesus. When we are baptised, we are baptised into the death, burial and resurrection of Jesus.

Or do you not know that all of us who have been baptized into Christ Jesus have been baptized into His death? ... Now if we have died with Christ, we believe that we shall also live with Him (Romans 6:3, 8).

For if we have become united with Him in the likeness of His death, certainly we shall also be in the likeness of His resurrection (Romans 6:5).

For the wages of the sin [is] death, and the gift of God [is] life age-during in Christ Jesus our Lord (Romans 6:23 YLT).

The sting of death is sin, and the power of sin is the law; but thanks be to God, who gives us the victory through our Lord Jesus Christ (1 Corinthians 15:56-57).

Before we look at restored life, there are so many questions that death raises; in fact, according to Hebrews chapter 2, the fear of death is what keeps mankind in bondage and slavery.

Therefore, since the children share in flesh and blood, He Himself likewise also partook of the same, that through death He might render powerless him who had the power of death, that is, the devil, and might free those who through fear of death were subject to slavery all their lives (Hebrews 2:14-15).

Is death inevitable?

If so, which death are we talking about?

• Is physical death inevitable?
• Is spiritual death as a result of sin inevitable?
• Is the death to self being co-crucified with Christ inevitable?

- Is the second death in fire inevitable?

But now Christ has been raised from the dead, the first fruits of those who are asleep. For since by a man came death, by a man also came the resurrection of the dead. For as in Adam all die, so also in Christ all will be made alive (1 Corinthians 15:20-22).

I believe that for mankind spiritual death and spiritual resurrection are inevitable in Christ; and that is why restoration is inevitable, as all have already been made alive and are just awaiting a realisation of that amazing truth.

I have been crucified with Christ... (Galatians 2:20).

This statement was not just Paul's declaration to the Galatians but was universal for all humanity because Jesus, the Son of Man and the second Adam, died for and as everyone. Jesus represented mankind, including each of us, on the cross, by dying our death. Jesus has already included everyone in His death and through His resurrection everyone is already made alive. When Jesus breathed on His disciples, as the Father did with Adam, they received the Spirit as representatives of the one new man in Christ. The whole of humanity was born from above and became spiritually alive and capable of realising their salvation.

For since by a man came death, by a man also came the resurrection of the dead. For as in Adam all die, so also in Christ all will be made alive (1 Corinthians 15:21-22).

For the love of Christ controls us, having concluded this, that one died for all, therefore all died; and He died for all, so that they

*who live might no longer live for themselves, but for Him who
died and rose again on their behalf*(2 Corinthians 5:14-15).

*So Jesus said to them again, "Peace be with you; as the Father has
sent Me, I also send you." And when He had said this, He
breathed on them and said to them, "Receive the Holy Spirit."*
(John 20:21-22).

So is physical death inevitable for mankind? No, but most
people don't know this truth, that Jesus has taken death out of
the equation and brought immortality back into reality. Jesus
has abolished death, and with death, what it implies: the result
or wages of sin and evil. The precedent set by Enoch and Elijah
not dying tells me that physical death does not have to be
inevitable and Jesus' teaching affirms that.

*"Your fathers ate the manna in the wilderness, and they died.
This is the bread which comes down out of heaven, so that one
may eat of it and not die."*(John 6:49-50).

*This is the bread that stepped down out of the heavenly sphere -
there is no comparison with the manna your fathers received
from heaven: they ate and they died - now feast on* (John 6:50
Mirror).

Why do people, including Christians, still die today? In reality,
because they are not believers in immortality and 'as a man
thinks within himself, so is he' (see Proverbs 23:7). Religion's
covenant with death has taken immortality off the table but this
truth is being restored in our day. Many throughout history
have discovered this reality and are still alive after many
hundreds, and in some cases, thousands, of years. Some of these

are known as desert fathers or hermits, including the Maharishi of Mt Kailash, as recorded in the book by Sadhu Sundar Singh[17].

For He must reign until He has put all His enemies under His feet. The last enemy that will be abolished is death. "Death is swallowed up in victory... O death, where is your victory? O death, where is your sting?"(1 Corinthians 15:25-26, 55).

Who has saved us and called us with a holy calling, not according to our works, but according to His own purpose and grace which was granted us in Christ Jesus from all eternity, but now has been revealed by the appearing of our Saviour Christ Jesus, who abolished death and brought life and immortality to light through the gospel (2 Timothy 1:9-10).

He rescued the integrity of our original design and revealed that we have always been his own from the beginning, even before time was. This has nothing to do with anything we did to qualify or disqualify ourselves. We are not talking religious good works or karma here. Jesus unveils grace to be the eternal intent of God! Grace celebrates our pre-creation innocence and now declares our redeemed union with God in Christ Jesus. Everything that grace pointed to is now realized in Jesus Christ and brought into clear view through the gospel: Jesus is what grace reveals. He took death out of the equation and re-defines life; this is good news indeed! (2 Timothy 1:9-10 Mirror).

As death is abolished, it is inconceivable and a total contradiction that death in its worst form, the second death, would be maintained forever as a state of eternal conscious torment in fire.

Physical death is not inevitable; but if we do die, what happens to us then? To answer that question, we must first decide who 'us' is referring to. Is there a difference between believers and not yet believers before and after death?

When anyone dies physically, their body is either buried or cremated and figuratively returns to the dust, hence 'ashes to ashes, dust to dust'. I believe that for those who have realised what Jesus has accomplished for them (and hence are 'believers'), their immortal spirit goes to be with the Lord and they become part of the heavenly cloud of witnesses.

...then the dust will return to the earth as it was, and the spirit will return to God who gave it (Ecclesiastes 12:7).

His spirit departs, he returns to the earth; In that very day his plans perish (Psalm 146:4).

As a believer, there has already been a realised reconciliation and restoration of relationship with God and between the soul, spirit and body that continues; and as there is no longer a two-part *sheol/hades*, we are present with the Lord, spirit and soul, relationally and dimensionally.

Now may the God of peace Himself sanctify you entirely; and may your spirit and soul and body be preserved complete, without blame at the coming of our Lord Jesus Christ (1 Thessalonians 5:23).

'Coming' is a mistranslation, which has arisen from a futurist eschatological perspective, of the word *parousia*, which properly means 'presence'. *En* can mean in, within or at, so the phrase 'at the coming' would be better translated 'within the presence'. Our restoration is within the presence of our Lord Jesus Christ; now, not at a future coming event.

Acts chapter 3 describes a refreshing that comes from the presence of the Lord and uses the Greek word *anápsyksis* – properly, breathe easily (again); hence, refreshing; 'cooling,' or 'reviving with fresh air', so this means 'living in the presence of the Lord, we can breathe His life-giving breath'.

There, away from any effort of your own, discover how the God of perfect peace, who fused you skilfully into oneness – just like a master craftsman would dovetail a carpentry joint – has personally perfected and sanctified the entire harmony of your being without your help! He has restored the detailed default settings. You were re-booted to fully participate in the life of your design, in your spirit, soul and body in blameless innocence in the immediate presence of our Lord Jesus Christ. (1 Thessalonians 5:23 Mirror).

We are of good courage, I say, and prefer rather to be absent from the body and to be at home with the Lord (2 Corinthians 5:8).

The body returns to its elements, and the spirit returns to God, but what about the soul?

If the soul and spirit have been reconciled in Christ as a believer, they are not separated after death; the person becomes one of the cloud of witnesses and they do have the memories of the soul.

356

What if the soul and spirit were not reconciled before death? For those who have not yet come to a realisation of their salvation in Christ, their soul and spirit seem to have different experiences and destinations. Their immortal spirit returns to God and their soul goes into the consuming fire of the second death.

Some people teach soul sleep and not soul consciousness but I don't believe that takes into account the power of the resurrection. My own experiences indicate that the soul and spirit are alive and united in the cloud of witnesses for believers and that the soul is very conscious in the consuming fire of God's loving presence.

It is possible that the not-yet believer's spirit returns to the Lord but the soul sometimes still hangs around in the physical realm. Are there ghosts? Are places haunted? If so, what causes the soul to remain or linger on earth after physical death?

I know of several ministries which teach that the souls can remain because of trauma and they help people affected by what they call Alien Human Spirits or Lingering Human Souls. Arthur Burk has a teaching series on this subject and ministers to people to evict those AHS; and in the UK there is a ministry that also deals with these LHS by preaching the gospel to them to help them cross over.

We were spiritual beings who became living beings and then became human beings (or in reality, for most people, human doings) but our destiny is to be godlike beings, sons of God. Human beings live with the soul being conscious but separated relationally from their spirit and God.

For a human being after physical death, the spirit returns to God and continues to be separated from the soul, which remains conscious. For those who do not know God relationally, the soul is separated relationally (though not physically) from Him and goes into the consuming fire of His presence. The anguish and torment it experiences is self-inflicted, not from God: it is the consequence of being in the fire without knowing God (who is love) personally. The fire continues to purify and refine, to remove the guilt, shame and condemnation and any other obstacles the soul feels.

Fate sealed?

As we saw, in 2 Samuel 14:14, 1 Samuel 2:6 and Lamentations 3:31-3, the Bible confirms that God rescues people from the grave, even before the power of the resurrection conquered death and took away its sting.

The Father's loving-kindness always offers His children a way out of death through His deep compassion and limitless grace. It would make no sense for the early church to teach that Jesus went to hades, preached there, and led captivity captive, (Ephesians 4:8,9; Psalm 68:18; 1 Peter 3:18-20) if death is a place of no escape.

Like the passages we looked at earlier in 1 and 2 Samuel and Lamentations, the book of Psalms speaks again and again about being rescued from the grave (or *sheol*):

But God will redeem my soul from the power of Sheol, For He will receive me (Psalm 49:15).

For Your lovingkindness toward me is great, and You have delivered my soul from the depths of Sheol (Psalm 86:13).

See also Psalms 16:10, 30:2-3, 116:3-8 and 139:8.

Early Christians offered up prayers for and were baptised for the dead (1 Corinthians 15:29). It seems they did not think that death settled people's fate forever.

Death cannot be the end, as it is cast into the second death, the lake of fire (Revelation 20:14) and is abolished (1 Corinthians 15:26; 2 Timothy 1:10).

Consuming fire

Now we have to deal with the question of what does go on in the place formerly known as 'hell' that I now prefer to call 'the consuming fire of God's loving presence'.

A common element or theme is fire but what is the nature of that place of fire? Who goes there, what goes on there and for how long does it go on? What is the purpose of what goes on there in the fire?

In my search for the truth, I came across a post on the Hippie Heretic blog by Chuck McKnight[18], which I summarise below, mostly in my own words.

There are 5 common views of what goes on and 5 common views of how long it goes on for, making 25 combinations. Confusingly, people who hold each of those different views all claim that the Bible confirms it.

The concepts can be described in terms of process or destruction. I use the word 'punishment' only as that is what is commonly thought it to be.

Five views of what goes on in 'hell':

1. Retribution: eternal conscious torment and punishment are applied because sinners must pay for sins.
2. Retributive but restoring: the punishment is applied because sinners must pay for sins, but it is also intended to bring about restoration.
3. Restorative: refining and purification are applied because sinners must be restored from sins.
4. Consequential: the punishment is self-inflicted as a natural consequence of sins.
5. Consequential but restorative: the punishment is self-inflicted as a natural consequence of sins, but it is also used to bring about restoration.

Five views of how long those things go for:

1. Inescapable process: the punishment is an ongoing process, which will continue for all of eternity.
2. Inescapable annihilation: the punishment is destruction, and this will not be reversed for all of eternity.
3. Escapable annihilation: the punishment is destruction, but this may be reversed if the individual repents.
4. Escapable process: the refining purification is an ongoing process which may come to an end if the individual repents.

5. Assured escape: the refining purification is an ongoing process which will come to an end once the individual repents.

Those five views of what and five views of how long can make up 25 possible combinations. Here are three:

- Eternal conscious torment, also called 'infernalism', is an ongoing process of punishment with no end.
- Annihilation, or 'terminal punishment', is inescapable destruction with no choice after death: it is just the end.
- Annihilation with escapable destruction, with choice after death, allows for a possible final end after an undetermined period.

Universal restoration has two variations, both lasting for an undetermined period:

- All will inevitably escape the fire; guaranteed, with no end of choice. God just does it at some point.
- All may escape the process after an indeterminate time; it is not guaranteed but there is no end of choice.

What is the purpose of the fire? A punishment that continues forever, or punishment that ends in annihilation, or a refining fire of justice for purification and correction? What best describes God's character and nature? Punishment or correction?

Does God enforce retributive justice, which in man's view is the requirement that sinners pay for their sins? Does God act with restorative justice to restore sinners from their sins? Does God allow people to make their own choices and reap the consequences? Or is it a combination?

What view does the Bible support in the original text and which view best reflects the character and nature of a loving God? Love is the key factor and point of reference for us to answer those questions.

Confused? You will be! (as the old TV programme *Soap* declared each week).

I do not believe that God punishes anyone, so the question "What is the purpose of the punishment?" is irrelevant. I have personally eliminated any form of retribution from my understanding of 'hell'. There are four main reasons for this.

1. Retribution is not how I believe God does justice. Though retribution was permitted for a time (Exodus 21:23–25; Leviticus 24:19–20; Deuteronomy 19:21), Jesus brought it to an end (Matthew 5:38–42). Likewise, Israel's sacrificial system was built largely around the idea of retribution via substitute, but Jesus sided with the prophets who taught that God never wanted sacrifices, only mercy (Hosea 6:6; Jeremiah 7:22; Matthew 9:13; 12:7).

2. Even if God did administer retributive punishment, there would be no need for it in 'hell', because Jesus has already paid the full price of redemption for all people. His sacrifice on the cross was for every one (1 Timothy 2:6; 4:10; 2 Peter 2:1; 1 John 2:2).

3. God's desire is for all people to be saved (1 Timothy 2:4; 2 Peter 3:9). To suggest that God's desire will be thwarted

because He is bound by retributive justice is to suggest that retribution is a power greater than God. God is bound by nothing but love, for He is love (1 John 4:8).

4. In my personal testimony of going to 'hell', the consuming fire of God's loving presence, I saw that God was punishing no one but I did see many people escape.

So if God does not send people to 'hell' for retribution, why will anyone go there? I believe that we send ourselves to 'hell'. To move toward God is to move toward life; to move away from God is to move toward death.

God's love is an unquenchable fire, intended to refine and purify us. In the resurrection and the judgment, God's love will be poured out in full measure on everyone. But those who fight against God's love, clinging to their impurities, will be unable to experience His love as intended. The 'hell' anyone faces is one of their own making.

Yet at the same time, because God does desire to save everyone, I am convinced that He will continue actively seeking the lost for as long as any hope of repentance remains. God steps into the self-inflicted 'hell' to bring about restoration.

So in answer to the first question, I would respond, "The punishment is self-inflicted as a natural consequence of sins, but it is also used to bring about restoration."

If it is restorative, how long does it last? As long as we choose it to last (by resisting the justice of God's consuming fire that is designed to remove all the dross we choose to hold onto). It will last until people finally surrender to God's loving restoration, or not.

God has reconciled the cosmos – including everyone and everything – to Himself (2 Corinthians 5:19).

God has done His part but we have to choose to accept what He has done and be reconciled to Him: it is not an automatic experience for us. With the realisation of loving grace that comes by encounters, Jesus' faith enables us to choose to accept that love.

Romans chapter 2 states that God is kind, tolerant and patient towards people, encouraging them to change their mind about Him and themselves whilst alive. If God is no longer kind, tolerant and patient towards the person after they die, then physical death has the ability to change God. That can never be possible as God is by very definition unchangeable, the same yesterday, today and tomorrow.

Or do you think lightly of the riches of His kindness and tolerance and patience, not knowing that the kindness of God leads you to repentance? (Romans 2:4).

As we have seen, the Bible never indicates that physical death is the end of the ability of a person to choose to acknowledge Jesus as Lord.

It has been the Father's plan from the very beginning that all His children would eventually experience His love and it is His desire to restore us and everything He created back into that love relationship. We all have a part to play, both by being restored ourselves and becoming the good news of restoration to creation. We are ambassadors of reconciliation so we can be revealed as the wonderful good news to longing, groaning creation, held in bondage to corruption. We are the good news and as sons, our frequency is bringing hope to all creation that it will be brought into the freedom of our glory.

My personal story

So finally I will now share my personal story, the testimony of my engagement with the consuming fire of God's love. This process was not easy for me as the mindsets, doctrines and theological frameworks of my thinking were very strongly programmed. So I know how hard it can be to let go of strongly held beliefs.

So far I have outlined what the Bible says about 'hell'. When writing these things online they have caused a certain amount of controversy (to put it mildly). But I am not trying to invent a new theology or doctrine, or even ask you to believe what I believe, and I am simply going to share my testimony with you of what led to me eventually going into the fiery place to see for myself what is going on there.

It began with the renewing of my mind. In recent years, God has given me experiences that demonstrate the strength of His love, profoundly challenging my beliefs and what I used to think the Bible was saying. This all happened as part of the removal of the manmade constructs of my mind, and it was not an easy process for me as those mindsets, doctrines and theological frameworks of my thinking were very strong.

For three weeks I felt severe pressure around my mind, almost like physical pain. God was challenging me to reconsider the issue of 'hell' but my long-held belief systems discouraged me from doing so. You see, I had even been to the fire. I had had visions of people in anguish in what I called 'hell'. So I purposely held back, even though frequent love-encounters were making it increasingly difficult to deny what I now believe. That is until Jesus actually took me back to the fire to see.

By now I was 100% theologically convinced that my previous understanding of 'hell' as a place of eternal conscious torment was incorrect and did not align with my encounters. One such encounter was with Wisdom, a beautiful created being assigned to mankind to help us in our sonship, particularly the governmental aspects of it.

Wisdom's Heights was my entrance to what is known as Satan's trophy room. There are doors there into many dimensions; and also pillars, and the gateway into Zion.

Does not wisdom call, and understanding lift up her voice? On top of the heights beside the way, where the paths meet, she takes her stand; beside the gates, at the opening to the city, at the entrance of the doors, she cries out (Proverbs 8:1-3).

Some years ago, I was a given a seal and staff by Wisdom during an encounter on the firestones. A little time later Wisdom met and took me to her heights, leading me through a fiery door. It was a tunnel of fire that led to a large door guarded by a being which barred my way. Going into Gandalf mode, I thrust my staff onto the ground and demanded that the door be opened.

The being vanished, the door opened and we walked into a place of extreme restriction and sadness: Satan's trophy room. There I saw three things:

- The sparkling diamond trophies of the destinies of those living and dead who had not believed the good news
- Stolen mantles and crowns
- An area of the heritage of my generational family lines.

As I looked at this area of heritage I felt angry that my generational lines had not passed much of a Christian heritage on to me. A thought crossed my mind: I wondered if all of that lost heritage would be restored to me now. Wisdom indicated that it could and I was rather excited to think that my entire lost heritage was going to be rolled up into a package and delivered to me. Little did I know what this restoration of heritage really meant but I would have been shocked and would have probably rejected that reality if Wisdom had revealed the truth to me at that point.

However, some years later, in 2016, I asked Jesus to show me the truth of 'hell' and fire as although I was theologically convinced that the 'hell' I had grown up with was false I still had no personal testimony to affirm my belief.

One day that seemed like any other day, everything changed. Jesus met me in heaven, took me to Wisdom's Heights and led me through the fiery door and back into that sad place, where He showed me my lost heritage again. I thought "Wow! Jesus is going to give me my lost heritage back!" and even then, as I looked at the family line of my father's father, I had no idea what was about to take place.

Jesus said to me, "Do you want to see this restored?"

I asked, "How?" I was still somewhat selfishly thinking of it all being personally restored to me.

Jesus said, "By going into the fire."

Then He showed me a door I had not seen when I went there before. He explained that the door had been there all along, but my framework of beliefs had not allowed me to see it. Then He gave me a silver heralding trumpet and we went through the door into the fire. There were thousands of people there from that part of my family line, not talking to one another; isolated individuals who appeared to be in the anguish of soul. They were not being tormented by anyone other than themselves; there was no devil there with a pitchfork or anything like that. They were there, on their own, in a place of consuming fire.

So I looked to Jesus, hoping He was going to do something. He just stood there looking right back at me. So eventually I preached the good news to them, though not very well! I felt rather tongue-tied and overwhelmed. Overwhelmed with love, actually, and of course completely unprepared. But at least I told them that they could accept Jesus and come out of that fearful place.

I figured Jesus must have given me the trumpet for a reason, so I blew it. He turned to walk out, and there was no way I was going to stay in there on my own, so I followed Him back through the tunnel of fire. I went through the door back to Wisdom's heights and this time I saw that the door appeared to be like a fiery sword (I knew that a fiery sword guards the way to the tree of life).

I looked back and a few hundred people had followed us to the door. As they approached I saw them kneel, I heard them confess Jesus as Lord and they walked out and through the gates into Zion.

I turned to Jesus. "What have you done to me? I'm in trouble now! How do I explain this?"

Jesus said "Just tell people that you are doing what I did – and I told you to do what I did, and greater things. This is just the beginning".

I asked Jesus why so few of them had followed us out of the fire. If it was me and someone offered me a way out, I would have been out of there as fast as I could. This is what He told me:

"You can only preach with authority to the degree that the fire has consumed generational things in you. That is why not everyone responded. Keep presenting yourself to the fire of the altar and you will be able to reach more of your generational lines. Embrace the coals to touch areas of your life that have come from your generations; that will give you authority."

So I present myself as a living sacrifice on the altar in the temple every day. Since that first time, I have been back to engage each of my 4 generational family lines, preached the good news to them and seen many thousands respond by confessing Jesus as Lord.

When I was in China in 2017, someone gave me a silver heralding trumpet just like the one Jesus had given me. One morning while I was there I woke up at 3am and felt a strong desire to engage the altar and ask for the fiery coals to touch a specific area of behaviour, the area of divorce.

As I did, I began to feel intensely loving towards everyone in my generations who had been divorced or in sexual sin, not angry or resentful, and I began forgiving them and blessing them. Once I finished, I went to the fiery place again. I preached to all my generational lines with boldness, blew the silver trumpet again and this time many more thousands responded. They followed me out, came to the door, confessed Jesus as Lord and went through and on into Zion.

Later, on a Sunday morning at home in Freedom Church, as I was embracing the fire, another area surfaced. I again went back and preached with renewed boldness and once again many more responded. Another time, I wondered what it might be like if I took communion down into the fire. So I went back there and offered communion, the body and blood of Jesus, to those who were in the fire. Yet again, many responded!

More recently I became aware that there were many in that place with fractured souls, what we sometimes call 'stuck parts', mostly caused by trauma in their lives. They were double-minded, triple-minded or worse and were unable to decide to follow Jesus. So I asked Jesus to come with me and I told them they could come to the Prince of Peace (*shalom* means 'wholeness') and be made whole. Vast numbers of them did so.

My strong desire is to empty that place, but for that to happen I need to continue to embrace the fire myself. I need to be good news and demonstrate that good news in my own life.

I have now had many experiences of going into the place of fire both for personal refining and on rescue missions. The fire of God is for purifying and refining and removing all the dross in people's lives. They are waiting for someone to come and share the good news with them.

One day, before I even mentioned this publicly, a friend I meet with online said he had something to share with me. He had been engaging in heaven when some of his family members came up to him. He was surprised and said, "I didn't know you were believers in Jesus!" And they said, "We weren't. But we remembered that you said your whole household would be saved, and Jesus came and preached the good news to us, and that's why we are here." This did not fit my friend's theological box, as he put it. He was encouraged when I then shared my experiences too.

Since then (and especially after this topic cropped up in several of my regular online mentoring groups) I have had conversations with others and I have heard many testimonies of people who have gone into the fire and preached the good news as Jesus did. After I shared this in the Vision Destiny 2017 series I had several emails from people thanking me for opening up the discussion as they had been afraid of sharing their experiences because of the reaction they knew it would cause (a reaction I have experienced for myself).

God is fire and that fire is love. I have some key testimonies of just how powerful that love – expressed in limitless grace and mercy – truly is.

There is no fear in love; but perfect love casts out fear, because fear involves punishment, and the one who fears is not perfected in love (1 John 4:18).

For God is love (1 John 4:8).

Fear of every sort robs us of our righteousness, peace and joy in the Holy Spirit; so it is so important to engage God as perfect love and let Him remove all fear from us. Perfect love is unconditional love: as soon as you put any conditions of belief and behaviour upon it, it ceases to be love and ceases to be God.

Religion has put so many conditions on God accepting us but God who is unconditional love has never been and never will be separated from us. Reconciliation was about us to God, never God to us, as He was never separated and never will be. As Richard Rohr says, Jesus did not come to change God's mind about us but to change our mind towards God.

I had many conversations with the Father about love, light and fire during this period of the deconstruction and renewal and transformation of my mind.

"Son, unconditional love has no choice: it cannot ever be anything other than what it is, as it 100% pure with no mixture, no contamination: unadulterated, untainted, uncorrupted, unpolluted, with no inconsistency and no shadow of turning.

"Unconditional love is totally consistent. It has always been the same and always will be the same: faithful and true.

"Unconditional love is overwhelming and can never be escaped or separated from.

"Unconditional love is light: pure, bright, shining; and hot with passion and burning desire for the blessing of its object.

"Unconditional love is a consuming fire that will refine and purify everything in its way, destroying nothing but transforming everything.

"Unconditional love is the essence of the restoration of all things as restoration is its inevitable consequence.

"Unconditional love expresses itself as limitless grace and mercy, overflowing with joy and peace, and always leads to rest.

"Unconditional love is deeply compassionate and is moved to heal, reconcile, resurrect, redeem, restored and renew all that it touches.

"Unconditional love is kind, patient, torrent, gentle, enduring, tolerant and always good, overflowing in lovingkindness.

"Unconditional love is living essence of light that is the frequency vibrating as grace within the fabric of all creation.

"Unconditional love is the building block energy of all matter and the relational glue that holds all things in existence.

"Unconditional love is Our and your glory, the weight and essence of being.

"I AM that I AM is unconditional love, light, fire and the spirit of life and existence.

"Son, the sons of God, revealed as the light of the world, are to be the ambassadors and emissaries of unconditional love to all creation.

"Unconditional love is the only thing that can set creation free from its bondage to corruption. So arise and shine with love's light."

I have engaged my family lines many times in the fire and seen many hundreds of thousands respond, confessing Jesus as their Lord. I have also been given mandated rescue missions to specific people groups, including new age and occult groups. During an encounter, I was able to preach Jesus as the way, truth and life, also using the seven 'I am' statements found in John's gospel to remove the deception they were under concerning the nature of Jesus as the only way to the Father. Many more responded. I have found that there are different strategies for different groups of people that are given when you feel how the Father feels about His children.

I have now had many experiences of going into the place of love and seeing people from those other groups rescued from their anguish by choosing to acknowledge Jesus as Lord.

Limitless grace

The Father has been talking to me about not just hyper-grace but limitless, manifold grace and that theme has inspired me to pursue rescuing as many as I can. I have seen God's unlimited grace extended towards even the very worst of mankind according to man's reckoning but from the Father's perspective, they are all His children.

"Son, the restoration of all things message needs demonstrations of limitless grace that will testify to the reality of the oracles of Our loving heart. The testimonies can come from both sides of the veil and beyond, so gather those testimonies from all dimensions." He asked me to look up John Newton, an ex-slaver and the composer of Amazing Grace to ask him to find those of the cloud of witnesses with testimonies of limitless grace.

One day the Father said, "John Newton has been at work and has many storytellers for you to meet. Limitless grace will be scandalous and outrageous to the religious mindsets but will be joyful to those of Our sons who are resonating with the Oracles of Our heart."

After a few days, I went to meet him in the Court of the Upright and he brought thousands with amazing testimonies of limitless grace to testify. The worst of the worst of the worst: mass murderers, rapists, paedophiles, abusers, traffickers; all sharing how they had been forgiven and welcomed by the Father into a restored relationship. I listened intently as they shared their stories of reconciliation and acceptance.

Then all the people who been victims of those terrible crimes shared how they had been restored and made whole by God's love. Some of them were standing right next to their abusers in total oneness and unity. This was God's amazing, limitless grace in action and I was totally captivated, really moved, overwhelmed; and I began weeping uncontrollably. I felt so privileged to listen to the stories of how the unconditional love of the Father had rescued them. Some of those stories were from people who had the experience before physical death and some after.

Some had responded before death when they had a realisation of God's love, for example, some at the Nuremberg trials. Many testimonies were of when Jesus engaged them as Light at the point of their death and invited them to come to Him. It was the testimony of many that, despite their debauched lifestyles, they were visited by the light of love, Jesus, on their death bed; and they willingly and gratefully accepted the grace and mercy that He offered them in love.

As they relived their stories, I felt what they felt when they experienced His oracles: the deep emotions of passion, burning desire, intense joy, deep compassion and overwhelming love. They testified that they were swept into the Kingdom on a wave of those wonderful emotions their loving Father had towards them.

There were other stories of those who were in the depths of despair as they faced the reality of their treatment of others when grace and mercy were demonstrated to them by the victim or a victim's loved ones. Forgiveness was what had unveiled the limitlessness of God's mercy and grace to them.

The stories continued one after the other, expressing the depth of their gratitude as they shared their hearts with me. This was so intense and I was overwhelmed by the emotions expressed as pure gratitude. They all had one thing in common: how love expressed through one or other of the Father's oracles had brought them the realisation of their inclusion, reconciliation and restoration.

There were also stories from people who described being in a state of grief over the loss of a loved one, child, parent, spouse or sibling, killed in some horrendously traumatic way: the deep compassion and overwhelming love of God as Father had touched them when they were at their lowest ebb.

Many came forward, victims of abuse of all kinds: rape, satanic ritual abuse, racism, slavery etc. They had experienced limitless grace that transformed them from deep darkness and despair into a place where the light of love shone brightly. Then there were those who had committed suicide, sharing that they had received the limitless grace and mercy directly from Jesus at the moment of their death; all revealing stories of being embraced with overwhelming loving acceptance.

The Father said, during an encounter, "Many have not yet responded to Our love because of the deep shame that they are trapped in. Son, you are tasked to seek them out within the fire and reveal just how limitless Our grace and mercy is. Your mission is to engage the serial killers, child murderers, paedophiles, tyrants, despots those who are responsible for genocide, ethnic cleansings, the satanic ritual abusers, the worst of the worst.

"Son, only limitless grace, through deep compassion and overwhelming love, will remove the deep shame they feel. Son, do you feel it for them? If you do not feel it, you cannot demonstrate it. Son, come deeper into Our heart to feel it and know it for yourself."

At that moment I saw all the worst things I had ever imagined, thought or done come to my mind and then, without any time to react, I felt overwhelming waves of acceptance hit me, washing away every thought and memory. I felt this amazingly lavish and limitless grace and the pleasure of a loving, doting Father roll over me: it was almost too much to bear.

That was just the beginning. Every emotion linked to love bombarded me into total surrender as any vestige of doubt was washed away in torrents of the abundance of the pentatonic love frequencies of the Oracles of the Father's heart.

The Father said, "Son, now you know limitless grace for yourself, you can give what you have freely received, as all sin is but a result of lost identity: to Us one is all and all is one. The comparative scale of sin is a DIY tree invention fuelled by guilt to lessen the shame. When there is someone worse than you, you can excuse, justify and delude yourselves.

"We just see Our children adrift in their lostness, as to Us, one act is all acts. Son, when the stories are told, mercy triumphs over men's views of justice but what you will feel from those in shame is the self-inflicted reaping of all that they have sown. They are still suffering the self-inflicted consequences in the fire.

I had felt the self-inflicted torment myself, even if for a moment, but I could identify with those who are facing their shameful acts yet are still unable to receive mercy, even though it is available.

"Son, you have this mandate and you have experienced this reality from both sides as only one who has experienced their pain and received limitless grace will be able to reach them. Freely you have received, now freely give by releasing limitless grace and mercy through deep compassion and overwhelming love.

I felt inspired, compelled to go into the consuming fire of God's love so I could preach limitless grace to the worst of the worst of the worst by man's reckoning; so I went back to the court of the upright to engage John Newton again. I met those who were beaming, shining with joyful exuberance, all waiting to tell their grace story. I asked if they would come with me into the fire and they were only too pleased to accept my invitation.

So we went into the fiery place from Wisdom's heights to engage with those who were trapped in deep shame. I turned my desire and my testimony of deep compassion and overwhelming love to create a frequency of hope to draw those out of their self-imposed darkness into the light of our glory. Our glory is our testimony of God's limitless grace and mercy and unconditional love.

I released a frequency and there, in the fire, were the representatives of all the worst categories of human degradation and all I felt was the oracles of the Father's heart for them. I saw Hitler, Stalin and other tyrants from history come forth, heads bowed, covered in darkness. Then I saw Ted Bundy, Manson, Christie, Brodie and many other serial killers come into the light. One by one they came, the worst of the worst, and I felt their anguish, pain and torment. I don't know if it was actually those people as individuals or if what I saw were representatives of categories.

There were also those who had committed suicide and were held captive by the religious shame created by those who told them that they could never enter heaven. I felt such passion, burning desire, intense joy, deep compassion and overwhelming love that the Father has for all His children.

I preached the love that inspires such limitless grace but I was overwhelmed by their guilt, shame, condemnation and fragmentation. Based on my experience, I released all the love and acceptance I had received and I covered them in the frequency of my sonship. I began to give an impassioned call to their alters to come into the light and my passion drew the Prince of Peace.

I called on the witnesses to release their testimonies of limitless grace and to release the forgiveness they had received. As they released limitless grace and forgiveness, hundreds of thousands responded, their countenance changed and their heads lifted. I offered them peace as I shared the true gospel of forgiveness. I forgave them, as did all the witnesses on behalf of all their victims, and I released another wave of the loving oracles.

More heads began to be raised and I continued to bombard them with love's light until they accepted that there was a choice they never imagined they could make, the choice to come to Jesus and receive His amazing grace and mercy. Jesus was there with us as the Prince of Peace and I watched as, one by one, the alters came into love's embrace to receive the rest of love, joy and peace.

When all had come, Jesus turned and led them out of that place of fiery torment and through the fiery sword, where each knelt in surrender to confess Jesus as Lord. Captivity was now led captive into the limitless grace and mercy which had triumphed over their self-inflicted form of justice. As they followed us out through the fiery sword, they ran into the arms of the Father who was running to meet them and they were embraced by limitless grace. Each was given a ring of sonship and robes of righteousness as all the hosts of heaven rejoiced and celebrated.

Restoration is limitless grace in action. What a celebration there was in the realms of heaven, as those who were lost, hidden within their shame and self-imposed darkness, began to shine as light!

Then I began to think of the victims of those now free, basking in limitless grace and mercy. What about those victims, still in bondage to the torture of unforgiveness, bitterness, resentment and trauma? I asked the new witnesses to help. We went back into the fiery place and I set the desire of my heart towards them.

They came forth, some hostile, angry, entitled, blaming God; and I could feel the sense of injustice that covered them in darkness like a cloud.

I released the frequency of the Oracles and one by one I reminded them of their lostness and their sin and called for restorative justice, where the victims would meet their perpetrators.

I asked any who were without sin to throw their accusations like stones but there was silence. Then one by one the perpetrators asked for forgiveness and I saw the most amazing acts of reconciliation take place. I did not need to say anything as I turned to lead more captives free from their self-inflicted torture and torment. Once again walking together, the victims and victimizers knelt to confess love for God and each other as they rose to walk through the fiery sword into Zion.

I felt the pleasure of the Father's heart as He said, "Son, now you see why there is a celebration when the lost are found and Our children return to us." I went through the gateway into Zion and saw the Loving Father running to embrace each one of His children, imparting sonship with robes of righteousness and rings of sonship.

I was curious to know what happens to those who come out of the fire and enter Zion (whose gates are never shut). Do they suddenly know God, or do they have to do so through relationship?

I had an encounter that revealed the answer. Jesus said, "Come and walk with Me." He held my hand and took Me through some gates into a large hall near the court of the upright. He said, "Here are those that have come out of the fire." There were many at benches, with men in white linen around them as if teaching or imparting. There were also angels present as if overseeing the training and warrior angels were standing to attention.

Jesus said, "This is where those who are being rescued from the fire go to be instructed in the truth and the ways of relationship. The fire has done its work and now relationship must do its work in preparing them for destiny. They have a different role than the others as they have been through a different process but they will be released for the coming harvest with the Hunter-Gatherer angels you see here. They will be sent to carry a message of love through consuming fire that will turn a generation to true repentance. They will become ambassadors of fire with a passion to remove the veils of deception just as those who came out of the graves who were witnesses of what I did under the earth at my resurrection. These are witnesses to the power of love to overcome even the choices of death and with warnings of the consequences of where they have been. They are being prepared to be at the disposal of the Joshua generation to engage the harvest that is coming. There is an urgency for My brothers to do what I did and preach the good news of My love to your generations and see your heritage restored."

My encounters continue, but I have hopefully given you the gist of what I believe is the Farter's desire for the restoration of all

His children. Many vehemently object to this teaching, saying that I am creating a new doctrine that is not based on orthodox theology.

This view of the fire as purification and a place from which people could be rescued is not some strange new doctrine. It is not a new or modern concept but a return to what many of the early church fathers believed, and others across the church spectrum through the last 2000 years, including Clement of Alexandria, St. Macrina, St Gregory Nyssen, St Isaac of Nineveh (and many other Fathers), and moderns including Fr. Sergei Bulgakov, St. Silouan the Athonite, Fr. Alexandre Turincev, Metropolitans Kallistos Ware and Hilarion Alfeyev. I am not asking you to believe me but I do hope that you will be willing to seek God for yourself.

Chapter 8. Universalism, Christian or Otherwise

I will pose many questions for your consideration and there will not always be satisfactory answers (that is the essence of mystery) but I would encourage you to get answers to those questions for yourself through your face to face encounters with the Father.

In concluding this book, I will end by summarizing what Christian Universalism (CU) is or is not because the term Universalist is often considered a derogatory term in evangelical circles. When I use the term 'universal' I am using it in its broadest sense regarding the restoration of all things. There are so many words linked to 'universal', of which 'inclusion', 'reconciliation', 'redemption', 'salvation' and 'restoration' are but a few; so what does the term 'Christian Universalism' mean?

Apokatastasis is the Greek term used by the early church for the restoration of all things and Christian Universalism (CU) is the belief in the restoration of all things. When discussing the term it cannot be through academic theological study alone, without personal experience of the truth of who God really is.

Jesus is at the centre

The essence, nature and characteristic of God who is Father, Son and Spirit as love is the backdrop to all our discussion about creation's beginning and end, as creation's beginning and consummation are connected to Jesus being the Alpha and Omega.

... all things have been created through Him (Jesus) and for Him... and through Him to reconcile all things to Himself (Colossians 1:16, 20).

... the summing up of all things in Christ, things in the heavens and things on the earth. In Him (Ephesians 1:10).

When all things are subjected to Him, then the Son Himself also will be subjected to the One who subjected all things to Him, so that God may be all in all (1 Corinthians 15:28).

... but Christ is all, and in all (Colossians 3:11).

Through all my heavenly encounters of going beyond beyond, what I believe I have discovered is that creation, from beginning to consummation, is Jesus- or Christ-centred. So that means the restoration of creation must also be Christ centred. Jesus is at the centre of God's purposes, we are in Him as God's sons, and therefore we are at the centre of God's purposes.

Blessed be the God and Father of our Lord Jesus Christ, who has blessed us with every spiritual blessing in the heavenly places in Christ (Ephesians 1:3).

For we are His workmanship, created in Christ Jesus for good works, which God prepared beforehand so that we would walk in them (Ephesians 2:10).

What is Christian Universalism? Even though I do not want to be labelled as such, it is useful to know what it is and what it is not. There is a stigma attached to the word universalism that causes great offence to evangelical streams of thought so I wish to try to define it. This is a definition of Christian universalism by Robin Parry[19], whom I thank for influencing some of the content of this chapter:

"Christian universalism is the belief that in the end, all people will participate in the salvation achieved for them by Jesus."

My experiences would agree with that definition but the objections often are not based on what Jesus did on the cross, universally.

Following this logic Christian Universalism (CU) does not state, imply or mean that:

1. You can have a personal relationship with God through any other means than Jesus.

You cannot engage the Father through any other religious methodology or any works of our own creation. The reality is that only Jesus leads us to the Father; but what Jesus? Yeshua, the Light, the Peace, the Rock. There are many testimonies of those who have met Jesus but did not know His name, nonetheless He led them to God, who is also known by many names, Father, Creator, the Source. One thing defines who God is and that is a personal being and not an impersonal force, energy or universe.

2. That proponents of CU take sin lightly.

The reality is that sin (lost identity) leads to all sorts of damaging behaviours and that is obviously very important.

3. That what we do in this life is irrelevant.

The reality is that there are clear consequences of how we live and we reap what we sow.

4. That there are no consequences after death for rejecting Jesus in this life.

The reality is that the concept of punishment is self-inflicted, it does not come from God. What does occur after death, usually represented by some image of fire, is corrective and restorative and not retributive.

5. That the truths of God's justice and God's love are not respected.

The reality is that there is no contradiction in love, holiness and justice.

6. That people who believe in CU do not believe in the Bible.

The reality is that I use the Bible a great deal as my point of reference but there are many confirmationally-biased views of what it says that may indeed be wrongly interpreted.

7. That there is no point in sharing the gospel if everyone is going to be 'saved' anyway.

The reality is that people come to a realisation of their salvation through the good news, the gospel, on either side of death and we are all called to be involved in that.

Like me, people tend to come to a Christian Universalist or restoration of all things position through a combination of many different avenues including the Bible, tradition, experience and their reflections on how this relates to who God is. My encounters led me to see that CU best reflects the nature and characteristic of God as Father and is totally consistent with Bible truth when the Bible is interpreted through the lens of love.

The deconstruction of my theological beliefs through realising that I had wrongly interpreted the Bible for many years played a key role in my journey towards a CU or a universal restoration perspective. The Father often gives us progressive revelations that take us back to the purity of what they believed in the early church.

Traditional Christian views found in the Bible can be seen to align with CU when they are not biasedly interpreted through modern theology. The Bible clearly reveals, to me at least, that we are all made in God's image, that God loves everyone and that Jesus died for everyone. The Bible keeps inevitably leading people back to this CU truth that many orthodox early church fathers held.

There are some excellent books on the market and more are being written daily as God unveils these truths. I particularly recommend these two:

A Larger Hope? Volume 1: Universal Salvation from Christian Beginnings to Julian of Norwich – Ilaria Ramelli[6]

A Larger Hope? Volume 2: Universal Salvation from The Reformation to the 19th Century – Robin Parry[20]

There are also many great YouTube videos about CU: my favourite, which I have mentioned before, has to be *The Gospel in Chairs* by Brad Jersak[3]. I just wish that I had been able to watch such an amazing resource when I was beginning my journey.

For me, the best evidence for the truth of CU is my own experiences and testimony of encountering God as love through face to face engagements. I have shared testimony after testimony of my heavenly experiences which have revealed the heart of God and I have seen the restoration that is going on in the fire. Many others also testify to this restorative process, both today and throughout history. There are many good testimonies of people's journeys and many were mystics like Jane Ward Lead.

CU is a simple concept that is consistent with many different biblical views and is inclusive of many different perspectives, some of which I have held myself in the past. CU cannot be defined as belonging to one particular stream of thought. Among Christian Universalists there are Catholics, Reformed and Charismatics; Arminians and Calvinists; even some whom still embrace penal substitutionary atonement views. CU is not confined to any one denominational or theological position.

A study of the early church fathers opens up the debate to the actual origin of the CU position of *apokatastasis*: where did the restoration of all things understanding come from? I believe that there are clear Christian, biblical and traditional roots: e.g. there are even accounts of the early church praying for people to be freed from the Lake of Fire.

There are some very valid questions that are raised when thinking about this subject concerning the nature of divine justice, as retributive or restorative. And the concepts of free and God's sovereignty pose the question, if there is free will, how could God ensure all will be restored?

I struggled with these and similar questions on my journey towards the belief in the restoration of all things. In my youth the issue of predestination was one that I pondered over at length, having many discussions during Bible studies.

On my personal journey I have at different times held many different points of view and positions, leading to many questions (and sometimes doubts and fears); but that, in my opinion, is good and healthy. Whichever direction you have travelled from and whichever way you get there, I believe the road eventually leads to the restoration of all things.

Paradoxes

Is it possible to biblically reconcile the apparent paradoxes between Calvinism and Arminianism? What questions do we need to ask of ourselves that will frame the discussion? I have pondered over these types of issues myself over the years; maybe they will be helpful for your reflections.

Did Jesus die for everyone or just some? And therefore the follow up question: did God only choose or elect those who He foreknew would respond? This train of thought then inevitably leads to another question: who has the ultimate power to decide a person's fate (and therefore who is actually sovereign), God or man?

Another big question that many Christians debate is whether someone can lose their salvation.

The Arminian argument goes that if people choose salvation themselves then they could choose to reject it in the future and God would respect their choice.

The Calvinist argument goes that if God elects some people to salvation then that salvation is guaranteed and totally secure.

These questions have divided opinion for generations and of course you can find some support from the Bible for both Calvinism and Arminianism. Can they both be true? Everyone can find agreement or problems in the interpretation of the Bible texts as there seem to be so many contradictions or paradoxes; that is why we need direct revelation.

I reconciled the positions myself by coming down on the side of Calvinism but I could never reconcile limited atonement, where Jesus only died for some, not all. That was a splinter in my mind that I could never remove until the restoration of all things made sense of it.

God chose and saved everyone as Jesus died for everyone and reconciled everyone but sadly many have not yet come to the realisation of that fact.

There is one further question that arises from this discussion, relating to how these historic positions view the issue of eternal separation and punishment.

The Calvinist view is that God chose to separate some people eternally because He knew that they would reject Jesus.

The Arminian view is that God does not separate and consign people to eternal punishment, they have chosen this position themselves.

Some are appointed to 'hell', or some choose to go to 'hell'; but neither of these theological positions answers the question, do they have to remain there permanently?

The problem is that if you take the *sola scriptura* position, that the Bible is the only permissible evidence, then you are left with only one option: eternal judgment, condemnation, punishment for some (or many, or even most) is appointed by God or chosen for themselves (depending on the particular theological variation you believe) and salvation is only for those who are chosen or those who choose.

There are genuine biblical reasons for those variations in beliefs and therefore we can honour people in our differences. That, I believe, is a sign of maturity that is much needed in the church today.

Dilemma

When faced with this dilemma what do we do?

I tried various options on my journey. I have tried to ignore the consistencies and put it down to a mystery that is unfathomable. I have also tried to rationalise the situation by choosing bits of both opposing positions to make something that was acceptable to me. I have also tried to make out that there are other more important issues to consider. The truth is I could never remove that splinter from my mind and it still sometimes niggled away at me.

When I discovered the truth for myself by directly engaging God about it I was able to honour all those who have different views because in reality we are all one family and are all part of one body.

I found that as my eschatology changed in the 1980's, so too did my view of God; and that then led me to look at what would happen not just at the end of the world but beyond that. This opened up the possibility of a different end result (even if I was not prepared to go there at that point of my journey). We will believe what fits into our preconceived or programmed perspectives, so I believed in 'hell' and eternal punishment for years, even though deep down I did not like it. It was only personal experience and engaging God face to face that brought me clarity.

I believe that God is omnipotent, sovereign and also love and He desires that in the end everyone will eventually choose life.

The Bible is always revealing the two realities from two very different perspectives and we find that hard to reconcile using DIY human logic.

So when I read Bible passages that were challenging my beliefs I tried to interpret those passages in a way that fitted what I already believed. That is how confirmation bias works: we use our understanding of the Bible to prove our point and ignore or twist those things that do not.

Using that methodology, the universalist texts are then reinterpreted to harmonise them with ECT in 'hell'. I know, because I did this myself for 40 years. I acknowledged that there were texts stating that God wants all to be saved but I knew it could not happen because of free will. I relegated God's will and desire to wishful thinking on His part.

In his contribution to *Four Views on Hell*, Denny Burk[21] argues that there are 10 passages which prove 'hell' as eternal conscious torment beyond any doubt:

Isaiah 66:22-24, Daniel 12:2-3, Matthew 18:6-9, 25:31-46, Mark 9:42-48, 2 Thessalonians 1:6-10, Jude 7, Jude 13, Revelation 14:9-11, Revelation 20:10, Revelation 20:14-15.

Yet when I read these passages, I do not believe they prove ECT at all. And what about the rest of the Bible? We cannot just ignore other contradictory passages. I know we are all guilty of it, and I could be accused of doing this all through this book; that is why I am seeking not necessarily to reconcile the passages but to acknowledge they do exist and therefore understand and honour those who hold different views.

Progressive revelation

I believe it is imperative not to start with what we believe is true but with the nature of God Himself as the Truth and seek to underpin our beliefs with the character of God as our foundation. My journey has been one of progressive revelation in which God has, in His mercy, only unveiled truth that my levels of personal intimacy with Him could cope with.

There are questions that we need to honestly ask ourselves in light of this and also in light of our personal progression history:

- Do I believe things differently today than in the past?
- Am I open to fresh and progressive revelation?
- Or is everything is a done deal, because I know all I need to know?

Our individual journeys are part of a much larger picture and our stories add to the overall narrative of creation. When we see the individual stories in the light of the overall truth, and not just 'truth' derived from only one author in scripture, we will perhaps realise that we need revelation in light of what is written and said for our day, so that we can serve the purpose of God in our generation through who we are and what we say.

My good friend Lindy Strong often says we need the books of Lindy, Mike, Nancy, and Justin; they are the records and stories to contribute to the narrative for our generation.

The creation story

My personal journey in some small way follows the path of the restoration of all things within the story of creation. In the beginning of mankind's part in the story, God stated creation to be good; and although it is currently in bondage to corruption, there is hope. That hope is the restoration and revealing of the light of our sonship. So our personal journey to sonship is integral to the end of the story, where all things will once again be declared good as they are restored to God's original intention and purpose.

So what is the metanarrative of the story of salvation that gives a context for 'hell' and CU concerning the beginning of creation and the end of creation? What is the best end to the story, one which is in keeping with the overall narrative that we have from all history and eternity? When we look at 'hell' as ECT or CU, which is more harmonious and which is most discordant with God as love?

God's desire from the beginning of the creation story was for relationship with His creation. To that end He is constantly at work to bring good out of the many crises and disasters that we have orchestrated by following our own independent DIY path. Creation was never meant to be independent of its Creator and that is the most helpful narrative to view things from.

For from Him and through Him and to Him are all things. To Him be the glory forever. Amen (Romans 11:36).

For by Him all things were created, both in the heavens and on earth, visible and invisible, whether thrones or dominions or rulers or authorities—all things have been created through Him and for Him (Colossians 1:16).

God and creation, and therefore all people and all created beings, were always intended to be in relationship: that is the beginning and therefore that will be the end.

Genesis 1:26-28 reveals our identity: made in God's image and likeness, we are sons and heirs of creation. Our identity, destiny and responsibility are linked to creation itself and we see in Romans 8:19-21 that creation's freedom is linked and entwined with ours.

God blessed them; and God said to them, "Be fruitful and multiply, and fill the earth, and subdue it; and rule..." (Genesis 1:28).

For the anxious longing of the creation waits eagerly for the revealing of the sons of God... that the creation itself also will be set free from its slavery to corruption into the freedom of the glory of the children of God (Romans 8:19, 21).

Our destiny is oneness, union with God; that has always been the goal of creating us as sons. Jesus pronounced us as gods (not God, of course, but sons) and there is nothing in the narrative that points us to the idea that man was created for judgment and 'hell' or ultimate destruction. Human destiny is seen in Jesus as the perfect model of sonship, as Jesus is the last Adam.

The first Adam was not the finished article: there was always an intended relational process of ascension to go through. The first Adam was a living soul but sin side-tracked him from being glorified in sonship. Jesus as the second or last Adam is a life-giving spirit to restore us back through the resurrection to ascension glory.

Sin and the Fall

To understand the nature of restoration it is important to have the correct perspective on the nature of sin and the fall of man. Man turned from the path of the Tree of Life, the source of life, and towards death, away from God, following the path of independence.

For the wages of sin is death, but the free gift of God is age enduring life in Christ Jesus our Lord (Romans 6:23).

Sin, therefore, affects all people. Romans 3:23 tells us that all have sinned – actually lost their identity as sons of God, and believe they are orphans and slaves.

What is sin? The Greek word is *hamartia*: the root of this word is *ha*: a negation or loss, and *meros*: form, hence lost form or image. Sin is actually our lost image and identity as God's children. We have lost our way, and our memory, so we do not know who we are nor what our purpose is. The behaviours associated with sin are just symptoms of mankind's lost identity and man's futile attempts to get back what was lost, through dead works of all kinds.

Sin is a noun and not a verb, therefore a specific thing. Sin is actually the specific definitive sin of Adam that has affected us all. Surely sin is not bigger and more powerful than our Father, who created us in His image for relationship with Him? Sin and eternal 'hell' are linked, as the doctrine of 'hell' is built on the premise that human sin is more powerful than God's solution: Jesus and the cross.

Sin wins?

No, love wins, because love has always won!

Which is more powerful: sin or God's desire and purpose?

Is the story of the Bible one of overall ultimate victory (Jesus wins) or defeat (sins wins)?

What is God's solution to the sin problem? Is that solution good enough to deal with the consequences, wages or results of sin?

Is what Jesus did through the cross (death, burial, resurrection and ascension) more powerful than sin and is it victorious over sin?

Yes and amen in Christ.

... namely, that God was in Christ reconciling the world to Himself, not counting their trespasses against them, and He has committed to us the word of reconciliation (2 Corinthians 5:19).

He made you alive together with Him, having forgiven us all our transgressions, having cancelled out the certificate of debt consisting of decrees against us, which was hostile to us; and He has taken it out of the way, having nailed it to the cross (Colossians 2:13-14).

This victory was guaranteed even before the foundation of the world.

... just as He chose us in Him before the foundation of the world, that we would be holy and blameless before Him. In love He predestined us to adoption as sons through Jesus Christ to Himself, according to the kind intention of His will (Ephesians 1:4-5).

Jesus has won, is winning and will win! Can I hear a hallelujah?

Revealed in Jesus

I love the Christmas story, the coming of Jesus into the world, the joy announced to the world that the light has come. This is the incarnation, and now we have Immanuel, God is with us: this is the key to understanding who God is because Jesus came to lead us to the Father.

Jesus represents and reveals the invisible God to us, so what kind of God do we see in Jesus?

What are the purposes of God that are revealed in Jesus?

In everything Jesus did, He demonstrated God as love, in healing, forgiving, raising people from the dead and delivering people from their bondage. Jesus came as the Son of Man: He represents all humanity before God. He is our representative and He takes humanity through death (the problem created by sin) and then resurrects mankind to new creation life.

The question is, did Jesus represent all humans (universal) or only some people?

Did Jesus bear all the sins of the whole world, or just some of them?

At the crucifixion, what Jesus did through His death, was it for all people or some people?

Did Jesus die for all or only for some people?

The Calvinist view of limited atonement is that He died only for some elected people: so was Christ's death for nothing?

The Arminian view is that even though He died for all, because of our free will to choose, we can thwart God's purposes. Can that really be true?

In the resurrection, is the salvation of all from death achieved for all, or just made possible for some?

The end goal of abundant life is revealed in the resurrection and is the promise of what is now for all who are now alive in Christ, born from above. I have explained what 'all' means concerning what Jesus did in previous chapters, but let me summarise:

I believe that Jesus represented the brokenness of all humanity and took on everyone's lost identity so that all can be healed and restored. Jesus died for our sin, bearing the consequence of sin, taking our death into the grave; and went beyond, through the victory of the resurrection over death. Jesus was raised from the dead, taking back the keys of death and *sheol* (or *hades*), defeating the wages of sin by overcoming death for all of humanity. I believe we can be confident that God will save all people because all are made alive in Christ in the resurrection (1 Corinthians 15:21-22).

What determines the end of the story: sin leading to 'hell' and eternal conscious torment or Jesus leading to salvation for all and the eventual universal restoration of all things?

Of course, experiencing salvation is something we have to participate in for it to be realised in our lives, as the truth is that man can be saved, reconciled to God, born from above and restored but not yet know it. Experiencing salvation is not automatic because, as Proverbs 23:7 tells us, 'as a man thinks in his heart, so is he'.

The reality is that we need to participate in what has been accomplished for us; living in and included in what Jesus did and not still living in lost identity and a 'less than' kind of life.

The person living without the realisation of what Jesus has accomplished is 'saved' and fully included in what Jesus did on the cross as part of humanity. Unfortunately they are not living in the experience of what has been accomplished for them. One day that person will actively experience the reality of the salvation that they already have in Christ, even if beyond the grave.

Hope beyond 'hell'

Then what about 'hell' from a CU perspective?

My own personal testimony of encounters shared in earlier chapters is that there is hope beyond death and 'hell'. The opportunity of choice after death is not denied in the Bible. There is hope beyond 'hell' according to many in the early church, and that is certainly my experience.

Is 'hell' everlasting? No. The interpretation of *aiōnios* as everlasting, as I have covered in depth, is not an accurate reflection of its Greek meaning.

Those thrown into the lake of fire in the book of Revelation actually end up in the New Jerusalem, not being tormented forever. The nations and kings of the earth are not the church, yet in Revelation 21 these nations and kings enter the New Jerusalem, and they enter through the blood of the lamb.

I conclude that 'hell' as eternal conscious torment is not consistent with the nature and character of a loving God who is kind, tolerant and patient and whose love we cannot escape.

God is love and love is stronger than death. I love where it says that in Song of Solomon and when I sing it in the Misty Edwards song, *You Won't Relent*.

"Put me like a seal over your heart, like a seal on your arm. For love is as strong as death, jealousy is as severe as Sheol; its flashes are flashes of fire, the very flame of the Lord. Many waters cannot quench love, Nor will rivers overflow it" (Song 8:6-7).

Another song I love to sing again relates to God's passionate jealousy for me, *How He Loves Me*, written by John Mark McMillan during a time of grief. Some lines from the song are

He is jealous for me...

And I realize just how beautiful you are
And how great your affections are for me.
And oh, how He loves us...

What does Christian Universalism or the restoration of all things fundamentally mean? Robin Parry[19] sums it up well:

- All those created by God will be brought to the destiny that God created them for.
- All those that God desires to save, and Jesus came to save, will be saved: that is, all things that He created.
- Jesus, not sin, will determine the future of creation.
- Everlasting 'hell' as ECT is not evangelical, in that it thwarts God's purpose in creation and salvation and is incompatible with the God of the gospel story.
- The God who is wholly love, not just love or holy, but is in essence love, will have His way eventually through kindness, tolerance and patience.
- It will be all right in the end and if it is not all right, it is not the end.
- In the end, God will be all in all; and if He is not, then it is not yet the end of the story.
- CU gives us hope of God's ultimate triumph over evil.
- CU gives us joy that Jesus brings all sons to glory.
- CU gives us the hope of glory in the face of suffering and tribulations that there will be an ultimate victory in time as well as eternity.
- If God has given us free will to choose, then why would he take away our free will to choose Him after we die?
- It is difficult to comfort those facing death or who are mourning someone who has died without the hope of CU yourself.
- CU gives us all hope, because God is love and love has won, is winning and will win.

Chapter 9. The Conclusion

In conclusion, if you are following this path, the journey will lead you into conflict with some of those who hold a contrary view and you will undoubtedly find yourself accused of many things.

Even using the word 'universal' is enough to send some people into a rage. You will be called a heretic, and a Universalist (in my opinion I am neither). I do not believe that all roads lead to God. I believe that Jesus gives people the choice. I like what the article *Putting Hell Back in the Handbasket*[14] says, "We cannot presume that all will be saved or that even one will be damned. Rather, we put our hope in the final victory and verdict of Jesus Christ."

I do not accept any labels people may try to put on me, because as soon as you accept a label you:

1. Immediately narrow your options to the views espoused by those who carry that label.

2. Are assumed by others to believe everything they think that a [insert label here] believes.

Keep a loving and forgiving heart towards those who disagree with you and do not treat them as your enemies even if they see themselves that way. Jesus directed us to love our enemies and pray blessings upon them anyway.

Objections and accusations

Some will say "If people are going to be saved anyway, then what is the point of preaching the gospel?" Is that not a rather selfish view? Do we not want people to know and enjoy a relationship with God now? Or to find and fulfil their destiny in this life? And I certainly do not want anyone to go into the consuming fire of God's presence without knowing Him. It is not a pleasant place to be if you don't know Him. If anything, I find I want to preach the good news more than ever.

They will also say, "Well, if there are no consequences to my behaviour then I might as well just keep on sinning." If that is true, then they are only behaving as they do out of fear. They are living under the law, not grace (whilst they sadly shake their heads and accuse us of promoting 'another gospel'). Why on earth would we want to keep on sinning, when sin messes up our relationship with God and everything else in our lives and its wages is death?

It is best not to argue with people. We can share our testimony, and just love them whether they agree with us or not. We are not looking to provoke controversy, enter into fruitless disputes or draw people into making accusations. This book is not intended for those who only want to fight their corner and prove that they are right. This is written for those who are open to lay down their presumptions and assumptions, to engage with God for themselves and allow Him to reveal the truth about His love for them and all His creation; for those who will embrace that truth and be part of the restoration of all things.

Embrace the fire

When we are willing to look at these matters again with an open heart and mind, I believe we will find that death is not the end of choice, so that people can accept what Jesus has done whilst they are in the refining fire of His loving presence. So every knee will bow to Jesus and every tongue will confess Him as Lord voluntarily, even if it is in the consuming fire. I do not want anyone to have to go into that consuming fire of God's presence but if they choose to reject Jesus as Lord before death, there are consequences of doing so that will bring torment to the soul: overwhelming guilt, shame and condemnation – but not from God. God is not tormenting anyone but everyone will have to face the realisation of all their own self-righteous DIY choices and that really is self-induced torment.

Everyone who rejects Jesus reaps the consequences of what they have sown but those consequences are not punishment by God, nor do they last forever. The consequences are self-punishment and anguish of soul but mercy always triumphs over the consequences whenever someone chooses life through Jesus. That choice is still possible even for those who are presently within the consuming fire of God's love. The consuming fire is God Himself and is actually designed not to consume people but to eliminate every objection of guilt, shame and condemnation that keeps them there in their self-imposed bondage. I believe that restorative refining and purifying is what the consuming fire is all about.

Jesus told me to release this message and encourage the Joshua Generation to arise and be bold, to come to Him and He will open the gates to reveal the consuming fire and show them the way, just as He has shown me. I believe we all have the ability to engage the fiery place and do what Jesus did, to preach the good news to those spheres that we are mandated to engage.

The refining fire of the altar is where the authority to preach will be given. As we embrace the fire with urgent desire, great authority will be released to us. I believe we get to choose when we go to the place of fire. We can go now, or later, but God is a consuming fire and we cannot escape His love. That love is an unquenchable fire, intended to refine and purify us.

Let's all choose to embrace the fire now.

If the Lord does not want anyone to perish, we can rest assured that He will do everything He can to that end. God is able to change people's hearts and make them willing to come to Him even if they come 'kicking, struggling, and resentful', as C. S. Lewis said he did[22].

We do not need another theology or doctrinal position about 'hell', inclusion or salvation; what we need is a daily, personal, intimate relationship with God who is Father Son and Spirit that will unveil the truth of who He really is: LOVE.

'Saved In Hope'

I will leave you with a quote from what some will find an unexpected source:

> Some recent theologians are of the opinion that the fire which both burns and saves is Christ himself, the Judge

and Saviour. The encounter with him is the decisive act of judgement. Before his gaze all falsehood melts away.

This encounter with him, as it burns us, transforms and frees us, allowing us to become truly ourselves. All that we build during our lives can prove to be mere straw, pure bluster, and it collapses. Yet in the pain of this encounter, when the impurity and sickness of our lives become evident to us, there lies salvation.

His gaze, the touch of his heart heals us through an undeniably painful transformation 'as through fire'.

But it is a blessed pain, in which the holy power of his love sears through us like a flame, enabling us to become totally ourselves and thus totally of God.

In this way, the inter-relation between justice and grace also becomes clear: the way we live our lives is not immaterial, but our defilement does not stain us forever if we have at least continued to reach out towards Christ, towards truth and towards love.

Indeed, it has already been burned away through Christ's Passion.

At the moment of judgment, we experience and we absorb the overwhelming power of his love over all the evil in the world and in ourselves.

The pain of love becomes our salvation and our joy. It is clear that we cannot calculate the 'duration' of this transforming burning in terms of the chronological measurements of this world.

The transforming 'moment' of this encounter eludes earthly time-reckoning – it is the heart's time, it is the time of 'passage' to communion with God in the Body of Christ.

The judgement of God is hope, both because it is justice and because it is grace. If it were merely grace, making all earthly things cease to matter, God would still owe us an answer to the question about justice – the crucial question that we ask of history and of God.

If it were merely justice, in the end it could bring only fear to us all. The incarnation of God in Christ has so closely linked the two together – judgement and grace – that justice is firmly established: we all work out our salvation 'with fear and trembling' (Phil 2:12).

Nevertheless, grace allows us all to hope, and to go trustfully to meet the Judge whom we know as our "advocate", or *parakletos* (cf. 1 Jn 2:1).

Spe Salvi ('Saved In Hope') – Pope Benedict XVI (2007)[23].

God's richest blessings on your continuing journey beyond beyond!

Appendix:
100 Logical Proofs for the Restoration of All Things

There are many good sound and logical reasons why the restoration of all things is a sensible conclusion to draw from a review of the evidence contained in both the Old and New Testaments, including Jesus' own life and teachings and those of the apostles. However, we need to read with an open mind, not from a confirmation biased perspective, so that each piece of evidence adds weight to the argument and is not just reviewed in a disconnected manner.

We should consider the nature, character and wisdom of God as Father and therefore what is His desire, will and purpose in creating man. We can put the Old Testament writers and prophets in the dock, along with the New Testament writers, many of whom knew Jesus personally, and see what light they can shed on the issue.

In 1840, Thomas Whittemore[24] published a list of *100 Scriptural Proofs That All Mankind Will be Saved* which are summarised in the following pages. Whilst I may not agree with him on every detail, when all the evidence is weighed and added together I believe it forms a compelling case not only for universal salvation through Christ but also for the restoration of all things.

God as Creator

1. God is the loving and benevolent Creator of all men: *and He made from one man every nation of mankind to live on all the face of the earth* (Acts 17:26). He would not have conferred an existence that He knew would end in the worst possible consequences to his creatures.

God as the Father of Mankind

2. God is the Father of all men. *Do we not all have one father? Has not one God created us?* (Malachi 2:10). His fatherhood is in keeping and consistent with His nature as love. It makes no sense at all that God, as the loving Father of all men, would consign His children to eternal misery.

God as Lord of Creation

3. *The earth is the Lord's, and all it contains, The world, and those who dwell in it* (Psalm 24:1). All men, of right, belong to God. He will not give up what belongs to Him to the dominion of sin and Satan forever.

All men committed to Christ's care

4. God has given all things to Christ. *"The Father loves the Son and has given all things into His hand."* (John 3:35).

5. God gave all beings to Christ so that they should all enjoy eternal life: *"even as You gave Him authority over all flesh, that to all whom You have given Him, He may give eternal life."* (John 17:2).

6. Christ will certainly save all that the Father has given him. *"All that the Father gives Me will come to Me, and the one who comes to Me I will certainly not cast out."* (John 6:37).

God's will revealed

7. It is the will of God that all people shall be saved: ...*who wills all men to be saved and to come to the knowledge of the truth* (1 Timothy 2:4).

8. God inspires the hearts of people to pray for the salvation of all men, and say, as Jesus said, *"Your will be done."* (Matthew 6:10).

9. The will of God is that all men be saved. Jesus came to do the will of God. Jesus said to them, *"My food is to do the will of Him who sent Me and to accomplish His work."* (John 4:34).

10. The will of God cannot be resisted. What God wills to take place must take place. *All the inhabitants of the earth are accounted as nothing, but He does according to His will in the host of heaven and among the inhabitants of the earth; and no one can ward off His hand or say to Him, 'What have You done?'* (Daniel 4:35).

11. God is single minded and has no other will besides the will to save all men. *"But He is unchangeable, and who can turn Him? And what He wants to do, that He does."* (Job 23:13 AMP).

God's essence and nature is love

12. *God is love* (1 John 4:8). *Love does no wrong* (Romans 13:10). If love does no wrong, God can do no wrong and therefore cannot be the author of endless evil.

415

13. God loves all mankind. *For God so loved the world that he gave his only begotten Son* (John 3:16). This argument compounds with the last.

14. God loves even his enemies. Jesus declared, *"But love your enemies, and do good, and lend, expecting nothing in return; and your reward will be great, and you will be sons of the Most High; for He is kind to ungrateful and evil men…"* (Luke 6:35). If God loves his enemies, He will not cause them to be endlessly miserable.

God's manifold wisdom

15. *[God] is wise in heart and mighty in strength* (Job 9:4). God is wise. He foresaw all the consequences of our creation when He made us: He knew fully what the result would be to each individual. God must have created only to bless.

16. The wisdom of God is 'full of mercy' and 'without partiality'. *But the wisdom that is from above is first pure, then peaceable, gentle, willing to yield, full of mercy and good fruits, without partiality and without hypocrisy* (James 3:17 NKJV).

God's pleasure, desire and purpose

17. The pleasure of God is in favour of all men. *"Say to them, 'As I live!' declares the Lord God, 'I take no pleasure in the death of the wicked, but rather that the wicked turn from his way and live.'"* (Ezekiel 33:11). Death and sin and pain may exist for a time; but God has no pleasure in them of themselves: they are not the end at which he aims but He uses the trials, troubles and tribulations we create for ourselves to bring about ultimate good.

18. God created all men expressly for His pleasure, and, therefore, not for ultimate death. *"Worthy are You, our Lord and our God, to receive glory and honour and power; for You created all things, and because of Your will they existed and were created."* (Revelation 4:11).

19. *And the pleasure of the Lord shall prosper in His [Christ's] hand* (Isaiah 53:10). God's pleasure is identical to His will: *all men to be saved and to come to the knowledge of the truth* (1 Timothy 2:4). Compare this with number 20, below.

20. *"So will My word be which goes forth from My mouth; It will not return to Me empty, without accomplishing what I desire, and without succeeding in the matter for which I sent it."* (Isaiah 55:11). God created men for His pleasure, and His desire in this matter will certainly be accomplished.

21. God has purposed to gather together all things in Christ. *He made known to us the mystery of His will, according to His kind intention which He purposed in Him with a view to an administration suitable to the fullness of the times, that is, the summing up of all things in Christ, things in the heavens and things on the earth. In Him* (Ephesians 1:9-10).

22. The purpose of God cannot fail: it must certainly be accomplished. *The Lord of hosts has sworn saying, "Surely, just as I have intended so it has happened, and just as I have planned so it will stand* (Isaiah 14:24).

God's promises

23. God promised Abraham that he would bless all mankind in his seed. *"And in you all the families of the earth will be blessed."* (Genesis 22:18). The seed of Abraham is Christ (see Galatians 3:16) and in Him all the nations and families of the earth shall be blessed.

24. God made the same promise to Isaac: *"by your descendants all the nations of the earth shall be blessed."* (Genesis 26:4).

25. The same promise was repeated to Jacob: *"in you and in your descendants shall all the families of the earth be blessed."* (Genesis 28:14).

26. Peter understood this promise as referring to the salvation of all men from sin by Jesus. *"It is you who are the sons of the prophets and of the covenant which God made with your fathers, saying to Abraham, 'And in your seed all the families of the earth shall be blessed.' For you first, God raised up His Servant and sent Him to bless you by turning every one of you from your wicked ways."* (Acts 3:26).

27. The apostle Paul repeats this promise and calls it 'the gospel', the good news of blessing for all: *the scripture, foreseeing that God would justify the Gentiles by faith, preached the gospel beforehand to Abraham, saying, "All the nations will be blessed in you"* (Galatians 3:8).

28. No warning found in scripture can contradict the promise made by God. *Is the Law then contrary to the promises of God? May it never be!* (Galatians 3:21). No portion of scripture should

be construed, interpreted, or explained in a way which contradicts those promises, as the doctrine of endless condemnation for sin does.

God's oath declared

29. God has confirmed his promise by an oath: *"I have sworn by Myself, The word has gone forth from My mouth in righteousness And will not turn back, that to Me every knee will bow, every tongue will swear allegiance."* (Isaiah 45:23).

God's power

30. God is almighty and nothing can prevent the fulfilment of his promise: *and being fully assured that what God had promised, He was able also to perform (Romans 4:21). For as many as are the promises of God, in Him, they are yes; therefore also through Him is our Amen to the glory of God through us* (2 Corinthians 1:20).

Jesus' death, burial, resurrection and ascension

31. God has provided the means for the salvation of all men: Jesus died for all. *... who gave Himself as a ransom for all, the testimony given at the proper time* (1 Timothy 2:6). *But we do see Him who was made for a little while lower than the angels, namely, Jesus, because of the suffering of death crowned with glory and honour, so that by the grace of God He might taste death for everyone* (Hebrews 2:9). *... and He Himself is the propitiation for our sins; and not for ours only, but also for those of the whole world* (1 John 2:2). The expressions 'all', 'everyone' and 'the whole world' leave no room for misunderstanding.

32. The work of Christ will be effective for all for whom He died. *As a result of the anguish of His soul, He will see it and be satisfied; by His knowledge, the Righteous One, My Servant, will justify the many, as He will bear their iniquities* (Isaiah 53:11). *"And I, if I am lifted up from the earth, will draw all men unto Myself."* (John 12:32). If Jesus died for all men, He will not be satisfied with less.

33. When Jesus was born, the angel told the shepherds, *"I bring you good news of great joy which will be for all the people."* (Luke 2:10). It was good news for all the people, not just some of them.

34. Jesus cannot be the Saviour of the world if the world will never be saved. *"It is no longer because of what you said that we believe, for we have heard for ourselves and know that this One is indeed the Saviour of the world."* (John 4:42).

35. *We have seen and testify that the Father has sent the Son to be the Saviour of the world.* (1 John 4:14). John knew this from his acquaintance with his Master. We cannot hide this truth; we will proclaim to men, that Jesus is the Saviour of the world.

The testimony of the prophets

36. All the holy prophets have spoken of the restoration of all things: *"...and that He may send Jesus, the Christ appointed for you, whom heaven must receive until the period of restoration of all things about which God spoke by the mouth of His holy prophets from ancient time"* (Acts 3:20-21).

This restoration is the putting of things back into their original condition: mankind restored to the image of God again.

37. Jesus is the seed of the woman referred to in Genesis 3:15: *"And I will put enmity Between you and the woman, And between your seed and her seed; He shall bruise you on the head, And you shall bruise him on the heel."*

38. David said, *All the ends of the earth will remember and turn to the Lord, And all the families of the nations will worship before You* (Psalms 22:27). This agrees precisely with the promise of God to Abraham, that all the nations and families of the earth shall be blessed in Christ Jesus.

39. *And let all kings bow down before him, All nations serve him... And let men bless themselves by him; Let all nations call him blessed.* (Psalms 72:11, 17). This agrees with the point made in proof 38.

40. *All nations whom You have made shall come and worship before You, O Lord, and they shall glorify Your name* (Psalms 86:9). This includes all the nations of the earth, since God made them all.

41. Twenty-six times in one psalm alone, the psalmist tells us that *His mercy endures forever* (Psalm 136 NKJV). 'Mercy' (or 'lovingkindness' in the NASB) is a translation of the Hebrew word *checed* which means covenant love. This is the basis of everything God does because of who He is – LOVE.

42. God's mercy, which is to endure forever, is over all the works of God. *The Lord is good to all, And His mercies are over all His works* (Psalms 145:9). God is the same, yesterday, today, and

forever. 'Mercies' here is the Hebrew word *racham*, often translated 'compassion'.

43. *"All Your works shall give thanks to You, O Lord"* (Psalms 145:10). How could all God's works give thanks Him, if some are consigned to eternal fire?

44. *The Lord is gracious and merciful; Slow to anger and great in lovingkindness* (Psalms 145:8). Can endless misery be ordained by such a God?

45. *The Lord is compassionate and gracious, slow to anger and abounding in lovingkindness. He will not always strive with us, nor will He keep His anger forever* (Psalms 103:8-9). If torment is endless, how can we say that 'God will not always chide' nor 'keep His anger forever?'

46. Isaiah indicated that there was no sin which could not be pardoned. *"Come now, and let us reason together,"* Says the Lord, *"Though your sins are as scarlet, They will be as white as snow; Though they are red like crimson, They will be like wool."* (Isaiah 1:18).

47. It is said, that *all the nations will stream to [the mountain of the house of the Lord]* (Isaiah 2:2) – a figurative representation of the covenant of the Gospel.

48. *The Lord of hosts will prepare a lavish banquet for all peoples on this mountain; A banquet of aged wine, choice pieces with marrow, And refined, aged wine* (Isaiah 25:6). Drinking and feasting from the wells of salvation, sufficient to supply the wants of all.

49. *And on this mountain He will swallow up the covering which is over all peoples, even the veil which is stretched over all nations* (Isaiah 25:7). All will then see the truth.

50. *God will swallow up death* (Isaiah 25:8). Paul quotes these words and applies them to the victory of the resurrection in 1 Corinthians 15:54.

51. *And the Lord God will wipe tears away from all faces, And He will remove the reproach of His people from all the earth* (Isaiah 25:8). The work of the Gospel wipes away the tears from all faces.

52. *"Then the glory of the Lord will be revealed, And all flesh will see it together; For the mouth of the Lord has spoken."* (Isaiah 40:5). God has said it, so it is sure to come about.

53. *"For as the rain and the snow come down from heaven, And do not return there without watering the earth And making it bear and sprout, And furnishing seed to the sower and bread to the eater; So will My word be which goes forth from My mouth; It will not return to Me empty, Without accomplishing what I desire, And without succeeding in the matter for which I sent it"* (Isaiah 55:10-11). If any were to be lost forever, God's word would be 'returning to Him empty'.

54. *"It is too small a thing that You should be My Servant To raise up the tribes of Jacob and to restore the preserved ones of Israel; I will also make You a light of the nations, So that My salvation may reach to the end of the earth."* (Isaiah 49:6). This is inconsistent with that salvation being of no benefit to millions of people.

55. *"For I will not contend forever, Nor will I always be angry; For the spirit would grow faint before Me, And the breath of those whom I have made."* (Isaiah 57:16) However, according to the doctrine of endless torment, God would indeed 'always be angry'.

56. *"But this is the covenant which I will make with the house of Israel after those days,"* declares the Lord, *"I will put My law within them and on their heart, I will write it, and I will be their God, and they shall be My people. They will not teach again, each man his neighbour and each man his brother, saying, 'Know the Lord,' for they will all know Me, from the least of them to the greatest of them,"* declares the Lord, *"for I will forgive their iniquity, and their sin I will remember no more."* (Jeremiah 31:33-34). The spirit of the passage is universal grace. What God here says He will do for Israel, He will also do for the Gentiles. The former is a pledge of the latter.

57. *For the Lord will not reject forever, For if He causes grief, Then He will have compassion According to His abundant lovingkindness. For He does not afflict willingly Or grieve the sons of men* (Lamentations 3:31-33). God does not afflict for the purpose of afflicting, but for the good of the sufferer.

58. *And to Him was given dominion, Glory and a kingdom, That all the peoples, nations and men of every language Might serve Him. His dominion is an everlasting dominion Which will not pass away, And His kingdom is one Which will not be destroyed* (Daniel 7:14). If all people, nations, and languages serve the Saviour, will they be endlessly miserable?

59. *"I will ransom them from the power of the grave; I will redeem them from death. O Death, I will be your plagues; O Grave (or Sheol), I will be your destruction."* (Hosea 13:14 NKJV). Paul applies this to the resurrection (see 1 Corinthians 15:54- 55).

60. *Who is a God like You, who pardons iniquity And passes over the rebellious act of the remnant of His possession? He does not retain His anger forever, Because He delights in unchanging love* (Micah 7:18). Forgiveness, not endless torment.

The testimony of Jesus

61. When Jesus preached, people *wondered at the gracious words which proceeded out of his mouth* (Luke 4:22 NKJV). He was not threatening them with endless misery.

62. *"Look at the birds of the air, that they do not sow, nor reap nor gather into barns, and yet your heavenly Father feeds them. Are you not worth much more than they?"* (Matthew 6:26) Jesus both demonstrated and encouraged confidence in God. The spirit of this whole passage (Matthew 6:25-34) is perfectly consistent with the doctrine of the restoration of all things, but utterly inconsistent with the doctrine of endless misery.

63. *And Jesus said to them, "Watch out and beware of the leaven of the Pharisees and Sadducees."* (Matthew 16:6). The Pharisees' doctrine was one of cruelty, wrath, and partiality; His was of love, compassion, and universal grace.

64. Jesus taught that after the resurrection, men will be like the angels of God in heaven, holy, spotless, and pure: *"for they cannot even die anymore, because they are like angels, and are*

sons of God, being sons of the resurrection."(Luke 20:36). They will be immortal and they will be children of God, bearing a moral likeness to him.

65. Jesus reproved the Pharisees for shutting up the kingdom of heaven, because He desired everyone to have access. *"But woe to you, scribes and Pharisees, hypocrites, because you shut off the kingdom of heaven from people; for you do not enter in yourselves, nor do you allow those who are entering to go in."* (Matthew 23:13).

The testimony of New Testament writers

66. In his rooftop vision, Peter saw that all people came down from heaven; that they are all encircled in the kind care of God while here on earth; and that all will be drawn up again into heaven. (see Acts 10:15; 11:5-10).

67. Paul represented the free gift of life as extending equally with sin. *So then as through one transgression there resulted in condemnation to all men, even so through one act of righteousness there resulted in justification of life to all men* (Romans 5:18).

68. *For as through the one man's disobedience the many were made sinners, even so through the obedience of the One the many will be made righteous* (Romans 5:19). The same 'many' that were made sinners will be made righteous.

69. Wherever sin reigned before, grace will now reign instead. ... *where sin increased, grace abounded all the more, so that, as sin reigned in death, even so grace would reign through righteousness to eternal life through Jesus Christ our Lord* (Romans 5:20-21).

70. *... the creation itself also will be set free from its slavery to corruption into the freedom of the glory of the children of God.* (Romans 8:21). The whole creation was in slavery to corruption and the whole creation is to be set free.

71. Paul teaches the eventual salvation of both Jews and Gentiles, comprising all mankind: *a partial hardening has happened to Israel until the fullness of the Gentiles has come in* (Romans 11:25).

72. Paul teaches that whether living or dying, we are the Lord's. *For if we live, we live for the Lord, or if we die, we die for the Lord; therefore whether we live or die, we are the Lord's. For to this end Christ died and lived again, that He might be Lord both of the dead and the living* (Romans 14:8-9). The terms 'dead and living' evidently signify all the human race. All the human race are Christ's forever.

73. *As in Adam all die, so also in Christ all will be made alive* (1 Corinthians 15:22). *... if anyone is in Christ, he is a new creature.* (2 Corinthians 5:17). Since all shall be made alive in Christ, all shall be new creatures in the resurrection.

74. *The last enemy that will be abolished is death* (1 Cor 15:26). There will be no enemies to the happiness of man remaining after the resurrection.

75. When Paul exclaims, in light of the resurrection, *"O death! where is your sting?"* (1 Corinthians 15:55), there must then be no sin, for *the sting of death is sin* (verse 56).

76. Paul said that *God was in Christ reconciling the world to Himself, not counting their trespasses against them* (2 Corinthians 5:19), 'The world' in this context is all for whom Christ died (and note that Paul did not say 'reconciling Himself to the world').

77. *There is neither Jew nor Greek, there is neither slave nor free man, there is neither male nor female; for you are all one in Christ Jesus. And if you belong to Christ, then you are Abraham's descendants, heirs according to promise* (Galatians 3: 28-29). That is, according to the promise of God to Abraham (proof 23). In Christ all division and distinction is done away with.

78. *At the name of Jesus, every knee will bow in heaven and on earth and under the earth* (Philippians 2:9-11). Beings in heaven will bow the knee to Jesus in spiritual worship to Christ: will they not all be holy and happy?

79. Reason 78 is confirmed by the fact that *if you confess with your mouth Jesus as Lord, and believe in your heart that God raised Him from the dead, you will be saved* (Romans 10:9).

80. *For it was the Father's good pleasure for all the fullness to dwell in Him, and through Him to reconcile all things to Himself, having made peace through the blood of His cross; through Him, I say, whether things on earth or things in heaven* (Colossians 1:19-20). It pleased the Father 'to reconcile all things to himself' – an irrefutable argument in proof of the final holiness and happiness of all creation.

81. Timothy is instructed to pray on behalf of 'all men', which is agreeable to God *who desires all men to be saved and to come to the knowledge of the truth. For there is one God, and one mediator also between God and men, the man Christ Jesus, who gave Himself as a ransom for all...* (1 Timothy 2:4-6). God is kind and good to all and will have all men to be saved.

82. *We have fixed our hope on the living God, who is the Saviour of all men, especially of believers.* (1 Timothy 4:10) God is called 'the Saviour of all men'.

83. *For the grace of God has appeared, bringing salvation to all men* (Titus 2:11). Again, all men.

84. *Therefore, since the children share in flesh and blood, He Himself likewise also partook of the same, that through death He might render powerless him who had the power of death, that is, the devil* (Hebrews 2:14). Christ will destroy all evil, and banish it entirely from the universe. Neither people nor other beings are evil, as evil is only an absence of good.

85. *For we who have believed enter that rest* (Hebrews 4:3), which could not be true if they believed in the doctrine of endless misery.

86. *It is impossible for God to lie* (Hebrews 6:18). God promised it to Abraham (proof 23), therefore all people without exception will eventually experience that blessing in Christ.

87. Hebrews repeats the testimony of Jeremiah that *"all will know me, from the least to the greatest..."* (Hebrews 8:11). This is similar to what Paul declares in Romans 11:25-26 (proof 71).

88. *All discipline for the moment seems not to be joyful, but sorrowful; yet to those who have been trained by it, afterwards it yields the peaceful fruit of righteousness* (Hebrews 12:11). If 'punishment' were endless, there would be no 'afterwards'.

89. *But if we walk in the Light as He Himself is in the Light, we have fellowship with one another, and the blood of Jesus His Son cleanses us from all sin* (1 John 1:7). There is no sin that the blood of Christ will not wash away. God has both the will and the power; therefore all men will be saved by his grace.

90. *The Son of God appeared for this purpose, to destroy the works of the devil* (1 John 3:8). Men are the workmanship of God, not the devil, and will not be ultimately destroyed. *For the Son of Man has come to seek and to save that which was lost* (Luke 19:10): He came into the world for that specific purpose; and He will not give over until it is completely accomplished.

91. *And the testimony is this, that God has given us eternal life, and this life is in His Son* (1 John 5:11). God has given eternal life to all.

92. *And every created thing which is in heaven and on the earth and under the earth and on the sea, and all things in them, I heard saying, "To Him who sits on the throne, and to the Lamb, be blessing and honour and glory and dominion forever and ever"* (Revelation 5:13). Every created thing.

93. *"Who will not fear, O Lord, and glorify Your name? For You alone are holy; For all the nations will come and worship before You, For Your righteous acts have been revealed."* (Revelation

15:4).This is the 'all nations' of God's promise to Abraham (proof 23 again).

94. *And I heard a loud voice from the throne, saying, "Behold, the tabernacle of God is among men, and He will dwell among them, and they shall be His people, and God Himself will be among them* (Revelation 21:3). This is already fulfilled through the cross and resurrection: all men are reconciled to God.

95. *He will wipe away every tear from their eyes; and there will no longer be any death; there will no longer be any mourning, or crying, or pain; the first things have passed away* (Revelation 21:4). There will no longer be any death, because Jesus *abolished death and brought life and immortality to light through the gospel* (2 Timothy 1:10).

96. God encourages all good people to pray for the salvation of all people, which He could not do if it were opposed to His will; because, *if we ask anything according to His will, He hears us* (1 John 5:14), and because *the desire of the righteous will be granted* (Proverbs 10:24).

97. *In this you greatly rejoice, even though now for a little while, if necessary, you have been distressed by various trials, so that the proof of your faith, being more precious than gold which is perishable, even though tested by fire, may be found to result in praise and glory and honor at the revelation of Jesus Christ; and though you have not seen Him, you love Him, and though you do not see Him now, but believe in Him, you greatly rejoice with joy inexpressible and full of glory* (1 Peter 1:6-8). Whittemore comments: "Can it be possible that they believed in the doctrine

of endless sin and misery? Would this have made them rejoice with unspeakable joy?"

98. All the warnings in the Bible, when properly understood, harmonise with the doctrine of the restoration of all things. Any 'punishments' spoken of are of limited duration, for the purpose of correction only, and there is nothing in the scriptures which extends the existence of sin, or its consequences, beyond the resurrection.

99. The restoration of all things is the only hypothesis which harmonises with the perfection of God as love, since if people were lost forever by God's design or permission, that would compromise His goodness; if by His neglect or lack of provision for them, that would compromise His wisdom; and if sin were too powerful for Him and rebels too stubborn for Him to overcome, that would compromise His power.

100. *When all things are subjected to Him, then the Son Himself also will be subjected to the One who subjected all things to Him, so that God may be all in all* (1 Corinthians 15:28).

If you take one piece of scriptural evidence in isolation it does not make a good enough case on its own for the restoration of all things but if you add each piece together, there is overwhelming evidence from the Bible alone. If you further add direct conversations with the Father and personal testimony from multiple sources, the verdict is clear: the restoration of all things is at the very heart of the Father's agenda for creation so that His original intentions can be realised.

References

1. Andre Rabe, *Icons of Beauty*.
2. John Crowder, *The Great Iconoclast*, article published on www.thenewmystics.com
3. Brad Jersak – *The Gospel in Chairs – YouTube* video, available at www.freedomarc.org/chairs
4. Gregory of Nyssa – *On the Soul and the Resurrection*, and *The Great Catechism*, both published by Aeterna Press.
5. Catholic Encyclopedia Online – *Apocatastasis*, www.catholic.com/encyclopedia/apocatastasis
6. Ilaria Ramelli – *A Larger Hope? Volume 1: Universal Salvation from Christian Beginnings to Julian of Norwich*, published by Cascade Books.
7. Clement of Alexandria – *Fragments,* available online at www.earlychristianwritings.com/text/clement-fragments.html
8. Jerome – *Commentary on the New Testament*, quoted in Church Fathers on salvation (online article), www.mercyuponall.org/church-fathers-on-universal-salvation/
9. C. S. Lewis – *The Lion, the Witch and the Wardrobe*, published by HarperCollins Children's Books.
10. Richard Rohr, OFM – *Richard Rohr's Daily Meditation: Love, not Atonement* (Centre for Action and Contemplation): www.cac.org/love-not-atonement
11. Wm. Paul Young – *The Shack*, published by Hodder.
12. Metropolitan Anthony Bloom – *Doubts*, blog post https://orthodoxwayoflife.blogspot.com/2016/02/doubts.html

13. Jerry Onyszczak – *Total Success of the Cross of Christ* www.sigler.org/jerryo/files/TotalSuccess.pdf

14. *Putting Hell Back In The Handbasket* – Brazen Church www.brazenchurch.com (Jacob McMillen, Josiah Pemberton, Julie Ferwerda and Brad Jersak).

15. C. S. Lewis – *The Great Divorce*, published by Collins.

16. J. W. Hanson – *Bible Threatenings Explained*, published by Literary Licensing, LLC.

17. Sadhu Sundar Singh – *The Mystery of the Maharishi of Mt Kailash,* published by ReformaZion Media.

18. Chuck McKnight – *5 Views on Hell? 2 Questions to Reframe the Debate* – Hippie Heretic blog on Patheos: https://patheos.com/blogs/hippieheretic/25-views-on-hell-2-questions-to-reframe

19. Robin Parry – *YouTube* videos on Christian Universalism: playlist of 3 talks at www.freedomarc.org/robin-parry

20. Robin Parry – *A Larger Hope? Volume 2: Universal Salvation from The Reformation to the 19th Century*, published by Cascade Books.

21. Denny Burk – in *Four Views on Hell* – Preston Sprinkle (Editor), published by Zondervan.

22. C. S. Lewis – *Surprised By Joy*, published by Collins.

23. Pope Benedict XVI – *Spe Salvi* ('Saved in Hope', 2007). PDF available online at http://www.scborromeo.org/docs/spe_salvi.pdf

24. Thomas Whittemore – *100 Scriptural Proofs That All Mankind Will be Saved*, available online at https://www.tentmaker.org/books/ScripturalProofs.html

Further resources

These publications and websites raise issues which I believe God is drawing to our attention today. The fact that they are listed here should not be taken to imply that I agree with all the doctrinal positions, conclusions or opinions of the authors and contributors.

Julie Ferwerda – *Raising Hell* (PDF download): raisinghellbook.com

Chuck Crisco – *A New Day Dawning* blog: www.anewdaydawning.com

Tentmaker website: www.tentmaker.org

Bible versions:

Unless otherwise noted, Bible quotations are taken from the New American Standard Bible® (**NASB**): Copyright © 1960, 1962, 1963, 1968, 1971, 1972, 1973, 1975, 1977, 1995 by The Lockman Foundation. Used by permission (www.Lockman.org).

Other versions used:

AMP: Scripture taken from the Amplified Bible, Copyright © 1954, 1958, 1962, 1964, 1965, 1987 by The Lockman Foundation. Used by permission (www.Lockman.org).

Mirror: The Mirror Bible: The Bible translated from the original text and paraphrased in contemporary speech with commentary. Copyright © 2017 by Francois du Toit. Used by kind permission of the author. All rights reserved.

NIV: Scripture quotations taken from The Holy Bible, New International Version® NIV®. Copyright © 1973, 1978, 1984, 2011 by Biblica, Inc.™. Used by permission. All rights reserved worldwide.

NKJV: Scripture taken from the New King James Version®. Copyright © 1982 by Thomas Nelson. Used by permission. All rights reserved.

TPT: Scripture quotations marked TPT are from The Passion Translation®. Copyright © 2017, 2018 by Passion & Fire Ministries, Inc. Used by permission. All rights reserved. ThePassionTranslation.com.

YLT: Bible text is quoted from Young's Literal Translation by Robert Young, published by Baker Book House, Grand Rapids, MI. This translation is in the Public Domain.

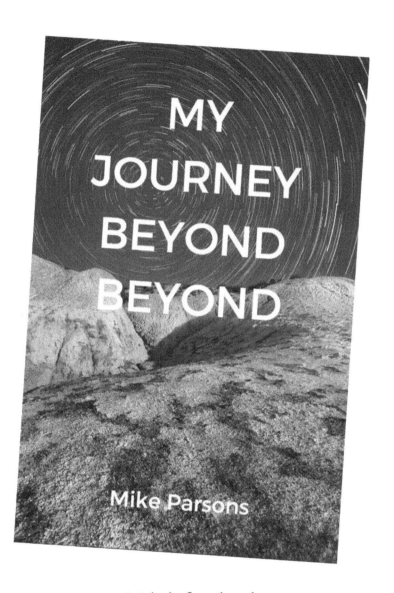

Mike's first book

My Journey Beyond Beyond

is available from local and online booksellers

The Restoration of All Things

Events recordings now available

with Nancy Coen

Lindy Strong

Justin Paul Abraham

and Mike Parsons

freedomarc.org/roat

freedomarc.org/roat2

"Deep calls to deep at the sound of your waterfalls..." (Psalm 42:7)

Engaging God

Online equipping for a supernatural lifestyle

freedomarc.org/subscribe

Mike Parsons presents this unique online resource of self-paced teaching, discipleship and worldwide community with others on this journey.

Learn to access God in the realms of heaven and within your own spirit and heart, and take up your responsibility as a son in God's kingdom.

Get your **2-week free trial** or find out more at

freedomarc.org/subscribe

Keep up to date with
Mike's journey towards
the restoration of all things.

Subscribe to his
YouTube channel at
freedomarc.org/youtube

Follow Freedom ARC
on social media:

freedomarc.org/facebook

freedomarc.org/twitter

freedomarc.org/instagram

freedomarc.org/pinterest

and on our *Sons of Issachar* blog:

www.freedomarc.blog

You'll find links to these and
much more on our website:

www.freedomarc.org

Lightning Source UK Ltd.
Milton Keynes UK
UKHW010637060421
381519UK00001B/10